The National

In the same series

THE NATIONAL

A Dream Made Concrete

PETER LEWIS

Methuen

First published in Great Britain in 1990
by Methuen London
Michelin House, 81 Fulham Road, London SW3 6RB
Copyright © Peter Lewis 1990

The author has asserted his moral rights

A CIP catalogue record for this book
is available from the British Library
ISBN 0 413 18570 2

Typesetting by Deltatype Ltd, Ellesmere Port, Cheshire
Printed in Great Britain by
St Edmundsbury Press Ltd, Bury St Edmunds, Suffolk

To the Memory of Laurence Olivier

Contents

List of Illustrations

The National's first director
Edwin Lutyens and Bernard Shaw
Lutyen's design for the first riverside site
Joan Plowright in Laurence Olivier's production of *Uncle Vanya*
Sean Kenny's sketch of his sweeping ramp for *Hamlet*, 1963
Edith Evans, Derek Jacobi and Louise Purnell in *Hay Fever*
Laurence Olivier in *Love for Love*
Rehearsing in 'the huts' for *Long Day's Journey Into Night*
Michael Hordern in *Jumpers*
John Gielgud and Ralph Richardson in *No Man's Land*
Denys Lasdun's model for the Shell site
About to move into the South Bank site
Olivier taking the stage of the Olivier on October 25, 1976
Albert Finney as Tamburlaine the Great
John Dexter at the National to direct *As You Like It*
Michael Gambon in Harold Pinter's *Betrayal*
The Oresteia of Aeschylus in the verse of Tony Harrison
The Rivals with Michael Hordern and Geraldine McEwan
Guys and Dolls, the National's biggest hit to date
Ian McKellen as Platonov in *Wild Honey*
Anthony Hopkins as Lambert Le Roux in *Pravda*
Judi Dench in Peter Hall's production of *Antony and Cleopatra*
Peter Hall and his successor, Richard Eyre

Preface and Acknowledgements

Although this book is the first detailed account of the first 27 years in the life of Britain's National Theatre, it is in no way an official history. The initiative in telling the story was mine. It was neither approved nor (as far as I know) disapproved by the theatre's Board or executive. It is the view of an outsider, whose work brought him into frequent contact with the theatre from its inception to the present day. An insider's view would be different. I have not had access to any of the minutes or records of the Board or administration, other than the annual reports and accounts, and my requests for further information were politely turned down.

This said, I would like to acknowledge the help I have received from members of the staff at the National and those who have worked there at various periods. Nearly all those I asked were helpful in contributing their part in the story. I am especially grateful to Lady Olivier (Joan Plowright) for throwing light on Sir Laurence Olivier's period as director and to his successor, Sir Peter Hall, for many conversations whilst he was at the helm and for permission to quote extensively from his published Diaries of the years 1972–79. The present director, Richard Eyre, and the executive director, David Aukin, were welcoming and helpfully frank and the head of the Press Office, Stephen Wood, patiently made my task easier in many ways.

My particular thanks to them and to all of the following who kindly spent time answering my questions: Lord Cottesloe, Lord Rayne and Lady Soames, chairmen past and present of the South Bank and National Theatre Boards; Lord Mishcon, Sir Derek Mitchell, John Mortimer, Sir Peter Parker, past and present members of the Board; Patrick Donnell, Peter Stevens, Michael Elliott, past general administrators; Sir Denys Lasdun, architect; and the following playwrights, actors, directors, designers, administrators, agents, writers and critics and backstage staff:

Maria Aitken, Lindsay Anderson, Alan Ayckbourn, Alan Bennett, Michael Billington, Lord Birkett, Michael Blakemore, Jules Boardman, Diana Boddington, Michael Bogdanov, Howard Brenton, Eleanor Bron, Michael Bryant, Bill Bryden, William Bundy, John Bury, Dame Judi Dench, the late John Dexter, Gillian Diamond, William Dudley, Frank Dunlop, Laurence Evans, Kenneth Ewing, John Faulkner, Anthony Field, Kon Fredericks, Michael Gambon, William Gaskill, Peter Gill, John Goodwin, Sebastian Graham-Jones, Gawn Grainger, John Gunter, Lyn Haill, Michael Hallifax, David Hare, Michael Harrison, Harry Henderson, Sue Higginson, Thelma Holt, Derek Jacobi, Robert Lang, Roger Lobb, Alec McCowen, Geraldine McEwan, Ian McKellen, Iain Mackintosh, Arthur Miller, Jonathan Miller, Stephen Mitchell, David Nathan, Trevor Nunn, John Osborne, Mary Parsons, Richard Pilbrow, Ronald Pickup, Tim Pigott-Smith, Stephen Poliakoff, Denis Quilley, Simon Relph, Michael Rudman, Peter Shaffer, Sir Roy Shaw, Neil Simon, Robert Stephens, Tom Stoppard, Lucy Stout, Jack Tinker, Dorothy Tutin, Kathleen Tynan, Michael White, Sir Hugh Willatt, John Wilson, Peter Wood, Nicholas Wright and Richard York.

Olivier Picks his Team

When Laurence Olivier's appointment as Director of Britain's forth-coming National Theatre was announced on 9 August 1962, nobody was exactly surprised. To most people at that date he was the obvious candidate. Four years earlier, he had confided to Kenneth Tynan that he was planning for the day when he would run the National Theatre, and he had told Max Adrian that he was thrilled by the prospect although it would make him 'the most hated man in England'.

On the night his appointment was announced, his fellow-actors at the Chichester Festival Theatre stuck a Union Jack postcard on his dressing-room door with the written message beneath, 'God Save Sir'. Olivier, arriving for the evening performance, stopped dead outside. According to a member of the company who was watching unobserved, he bowed his head and said 'Please, God, help.' It was a humility not characteristic of him, at least not when people were looking.

Olivier was at this point unquestionably the most widely admired classical actor in England. Two achievements had established him as such in the mind of the nation at large: his Shakespeare films of the late forties and fifties, and the legend that clung to his performances with Ralph Richardson at the Old Vic in 1944–6. Other names could be, and were, put forward as candidates to bring a national theatre to birth . . . John Gielgud and Anthony Quayle, both experienced as actor-managers, and, among directors, Tyrone Guthrie, the Old Vic's unpredictable fiery comet who had fizzed off to another continent, or Peter Brook and Peter Hall, representing the new generation of Shakespearean directors of originality and audacity. It was a theatrical golden age, not equalled since, and the choice was considerable. But Olivier shone with a special nationalistic light for his quality of command. He still trailed clouds of glory in the mind of the public which had reacted to his Agincourt-winning performance in *Henry V* by standing up and cheering in the cinema in 1944.

For all its remembered glories, Olivier's career had been in the doldrums, by his standards, in the fifties. His management of the antique, charming but unsafe St James's Theatre had ended in loss, and his film career had been reduced to playing the Ruritanian prince to Marilyn Monroe in *The Prince and the Showgirl*. His marriage to Vivien Leigh was under great strain in private, while in public they continued to play the role of the theatreland's royal couple. Also, he was bored with his position at the head of the theatrical establishment and fearful that his sort of theatre and his sort of acting were being left behind. The new wave of theatrical advance was taking place at the Royal Court, not at the St James's or even at Stratford, where he had been guest-starring as Macbeth and Titus Andronicus (the latter directed by Peter Brook). 'At that time I had reached a stage in my life that I was getting profoundly sick of – not just tired – sick,' he wrote in a book of tributes to the Royal Court on its 25th anniversary in 1981. 'What I felt to be my image was boring me to death. And now, suddenly the miracle was happening. I began to feel the promise of a new, vitally charged, entirely unfamiliar Me . . . a conviction that I now belonged to an entirely different generation.'

He had gone to the Royal Court to play *The Entertainer*, joining the group of writers and actors that gathered round the eminent but unstuffy George Devine, its artistic director. Archie Rice proved to be his liberation. John Osborne's down-at-heel, cynical and hollow music-hall comedian was a tailor-made vehicle for a certain side of Olivier which had been suppressed for years – his anti-Establishment side. ('There must have been something of Archie in me all along,' he said.) It also liberated him for the first time in years from acting with or directing Vivien Leigh. In her place he shared the play with Joan Plowright. She was then emerging as a new, Royal Court kind of star. 'For the first time at the Court, I found my own voice as an actress and an exhilarating sense of purpose which had been sadly lacking elsewhere.' She was not the sort of actress to be much impressed by Olivier's fame. At their first meeting in George Devine's office in 1956, he had thought her smile had more than a hint of mockery about it. 'I divined that I stood for everything that the young generation at the Royal Court would find most objectionable and everything that was most odious to a girl of this generation of actors who had come from North Lincs. I was titled, necessarily self-satisfied, pompous, patronizing, having obviously come to visit in a spirit of condescension.' Joan Plowright's reaction more or less bore this out. 'A lot of us were suspicious when he came to do *The Entertainer*. We were opposed to all he represented. But all that vanished at the first rehearsal.'

They fell in love during the run of *The Entertainer* and after at first

2

concealing their love affair (for both were married) from the hounding Press, Olivier and Plowright were able to marry in 1961. From then on her enthusiasm for the new realism and its exponents was to be a powerful influence on his career and especially on his policy for the National. The daughter of a local newspaper editor in Scunthorpe, she was given to such down-to-earth pronouncements as 'I look on acting not as a glamorous profession but as a job'. It was as Beatie Bryant, the country girl in love with culture in Arnold Wesker's play *Roots*, that, said Olivier, 'she knocked me right off my feet'. Although twenty-two years his junior, 'Joanie' was, he once admitted, the sort of maternal figure for whom he had been searching ever since his mother's early death when he was thirteen, as well as the actress he most admired.

In 1962, knowing that the National Theatre might be started at any time, he accepted an invitation to become Director of the new Festival Theatre at Chichester, which had the widest thrust stage to be found anywhere in the country. Plainly he wanted to demonstrate anew his capacity to run a successful company, but his choice of Jacobean plays, *The Chances* and *The Broken Heart*, which were meant to display the vast open stage's versatility, flopped with both critics and public. This provoked Kenneth Tynan, normally an idolater of Olivier's acting, into the sort of personal attack he had usually reserved for Vivien Leigh. In 'an open letter' to Olivier in *The Observer*, he suggested that Olivier was not up to running the company and playing the leading roles as well. '*Uncle Vanya* opens tomorrow. Within a fortnight you will have directed three plays and appeared in two leading parts. It is too much.'

Luckily, the opening of *Uncle Vanya*, at which Tynan's arrival was jeered by his fellow critics, put paid to criticism. Oliver's production is still believed by those who saw it to be the best *Vanya*, possibly the best Chekhov production, yet mounted in England. It came as near to perfect ensemble playing as can be expected of mortal actors, chief of whom were Michael Redgrave in the title role, Olivier as the visionary doctor Astrov, and Joan Plowright as Vanya's niece Sonya, devoted to both of them. It was a rare instance in Olivier's career of his offering a rival actor of equal stature a role perhaps better than his own. The last act was heart-stopping and plaintive chamber music played with such exquisite timing that it seemed to stop the audience's breathing. The failures of the other productions were forgotten in the unexpected acclaim for this one. Olivier decided, naturally enough, to keep it in readiness for the next season at Chichester and beyond that for his first season at the Old Vic.

Before the Chichester season ended, his appointment as Director of the National Theatre was publicly announced. Soon afterwards he

3

received a letter from Kenneth Tynan, proposing himself for the job of *dramaturg*. Typically, Tynan made no apologies about his recent attacks. Olivier showed the letter to his wife with the words, 'How shall we slaughter the little bastard?' Joan Plowright defused his reaction by pointing out that for Olivier to employ Tynan would be to remove the most readable, influential and potentially damaging critic from a position where he could attack the new venture as he had attacked Chichester. 'It didn't take me very many minutes to see that,' said Olivier. He swallowed his resentment and wrote back that Tynan's suggestion was most welcome 'and one that I'd thought of myself already'. He added, with transparent guilelessness, 'God, *any*thing to get you off that *Observer*!'

This was a remarkable *volte-face* for a man as choleric as Olivier could be. Tynan's gift for catching the quality of an actor's performance in words had often been lavished on Olivier in the past, but he had been consistently cruel about Vivien Leigh's inadequacy to play opposite him. 'She remains sweet' was his belittling verdict on most of her roles, 'but when you have said that a half a dozen times you have said everything.' Olivier might by now have ceased to care so much about these wounding put-downs of his former wife. But he always regarded critics as enemies, a 'necessary evil' at best, as I can testify as a lowly member of the species who was first introduced to him at a theatrical party. Some awe-struck phrase about having for so long admired him without having met him came to my lips. He gave me the look that, as Richard III, he had given Buckingham: 'We can leave it like that if you like,' he said and passed on.

In Tynan, he had appointed the longest-serving member of his team and in the long run the most influential one after his wife. Associate directors came and went, but Tynan, despite behaviour that made the Chairman of the National Theatre Board, Viscount Chandos, go purple and demand his dismissal, survived all the crises so long as Olivier was there to save his skin. He was not a popular choice in the acting profession. All through Olivier's years as Director, actors would complain that he had been unwise in his choice of advisers – by which they mainly meant Tynan. The two men had an edgy relationship which never turned into close friendship, partly because Tynan kept his distance as hero-worshipper, acolyte, keeper of the flame, partly because Olivier felt uneasy that Tynan was intellectually his superior. He needed Tynan. He needed the advice of a well-read, well-travelled theatre connoisseur who knew what was going on in contemporary European and American theatre. He needed him as a recommender of plays for the repertoire and of parts for himself, as a public spokesman for the company – Olivier tied himself up in turgid, convoluted prose –

4

and as a house critic whose assessment of a production would be all the more valuable to hear before it opened to the public.

After one of Tynan's in-house criticisms which, in this case, upset the much respected George Devine, Olivier wrote him a shrewd character assessment: 'I like having you with me, apart from it rather tickling me to have you with me, but you can be too fucking tactless for words. It may be that such criticism as you received when you were young did not hurt you much or it may be that you've had so much of your own back since that it has all got obliterated.' Tynan saw Olivier as 'complex, moody and turbulent. Deep in his temperament there runs a vein of rage that his affable public mask cannot wholly conceal,' he noted for his own edification. 'The volcano remains active, the eruption forever imminent.' Two such volatile and complex people harnessed together, both easily triggered into impulsive action, promised stormy passages ahead.

Kenneth Peacock Tynan had carved himself a remarkable career by the sheer application of his wits, his cheek and his flamboyant personality. From an obscure start as the illegitimate son of a provincial lord mayor, he made his way from a Birmingham suburban background, via Oxford – where he made himself the best-known undergraduate of his generation mainly by relentless showing-off – to the position of the most eagerly-read theatre critic since James Agate, to whom he had written fan letters as a schoolboy. Though his own early attempts at acting had been ill-starred (he had appeared in Alec Guinness's unsuccessful *Hamlet* as the First Player), he had an instinctive appreciation of good acting in others. His theatre notices can still bring back performances of thirty and forty years ago and make them live afresh in the reader's imagination, although they were adorned with unnecessary quotations from remote authors or obscure works, to reflect credit on his own wide reading. His weaknesses were vanity, calculated exoticism, excessive hero-worship and a compulsion to *épater les bourgeois*, which seemed to inspire his socialism. He was also an omnivorous glamour-hunter, consuming much energy in adding to his oddly mixed bag of celebrity acquaintances: movie stars like Orson Welles, a bullfighter, Antonio Ordoñez, comedians like Danny Kaye, cabaret performers like Marlene Dietrich and, in latter days, Noël Coward. All of their various talents, one felt, were as important to him as Laurence Olivier or the playwright he championed *ad nauseam*, Bertolt Brecht. To his credit was his enormous fund of enthusiasm, his determination to transcend the narrow, parochial outlook of English culture, and his long and ardent campaigns to abolish stage censorship, to encourage state subsidy and to shame the English into getting their long-proposed national theatre actually built. In 1956 he castigated the inaction: 'Must it again be urged that Britain is the only European country which lacks a national theatre? And that the public money which gave us a visual library, the National Gallery, is needed to provide a living library of plays?' In joining Olivier, he too was fulfilling one of his dearest ambitions.

Olivier's first choice for the man to be his second in command was an irony in view of what happened later: Peter Hall. While they were working together at Stratford in 1959, on the production of *Coriolanus* in which Olivier was directed by Hall, he confided in Hall that he had been approached (by Lord Chandos) to run the future National Theatre: would Hall be his Number Two? Hall, who was to run the Stratford Memorial Theatre with a new permanent company (soon to become the Royal Shakespeare Company) the following year, not surprisingly turned down this vague offer: 'Sorry, Larry, I'm immensely flattered but I'm going to make it on my own as Number One.' Olivier also asked George Devine, Director of the Royal Court Theatre and of the English Stage Company. Like Hall, he was unwilling to serve as Number Two and was too wedded to his own enterprise to leave it. But the Royal Court connection profoundly influenced Olivier when he set about recruiting his team that summer. If he could not have George Devine, he would have two of his right-hand men, directors William Gaskill and John Dexter. The first was an earnest and pale graduate to the theatre from Shipley in Yorkshire and Oxford, the second from an industrial background in Derby. 'George Devine had opened the way for me and I knew he wouldn't mind if I purloined some of his best talents for my new enterprise,' wrote Olivier.

'It was a bright idea of his to get both of us as the two of us were very close and wanted to go on working together,' Gaskill remembered. 'Those early days were very exciting and enjoyable. We felt we could do anything, we could have any actors we wanted, there were no bounds to what could be done.' Gaskill had first made his name by directing the absurdist plays of N. F. Simpson and *Epitaph for George Dillon*, a play by John Osborne and Anthony Creighton. He was a committed disciple of Bertolt Brecht. Dexter had devoted much of his time to producing a series of plays by Arnold Wesker. Both of them had shared Devine's objective of making the Court a writer's theatre in which the staging centred on the play with no distracting decorative flourishes.

Olivier surprised and hurt his old friends and associates in the profession by ignoring them when he recruited his first company. 'He wanted to make a completely clean sweep of the actors who were in his life before,' said John Dexter. 'He wanted a new team.' This chimed in neatly with the ideas of Dexter and Gaskill, who naturally wanted to bring with them some of the actors they had worked with successfully at

6

the Court: chief among them in the first year were Colin Blakely, Frank Finlay, Robert Stephens and Joan Plowright, to be followed the next season by Albert Finney. They were examples of the new type of player whom Olivier was anxious to identify with his new company. 'The Royal Court had produced a new breed of actors and directors,' he wrote. 'Most of them were part of the influx of regional talent in the 1960s. They had a reality, inventiveness and spontaneity which brought richness and variety to the stage. They made the sort of company I had round me at the St James's look a wee bit old-fashioned.'

It was not enough to produce a miniature version of the Royal Court company. He spread his net a good deal wider. He recruited the veteran Max Adrian, for example, with the none-too-respectful invitation, 'We need some old character tats like you.' And he invited Michael Redgrave to stay on, to play not merely Uncle Vanya but a range of leading roles. Maggie Smith, whose reputation was then that of the most promising light comedienne in the West End, was recruited because Gaskill insisted that he could not do Restoration comedy without her. The three directors ranged the country looking for young actors of promise who would start as walk-ons and perhaps develop into featured players. On a visit to a matinée at Birmingham Rep Olivier spotted Derek Jacobi. Auditions yielded Michael Gambon, who had carried a spear on tours of Ireland with Michael MacLiammoir. At twenty-three Gambon was, he says, so unaware of theatrical history that he saw nothing presumptuous in doing as his audition piece the opening soliloquy of *Richard III* with which Olivier had hypnotized audiences of the wartime Old Vic company in 1944–5. During the speech he flung out a hand and cut it on the edge of some scenery, finishing with blood leaking from the injury. Olivier sent him away to be bandaged and offered him work. Other young actors taken on as walk-ons included Anthony Hopkins, Edward Petherbridge and Michael York. The money offered was meagre, a basic £14 a week plus £1 per performance. Salaries were not princely at any level. John Dexter worked as one of the ruling triumvirate for £60 a week. Ken Tynan earned an average of £46 a week for ten years as Literary Manager. Olivier himself had taken a voluntary cut to £60 a week at Chichester and received about double that amount as full-time Director of the National Theatre. This was at a time when in commercial theatre work (not films) he could command £400–£500 a week.

Nor were offices on a scale that might be expected of a national institution. They consisted of a row of site-contractors' huts of wooden weatherboarding erected down the centre of Aquinas St – more an alley than a street – some ten minutes' walk from the Old Vic Theatre itself. The surroundings still resembled a wartime bomb-site – there were nettles, brambles, rubble and wild cats, which found their way under the wooden flooring. At one end of 'the huts' was a large, cold rehearsal room, then a row of cramped offices, opening off a central corridor which ended in the 'Boardroom'. The partition walls were far from sound-proof. 'You couldn't have a private conversation,' Dexter recalled. 'We would wander into each other's offices and make constant contact. You could casually take the pulse of the place. As a working atmosphere, it was perfect.' It was too cold in winter, too hot in summer and leaked in the rain. It was impossible to find without a good deal of practice. A guide was provided for important visitors arriving at the theatre for the ten-minute trek through the urban jungle of Waterloo with its street urchins and meths drinkers. In retrospect these spartan surroundings have acquired fond, romantic associations of cheerfulness in adversity, as in war. John Mortimer saw the scene in terms of Agincourt with Olivier 'stalking the prefabs' on the eve of battle. To Kenneth Tynan the frequent emergencies resembled an RAF station. 'One has the sense of participating in the theatrical equivalent of the Battle of Britain,' he noted with pleasure at the time. To Jonathan Miller, the huts were like a Royal Navy shore barracks where Olivier acted like the captain of the ship. 'He loved the thunder of feet on the companionway. He was always speaking down the tube . . .' People now remember not the cold, cramped inconvenience but the camaraderie and the wild blackberries, which ripened outside the windows and were collected gratefully by the homegoing staff. It was humble but it was home.

When the artistic directorate met, it seemed a matter of little difficulty to choose the repertoire for the first season. 'We settled most of the plays between the soup and the savoury at lunch at the Queen's Restaurant,' said Dexter. Among them were *The Recruiting Officer*, *Hobson's Choice*, *Othello* and *The Master Builder*. To these were added the Chichester productions of *Uncle Vanya* and *St Joan*. To open the theatre, the obvious choice was *Hamlet*. Olivier said he was going to do the first production himself. 'No one's going to like it – they never do,' he said. The casting of Peter O'Toole as the Prince went down badly with Olivier's colleagues, Dexter and Gaskill, who opposed the whole idea of engaging star performers. O'Toole's reputation mainly rested on the film role of Lawrence of Arabia. He was due to make another film almost immediately, so there was no question of him staying on. It was, among other things, window-dressing to guarantee opening publicity. The cast surrounding him was extremely strong, although at the time some were not yet well-known names – such as the Horatio (Robert Stephens), Laertes (Derek Jacobi), Fortinbras (John Stride), and First Gravedigger (Frank Finlay). Among the Elsinore sentries was a

23-year-old Michael Gambon. The first rehearsal was called at the huts in Aquinas St where champagne was served. Gambon arrived two hours early, wearing a very expensive pair of suede shoes from Bond Street to give him confidence. Peter O'Toole arrived 'looking like a god with bright blonde hair'. Olivier was in his usual double-breasted business suit and boardroom spectacles. 'I was completely overawed,' said Gambon. 'We all felt that we were part of something big. There was a great deal of kudos in just being there . . . What I mainly remember of the season is fear and the thrilling presence of Olivier. There was competition between the spear-carriers. We would try to time our walks along the theatre corridors to coincide with his.'

The Old Vic had had its roof destroyed during the wartime bombing. It had been re-opened in 1950 for some notable Shakespeare seasons. Now the gilt gave way to grey, reminiscent of the austerities of the Royal Court. There was a new proscenium, a new electrically-operated front curtain and a new forestage, projecting into and rather spoiling the auditorium. The alterations caused miserable conditions for rehearsals on stage. 'The whole place was still littered with rubble and there was a bloody enormous hole in one wall which allowed the wind to blow straight in from Waterloo Road,' Max Adrian, who played Polonius, remembered. 'To add to the problems we had a very complicated, overpowering set by Sean Kenny, a delightful Irishman. I said to him after falling over bits of the set for the hundredth time, "I suppose this is your revenge on the English." '

Sean Kenny was the fashionable stage designer of the day, who had made his name at Joan Littlewood's Theatre Workshop. His hallmark was the use of complex wood and metal structures, which sometimes took over the production, as was the case here. A curved metal ramp steeply raked up to a bridge to suggest a very schematic Elsinore was set on a revolve which sometimes gave up revolving under its weight and had to be pushed round by the actors hidden behind it. 'The whole stage was taken up by a massive spiral rock which writhed about and groaned between scenes, shutters opening and closing and sections twisting upon other sections, simply to make the great lump look different,' wrote the *Scotsman* critic, Ronald Mavor. 'After each seismic convulsion a little bit of the play would appear, only to be stopped by another one.' Olivier spent the run of the production wearing evening dress so that he could go before the curtain when necessary to ask for the audience's patience between of technical problems or delays. The new electric motor for the curtain also misbehaved. Olivier would discard his dinner jacket and go up to the fly gallery to help the flymen wind up the tabs by hand.

With all these technical worries it is not surprising that the run-up to the opening was unusually fraught. O'Toole was living up to his wild reputation by larking about, on stage and off, and took little notice of Olivier's direction. 'He shambled about at rehearsals, smoking a cigarette and telling jokes,' according to his Horatio, Robert Stephens. 'He was as thin as a stick insect and Hamlet demands enormous energy.' O'Toole showed no lack of energy in his duel with Laertes, however. 'I had to fight for my life every night because he wouldn't stick to what we had rehearsed,' Derek Jacobi recalled. 'If he gave me a wink, and he usually did, this wild Irishman, it meant a very hard fight. It was dangerous. It was even dangerous to be sitting in the front row when he flashed out his sword like Douglas Fairbanks.' Nevertheless O'Toole called the first night 'the most humbling, humiliating experience of my life. As I went on I suddenly knew it was not going to be any good.'

Another unhappy member of the company was Michael Redgrave, playing Claudius. He was upset when Olivier, giving the cast notes, said to him in front of the rest, 'When you played Macbeth you strode on and looked as though you were saying "Fuck you, I *am* Macbeth." When you come on now you look as though you're apologizing to the audience. As Claudius you are dim.' For Redgrave it was to be a season spent in terror of losing his memory. 'For the first time I was appalled at the thought of going on stage. I used to dread the car coming to take me to the theatre,' he told me. 'I didn't enjoy playing the King in Larry's, I thought, ghastly production – but I still think I could have made a good King.' Later on he wrote: 'I remember only a great feeling of tiredness. I frequently caught myself fixedly staring at the same object. I began to think that I was ill.' Long afterwards he realized that his agitation was a symptom of the onset of Parkinson's disease.

So on 22 October 1963 the National Theatre was at last born. In spite of the foreboding, the curtain went up and down smoothly, the revolve did not stick, the duel caused no injury and the response was – if not wildly enthusiastic – politely encouraging. The reviews were respectful, dutifully praising the company as having passed a test-piece, welcoming its existence rather than its achievement. Nobody said it was dull but nobody was overpowered by the interpretation. Olivier was heard to observe that it was about the worst production he had ever done and now they must get down to some serious work. After a mere twenty-seven performances, O'Toole departed to film Conrad's *Lord Jim* and that was that. It was a *Hamlet* seen by few. It left its mark in theatrical history purely because of what it signified, that after 115 years of fruitless discussion, Britain had a national theatre open for business.

The tortuous history of the campaign to bring this to pass is described in other places and a resumé must suffice here. The idea had been mooted as long ago as 1848 in a tract by Effingham Wilson, a London publisher. It had been advocated by people as different in temperament as Matthew Arnold, whose reaction to a visit by the Comédie Française in 1880 was to demand a Comédie Anglaise, and Winston Churchill who demanded in a speech in 1906: 'Think with what excitement and interest this people witnesses the construction of a Dreadnought – what a pity it is that some measure of that interest cannot be turned in the direction of launching a National Theatre!' That was the year in which the actor-playwright Harley Granville-Barker and the critic William Archer were collaborating on their 'Scheme for a National Theatre', which was published in 1907 and attracted the support of many public figures, most notably Bernard Shaw. Money was raised and plans laid for making the Shakespeare tercentenary in 1916 the occasion for its foundation, but the First World War killed that idea. In 1930 Granville-Barker published revised estimates and his prescription for a national theatre and in 1937 money was found to buy a site opposite the Victoria and Albert museum in South Kensington. Bernard Shaw took symbolic possession of it, Sir Edwin Lutyens prepared designs, but once again war swept all the plans away.

By the end of the war, however, the Old Vic company under the joint direction of Olivier, Ralph Richardson and John Burrell had become so pre-eminent in their seasons at the New Theatre (the Old Vic itself being bombed) that for a time there was a lively expectation that the company would be declared a national company and a home built worthy of it. Lord Esher, who became Chairman of the Old Vic governors in 1948, persuaded the Labour Chancellor of the Exchequer, Sir Stafford Cripps, to authorize £1 million of public funds to enable a national theatre to be built, and in 1949 the National Theatre Bill was passed by Parliament, without a vote, authorizing the money. The site now designated was on the South Bank, most of which had been reduced to still-vacant bomb-sites. That year Olivier, Richardson and Burrell left the Old Vic company. Thinking actors too unbusinesslike and unreliable as heads of a national institution (and too liable to leave the helm in order to go off and act elsewhere), Lord Esher had sacked them and appointed a permanent administrator, Llewellyn Rees of the newly-formed Arts Council, in their place. It was an astonishing decision. Olivier's reaction on receiving Esher's cable the previous year, dismissing him in the middle of a hugely successful tour of Australia with the company, was to become hysterical with laughter. He cabled back: 'I feel like a pioneer disowned by his countrymen in the midst of a very distant campaign.' If Olivier and Richardson were not the right sort of men to run a national theatre which, said Lord Esher, 'cannot be administered by men, however able, who have other calls on their time and talent', the Old Vic governors soon fell prey to squabbling factions and did not look the right sort of organization to run a national theatre either. When a theatre producer, Stephen Mitchell, complained of their theatrical inexperience in the *Daily Telegraph* – 'It is disturbing that people so little qualified should be responsible for our highest artistic endeavours' – Lord Esher replied from a dizzy height that the governors 'are chosen of set purpose outside the profession, on the principle that independent and intelligent minds, free from both profit and prejudice, should control public enterprise'.

It was soon clear that their minds were also free of any practical grasp of how to bring a national theatre into being. After much high-minded and amateur bungling, the project was put back in the drawer. Queen Elizabeth, in 1951, the last year of her husband George VI's reign, had laid the foundation stone on the South Bank, then being revived as the site of the Festival of Britain and the new Royal Festival Hall. But 1951 also saw the demise of the Labour Government which had passed the Act. Winston Churchill, who had been so enthusiastic about the launching of this theatrical dreadnought in 1906, became a peacetime prime minister and did absolutely nothing to get it any further down the slipway. Probably he had forgotten all about it. Throughout the fifties the inaction was prodded by Tynan in articles in *The Observer* and, in a suitably theatrical gesture, by standing in top hat and black mourning bands beside the now much-moved foundation stone on the South Bank, which seemed to be in no danger of being joined by a building.

The Joint Council of the National Theatre and the Old Vic, consisting for practical purposes of Oliver Lyttleton, now Lord Chandos, and the same Lord Esher who had so loftily dispensed with Olivier's services at the Old Vic in 1949, invited him to become a National Theatre trustee. A proposed amalgamation with the Shakespeare Memorial Theatre company was half-heartedly pursued in 1961. The Joint Council submitted some rather vague plans for a National Theatre company divided into four groups – at a theatre yet to be built, at Stratford, at the Old Vic and on tour. Then the bombshell fell: the Government, in the person of the Chancellor of the Exchequer, Selwyn Lloyd, suddenly announced in March that it had decided there would be no national theatre. It was not prepared to spend the million pounds authorized by the National Theatre Act after all. Instead, it would provide £400,000 a year as subsidy to the regional theatres, notably the one at Stratford-on-Avon. At this point it looked as though the Royal Shakespeare Company had decisively stolen a march on the national theatre campaigners. It had already established its London base at the Aldwych and got itself a royal charter. It was acting as if it were *de facto* a national theatre company. And now it had promises of state subsidy. Nobody really believed that the Government would subsidize two major companies both playing the classics on either side of Waterloo Bridge. Peter Hall was campaigning strenuously for a subsidy of £124,000 – an enormous figure – by threatening to close down if it was not granted. On his side, Olivier could see what a threat the RSC's London operation posed to hopes of getting a government grant for a national theatre.

The national theatre lobby, which appeared to have lost to Stratford, then swung the battle in its own favour by a sudden alliance with the then London County Council, led by the Socialist Isaac Hayward. Selwyn Lloyd was told that if the Government gave its million pounds, the LCC would give a million too – indeed it would give more, £1,300,000, the product of a penny rate – to help build a national theatre. Selwyn Lloyd changed his tune and suggested that there should be a larger scheme to build a national theatre *and* opera house (as a new home for the Sadler's Wells Company), to which the Government's £400,000 a year subsidy would be devoted. Suddenly Stratford was out in the cold again, except as part of the proposed national theatre.

Stratford's reaction to this was to pull out of the scheme and out of the Joint Council in January 1962. It saw its autonomy threatened with extinction. Peter Hall was not anxious to be subordinate to Laurence Olivier, nor was the RSC prepared to accept the role of the National Theatre's second team. The rivalry for supremacy between the two institutions which was engendered then was to endure, like a lingering illness that flares up at times of crisis, during subsequent years. From this time onwards there was little love lost between Olivier and Hall. During the well-orchestrated public campaign to get a subsidy for the RSC (without which it could not continue in London) Olivier remained conspicuously silent, a silence which was interpreted to mean that he would not be sorry if the RSC had to withdraw from the Aldwych. The high point of confrontation was reached in October 1962, when Olivier, on a visit to Stratford, suggested that for three months of the year the future National Theatre should open its doors and auditorium to the RSC so that it could perform there. Was this the generous offer of a toehold for the RSC in London, in the event of its being refused a grant, as Olivier maintained? Or a devious plot to make sure that the RSC's existing competition in London was closed down, as the RSC's chairman, Sir Fordham Flower, believed?

It is impossible to know what was actually said at the disputed meeting. What followed closely upon it was the announcement by the Chairman of the Arts Council, Lord Cottesloe, that the RSC would receive a subsidy of £47,000 for the following year, 1963–4, with a warning: if the RSC chose to operate on a 'National Theatre level', that was no guarantee that it would be subsidized at that level. The National Theatre's first subsidy, for the same year, turned out to be £130,000 from the Arts Council, plus another £100,000 from the London County Council. The total was almost five times as large as the RSC's, and it was to run one theatre, not two. The pecking order, in the eyes of the authorities, had been spelt out.

Artistically speaking, however, the Royal Shakespeare Company was going to be hard to beat. When the National opened with its less than triumphant *Hamlet* in 1963, the Stratford company had just made theatrical history with its trilogy, *The Wars of the Roses*, which was being hailed as the pinnacle of Peter Hall's achievement so far. It was to be staged at the Aldwych in 1964, the 400th anniversary of the birth of Shakespeare. At Stratford the RSC were about to go one better to mark the quartercentenary of their house dramatist: the complete cycle of history plays from *Richard II* to *Richard III* was to be mounted for the first time. Meanwhile the first World Theatre Season was announced at their London home, bringing leading companies from all over the world to the Aldwych. The RSC's reputation for excellence was worldwide because of its tours in Europe and America. With it went a reputation for doing plays of political controversy and provocation, especially the *Marat-Sade* by Peter Weiss, directed by Peter Brook.

Olivier and his co-directors had cause to worry that their rivals were looking more like a national theatre than the real thing did. For 1964 they had to pull out something special. Olivier reluctantly nerved himself to undertake a part which he had always avoided and which Tynan had been urging on him since they joined forces: the title-role in *Othello*.

1964–7: Scaling the Andes

Of the five great Shakespearean tragic heroes, Hamlet, Macbeth, Antony, Lear and Othello, Olivier had come last to 'the black one'. Anthony Quayle, he said, had warned him against it. 'The most difficult ones to bear are the ones who complain all the time. How many ways are there of saying, Oh! Oh!? Othello is all of that and you have to black up for it as well.' Olivier also remembered playing Iago at the Old Vic in 1938. 'Ralph Richardson's Othello was as boring an Othello as has ever been and I was in like a jackdaw, stealing the goodies . . . It's Iago's piece.'

Most daunting to Olivier's mind was his belief that he had not got the voice for the part. He was known for his high notes rather than low ones. The voice, he said, had to be a 'dark, violet, velvet bass'. He decided to get to the rehearsal room beside his office in the huts early in the morning and lower his voice by roaring like a bull when no one was there to hear. He went to the gym to build up his physique and jogged along the seafront at Brighton. He began preparations six months before the opening date, set for Shakespeare's 400th anniversary, 23 April 1964. Being Olivier, his first concern was to work out the appearance and the walk and movement of his character. He would have none of the 'coffee-coloured compromise' of a North African Moor. 'I hope you agree with me that he's black?' he said to John Dexter, who was directing him. 'If Shakespeare had meant brown he would have said so.' He wanted to walk 'like a soft, black leopard' but it was only when he was barefoot and put his whole weight on each foot in turn that he found a lithe, lilting walk with swaying hips that satisfied him. For the character of the man who believes, incredibly, that he is 'not easily jealous', he found the key in his narcissism: 'He is the greatest exponent of self-deception there has ever been.'

Olivier stunned his director, Dexter, and the rest of the cast when they met for the first read-through. Normally, actors do not attempt any sort of performance at a read-through: they stumble along almost as if wishing to demonstrate that they are not yet trying for any kind of characterization. 'Into this polite gathering Olivier tossed a hand-grenade,' noted Tynan. 'He delivered the works – a fantastic, full-volume display that scorched one's ears . . . seated, bespectacled and lounge-suited he fell on the text like a tiger . . . We were learning what it meant to be faced with a great classical actor in full spate.' And the voice which Olivier had produced had deepened its compass by several notes, almost an octave. He himself thought he embarrassed his fellow-players by ranting and raving in the rehearsals, deliberately trying out extravagant effects, not caring that he went well over the top at times. 'It saves a hell of a lot of time,' he explained in retrospect. 'Often by mistake you stumble on something, an accident happens, and there it is . . . the man you want. That's him.'

Olivier's first entrances were often the most calculated moments of his performance. As Richard III he came on upstage at the back of the set, unlatched a gate and advanced in almost leisurely fashion upon the audience. It seemed minutes before he spoke and before he did, his walk, his mien, the mischief darting from his eyes over the long nose, had already signalled what sort of a man he was. By the time he said, quite lightly, 'Now is the winter of our discontent . . .' all were transfixed by his spell. As Othello, he sauntered on in bare feet and white robe, privately preoccupied, toying with a rose, fingering its long stem, full of self-confidence and high sexual voltage. His eyes rolled upwards, revealing their glistening whites with a tiny shock, and his thin moustache curved proudly downwards. His voice rolled out with thickened consonants and deep-throated long vowels between lips the colour of blueberries. His face and hands glistened like the broad gold necklace with its primitive crucifix that he would later tear off and hurl away. He gave off, as with his Richard, the sensation of acute danger. It built up during the play to actual fear as he turned into a more and more destructive primitive force: breaking down his façade of nobility to reveal a naked beast out of control, to the alarm of his two successive Desdemonas, Maggie Smith and Billie Whitelaw. 'It was like being on stage with a Force Ten gale,' said Whitelaw.

Most critics and audiences responded to Olivier's elemental powers unreservedly. 'It's an anthology of everything that has been discovered about acting in the last three centuries,' declared Franco Zeffirelli. 'It seemed to set the seal on his career and guaranteed his place with Garrick, Kean and Irving,' wrote Richard Findlater. But this was by no means a unanimous opinion. There was heated controversy about the Negro interpretation. Was it a caricature both of blackness and of Shakespeare's intentions? There was also the deliberately chosen imbalance with Iago. By casting Frank Finlay, a growing actor but one whose only previous experience in Shakespeare was as First Grave-digger, Olivier had made sure that his Iago would not walk away with the play (Iago is the longer part) as he once had done. 'I wanted an honest-to-God NCO,' he said. There was none of the finely balanced rapport that Olivier had achieved in *Uncle Vanya* with Michael Redgrave. It was this sort of consideration that led John Osborne to describe his performance as 'unspeakably vulgar' and to say 'he is the only actor who would have the courage to do something dreadful like his Othello, once he had made up his mind'. Tony Richardson called it a 'degrading image of a NEGRO in capital letters' and Sybil Thorndike thought he missed the deep agony in the part. 'I don't think he can ever do agony.'

This was also what was said by some of those who found that the performance failed to live up to their expectations. It was always a technical *tour de force*. But, on some occasions, some people found it unmoving. 'Sir Laurence can move every muscle at will – I regret he could not move me,' wrote the *Sunday Telegraph* critic, Alan Brien. It is possible that his preparation had been, like his two-and-a-half-hour make-up, so thorough and elaborately worked out that he sometimes turned in an exhibition piece. It was by any comparison an exhausting physical feat. As he admitted, 'I really felt I was useless in the office the next day – as if I'd been run over by a bus.' No doubt there were days when he could not, as Sybil Thorndike said, 'do agony' as well.

Everyone wanted to see it, so he became the prisoner of the role, with little prospect of being able to bring the production to an end. It was doing wonders for the National Theatre's box office and for its prestige. A ticket became the most difficult piece of paper to get hold of in Britain. There were all-night queues round the theatre for returned or unreserved seats. Distinguished foreign visitors were turned away. Leading actors appearing in West End shows wrote to ask Olivier to give a special matinée performance so that they could see him. In the first season he gave three performances a week, in the second he limited it to two. Attendances rose in the National's second season, with *Othello* in the repertoire throughout, to 96 per cent of seats sold. The capacity of the Old Vic, 878 seats, seemed quite inadequate. In 1965 the production was filmed in three weeks in a studio, almost exactly as played. Immediately afterwards it was toured to Moscow and was met with fifteen minutes of applause. In Berlin the clapping went on for thirty-five minutes.

Six months into the run, Olivier began to get the first attacks of the stage fright that was to dog him for five years with the fear of not being able to remember his lines. Curiously, it first struck him when playing

Ibsen's Solness, in *The Master Builder*, a role he had taken over from Michael Redgrave because he was smitten with the same fear and had left the company. But it spread from that role to others, including Othello. He confided to Robert Stephens, 'All my life I have known I could stand on a stage and command an audience, but now I am starting to dry. I'm frightened my memory will go in other parts.' Othello was withdrawn from the repertoire after two and a half years. This master of the soliloquy could not bear to be left alone on stage. He begged Finlay to stay in the wings where he could see him. 'Without warning this seventeen-year-old's stage fright would seize hold of me,' Olivier said later, 'The audience went round and round. It was a dreadful thing to happen to a chap of sixty.'

While *Othello* was drawing the town, Olivier, urged on by Tynan, was eager to repay a debt to Noël Coward by promoting his work to its rightful place among the modern English classics: he invited him to direct *Hay Fever*, the comedy which Coward, as a very new playwright, had written in three days in 1925. Olivier owed a great deal to Coward, who had cast him in the first (1930) production of *Private Lives*, and looked on him as his mentor – the man who had cured him of giggling on stage and 'the first man who took hold of me and made me use my silly little brain and made me read'. Since the war, Coward's plays and musicals had failed regularly and he had turned himself into a cabaret entertainer. The tide of unfashionableness had just begun to turn. *Private Lives* had been successfully revived in the West End and the word 'classic' had been applied to it. Now, seeing Tynan in a Mayfair street, Coward responded to the National's invitation by leaning out of the window of his Rolls-Royce and saying, 'Bless you for admitting that I'm a classic. I thought you were going to do nothing but Brecht, Brecht, Brecht.' In September he invited Edith Evans, who was to play Judith Bliss, to his home in Switzerland to read through the play with him. He thought her 'perfectly brilliant. To have a really great actress to work with will be thrilling. She may be tiresome (particularly with other actors) but she will deliver the goods – and what goods! Perfect timing and every comedy implication in its place. The fact that she is – in years – too old for the part could not matter less.' Dame Edith was, in fact, seventy-six.

Never one to underestimate his deserts, Coward prefaced rehearsals in London with an uncharacteristic touch of modesty and well-turned flattery: 'I'm thrilled and flattered and frankly a little flabbergasted that the National Theatre should have had the perceptiveness to choose a very early play of mine and to give it a cast that could play the Albanian telephone directory.' The Bliss family led by Dame Edith consisted of Louise Purnell, Anthony Nicholls and Derek Jacobi, while their hapless guests were played by Maggie Smith, Robert Stephens, Lynn Redgrave and Robert Lang. Rehearsals went like a breeze. October came, with a Manchester opening booked for the last week of it. By now Dame Edith was 'floundering' over her words. If only she had learned them before rehearsals began, Coward reflected crossly. She was no longer described in his diary as 'a great actress' but as a 'stubborn old mule'. But he still took her difficulties with a light touch. When she persisted in misreading one of her lines as 'On a *very* clear day you can see Marlow' Coward, after many patient corrections, snapped: 'Edith, the line is "On a clear day you can see Marlow". On a *very* clear day you can see Marlowe *and* Beaumont *and* Fletcher.'

Things got worse, not better. 'She never really knew the part,' Robert Stephens recalled. 'She came in one morning and talked complete rubbish. "I knew it backwards last night," she moaned. "And you're doing it backwards this morning," was Coward's reply.' She found endless fault with the sofa she sat on and demanded alterations. Diana Boddington, the stage manager at the Old Vic, remembered, 'At one point they were all on their knees, Larry and Noël and the designer, cutting bits out of it with scissors at her orders.'

The crisis struck on the Sunday of the dress rehearsal at the Opera House, Manchester. Dame Edith travelled up on the train with her old friend, Gwen Ffrangcon-Davies. En route she worried more and more about her lines, especially the line 'Anyone would think I was eighty, the way you're treating me.' She knew she was indeed nearing eighty. She was clearly too old to say it. Miss Ffrangcon-Davies was despatched to break the news that Dame Edith would not play the dress rehearsal: she would not be playing all week. When Coward was told the news in his hotel suite he adopted stern methods. 'We decided to give the Dame hell. I went upstairs and told her she was a disgrace to herself, the theatre and Christian Science,' he wrote afterwards in his diary. 'He said that he shook her like a rat and told her that she had got to get on that stage or she would never go on a stage again,' said Robert Stephens. The dress rehearsal was funereal, according to Coward. After it was over, Coward told her she could go back to the hotel and the play was run through again with Maggie Smith, who had understudied the part. When Olivier arrived in Manchester to see the first night, Coward greeted him with: 'Larry, boy, you've got to fire Edith tonight.' After seeing her performance in which she was 'fluffing about quite lost and at random', Olivier went round to the dressing-room to bluster it out with her. Beside her make-up tray he noted a pair of eyelashes, unworn. 'Why didn't you wear these?' he demanded. 'Well, dear, I didn't want to think of it as a performance!' was the Dame's extraordinary reply. Olivier gave her until the Thursday to improve. By that time she had

19

gained a grip on her part, but he was losing his on the part of Solness in *The Master Builder*, from which the similarly afflicted Michael Redgrave had withdrawn. It seemed ironic that three of the most illustrious and experienced English actors of the century, Edith Evans, Laurence Olivier and Michael Redgrave, should all be struck down at the same time by the same fear-provoking loss of memory, which was largely, no doubt, due to age.

The play opened at the Old Vic the following week, to rave notices. The box office was besieged. Dame Edith soon perked up after the first night was over. 'With vague swoopings and cooings she dives from sofa to piano like a huge cuckoo,' wrote Ronald Bryden in *The Observer*. Initially the other performances had helped to save the day, notably Maggie Smith's glacially cool flapper, twirling her long bead necklace and outsize cigarette holder. Years later, gazing at a blown-up photograph of the late Edith Evans on the wall, I remarked to Noël Coward: 'There's Dame Edith in the period when she could still remember her lines.' Coward's reaction was unforgiving: 'There never was such a period,' he snapped.

During its second season the National presented its first new play by an English author, Peter Shaffer's *The Royal Hunt of the Sun*, the story of the conquest of the Incas by a mere 167 Spanish soldiers led by Pizarro. Shaffer wrote it out of a desire to re-create epic theatre in England. It had been rejected by the commercial theatre impresario, Binkie Beaumont, to whom it was submitted first, largely because of the stage direction, 'The soldiers now climb the Andes'. John Dexter picked it out from a pile of scripts lying on Olivier's desk. He was looking for a play to show off the company in an experimental fashion and he had found it. It required not only the ascent of the Andes but the slaughter of several thousand Incas and the plundering of untold amounts of gold, as well as the ritual killing of the Inca king, Atahualpa, the sun-god's divine and supposedly immortal representative on earth. All this was to be brilliantly executed in a series of intensely dramatic *tableaux vivants*. The combination of Dexter's direction, the set and costumes by Michael Annals and the music of Marc Wilkinson created an experience of total theatre which was unforgettable to those who were susceptible to it (not everyone was). A huge metal medallion hanging on the back wall opened outwards into petals to form a golden sun with the Inca, sovereign of Peru, masked, crowned and dressed in gold in its centre. In a virtuoso performance, Robert Stephens developed a high-pitched voice and consonantal delivery which was eerily effective for a man who believed he was a god. Claude Chagrin, the French mime artist, was responsible for the ascent of the Andes (ritual steps set to eerie, cold music made of the whine of musical saws). The slow-motion massacre of waves of Indians culminated in the ejection of a huge blood-red cloth, flooding out over the stage like a river from the centre of the golden sun.

In the final moments of the play, Pizarro, the grizzled, unbelieving general played by Colin Blakely, waits with the body of Atahualpa, whom he has reluctantly allowed to be executed by garotting, for the first rays of the sunrise which the Inca believed would resurrect him. Round them stand Indian priests robed in black and wearing great golden funeral masks, turning their triangular eye-slits expectedly up to the sky, awaiting his resurrection. The audience's dismay as the beam of light failed to stir the Inca's body was audible. People swore afterwards that they had seen the masks change expression from hope to despair.

Robert Lang, as narrator, concluded the play with a bitter epitaph: 'So fell Peru. We gave her greed, hunger and the Cross: three gifts from the civilized life.' It was not an intellectual play – it was mistaken for one by some critics – and its language at times grew pretentious, but it was an unfailingly effective exercise in spectacle and showmanship, which only the National or the RSC had the resources to mount. It was the most popular production, apart from *Othello*, in the National's repertoire for the first five years.

To the disapproval of his co-directors, Gaskill and Dexter, Olivier brought in guest directors from other countries to broaden the scope of his acting company. Franco Zeffirelli, though known primarily as a film director, had amazed Old Vic audiences back in 1960 with a *Romeo and Juliet* that lived and breathed Italy, his elaborate set conjuring up a Verona whose atmosphere could almost be smelt. It seemed logical that he should interpret another of Shakespeare's Italian plays, *Much Ado About Nothing*, which he saw as broad Sicilian comedy set in a fairyland of twinkling lights. He generated a magical carnival atmosphere. His costumes presented the men as gorgeously over-decorated toy soldiers, all moustachios, epaulettes, sashes and stars. His frenzied production served to illustrate the theory that there was no scene that could not be improved by a bit of outrageous clowning. 'Zeffirelli even wanted us to play the church scene and the renunciation of Hero for laughs,' said Robert Stephens, who was Benedick to Maggie Smith's Beatrice, in the first of their many partnerships. The actors demurred at this. In the last days of rehearsal Olivier suggested that all the Sicilians except Beatrice, Benedick, Claudio and Hero should put on ice-cream-seller Italian accents, to match their moustaches. Albert Finney, strapped in a corset, was given a cigar and a Spanish accent as Don Pedro. Frank Finlay as Dogberry appeared to have no neck at all. Hero's disgrace at the altar and Beatrice's line 'Kill Claudio' fitted uneasily into this atmosphere of farce. The shock change of mood that Shakespeare had contrived went for very little. The public crowded in to enjoy Zeffirelli's inventiveness although, as Noël Coward remarked, its enjoyment had little to do with Shakespeare.

The next success was a comedy of quintessentially English manners, Congreve's *Love for Love*, which opened, foolhardily enough, in Moscow on the back of the triumphant reception for *Othello*. The Muscovites watched it in dumbfounded silence: such extravagant Restoration peacocks came from another planet as far as they were concerned. It was a connoisseur's dish. The production by Peter Wood was unerringly cast, down to the servants. On the play's ten gorgeous character studies the National lavished the acting strength of what was then an extraordinarily strong team. Geraldine McEwan, a new addition to the company, was the heartlessly provoking Angelica. Lynn Redgrave, as Miss Prue, seemed the incarnation of the eager but cunning bumpkin with dairymaid thighs whose wooing by Sailor Ben, the rude, seafaring son, showed off Colin Blakely's rolling walk, bovine Hogarthian smile, and attempts to score as a wit, raising a finger to mark what he believed to be another telling stroke of it. It was a measure of the talent available that when he was replaced, it was by Albert Finney, another newcomer. John Stride was the lovesick but manly Valentine and Robert Lang developed the peripheral part of Scandal, the malcontent, into a memorable study of self-wounding cynicism. The older characters were in the safe hands of Joyce Redman, Madge Ryan, Anthony Nicholls and Miles Malleson, chins a-tremble as old Foresight, in the style of which he was past-master. And for the minor part of the ageing lecher, Tattle, why, the company could spare Laurence Olivier, the Olivier of wig, lace and cravat, in contrast to the Olivier who was performing Othello on alternate nights. Peter Wood proved himself a knife-sharp director of affectation-free Restoration comedy, and kept the ensemble balanced despite the fact that Olivier acted with an upper lip wrapped lasciviously over protruding teeth which invested the word 'barbarous' with rubbery lubricity.

Into the atmospheric street scene designed by Lila de Nobili, one entrance was unforgettable – that of Olivier's Tattle climbing backwards out of a lady's bedroom window in the house that overlooked the little square. He slithered down the sloping roof of the pillared bay below, and dropped on to the top of a narrow wall, along which he proceeded to totter on his high Restoration heels before jumping safely into a tall basket chair, where he discovered that his calf-padding was now the wrong way round. It was typical Olivier virtuosity. 'You didn't direct Olivier, you made room for him,' said Wood. 'You could unlock the garage door and give him the key to the car. But you interfered at your peril.' Nevertheless, there were times when the great man had to be, and could be, restrained, both as Tattle and as the swaggering Captain Brazen in *The Recruiting Officer*, directed by William Gaskill in 1963, the first great success that the company mounted. These two productions revolutionized the playing of Restoration comedy. They banished the tradition of face-patches and fans, mincing walks and affected delivery which had passed for Restoration 'style'. Instead the plays emerged as typically English comedies of warmly-observed human nature in real situations. Both productions were hugely popular and gave to the classics the re-thinking that it was part of the function of the National Theatre to give. 'It is a piece of team-work of which people will say, years hence, "But did you see the National's *Love for Love*?" ' I prophesied at the time. It was followed by a lesser piece lovingly restored until it glowed like a Victorian oleograph – Pinero's affectionate study of a company of old-style ham actors, *Trelawny of the Wells*.

Early in 1966 the company was put in the hands of its second foreign director. This was Jacques Charon, veteran actor and director of the Comédie-Française, who was invited to present Feydeau's *A Flea in her Ear*, in an adaptation by John Mortimer. At the Comédie, Feydeau ranks almost with Molière and is presented with as much careful and detailed polish as his meticulous stage directions demand. It was in that spirit that the actors were schooled by Charon. But at what speed! The company attained a dizzying prestissimo in the second act, set in the hotel of assignation, that made English farce look pedestrian. The hectic traffic on the staircase and the revolutions of the bed against the pivoted wall which, at the touch of a button, swung round to substitute the bed from the room next door made one breathless. In the doubled role of the deceived husband and the put-upon night porter at the hotel which he visits to look for his wife, Albert Finney discovered a new comic persona as a victim and executed some brilliant falls. Edward Hardwicke gave one of the funniest performances as the young man deprived of his artificial palate and reduced to incoherence just when he hopes to score a conquest. Geraldine McEwan, who played the suspicious wife who is only visiting the hotel to check up on her husband and is then forced to defend her virtue, remembered the precision with which Jacques Charon moved and placed every character. 'Having little English, he would demonstrate what he wanted and was so funny doing it that I felt I could never match him.'

The company proved their versatility in farce by following Feydeau with *Black Comedy*, a home-grown addition to the repertoire which was partly improvised in rehearsal. Kenneth Tynan commissioned it from Peter Shaffer over a lunch in which Shaffer described a scene in the

Peking Opera which he had seen in which a warrior and a bandit fight a duel in the dark, only the stage is brilliantly lit. 'I said I had long wanted to do a play about a party which begins in darkness and then, when a fuse blows, the stage is flooded with light. Ken dragged me to see Olivier, to whom I protested that I hadn't yet got a play reversing light and darkness. Larry fixed his eye upon me and said "It's going to be brilliant" – and with that he had gone. I went away and got very stuck. They rang me in New York to say the play had already been advertised and there was a big response at the box office. At that point I had two pages of script. I had some very bad days, wondering how to keep the play going and sustain the joke for the required length.'

In the author's initial absence (he was contracted to write a film in America) the cast had been exercised by John Dexter in exploring how people behave and move in pitch darkness. They wore blindfolds. They found that blindness made them crouch. One, Derek Jacobi, would move by patting each outstretched foot on the ground to test it first. Another, Louise Purnell as the cut-glass debutante girlfriend, tottered with her wrists raised in front of her face, pushing against the darkness. It was a comedy of gesture and it owed most of its brilliance to this observation of spontaneous human behaviour in an extreme situation. It was a hit from the start. The first night of its try-out at Chichester (still run as an annexe of the National in its first two seasons) rewarded Peter Shaffer with every comedy-writer's dream experience. The man in the seat in front of him ('a large, egg-shaped person like Edward Lear') fell out of his seat into the aisle, beat the carpet with his fist and began calling out in a weak voice, 'Stop it! Stop it! Oh, please stop it!' 'I cannot remember a more pleasing thing happening to me inside a theatre,' said Shaffer.

By now the National Theatre company was not only established but was reaching a pinnacle, both in standards of acting and production and in popular appeal. The problem was getting in to see it in a theatre that seated 878 people. In an attempt to meet unsatisfied demand the company moved into the West End for a season of ten weeks at the Queen's Theatre with a repertory of *Othello*, *A Flea in her Ear*, *The Royal Hunt of the Sun* and *Black Comedy*. The latter was half of a double bill with Lope de Vega's bewildering and hitherto unperformed play of incest, violence and crucifixion, *A Bond Honoured*, adapted (nobody knew how freely) by John Osborne. Previously, it had been teamed with *Miss Julie*, performed all too briefly by Maggie Smith and Albert Finney.

It was not only London that wanted to see the company. Each year from 1964 onwards it had split into two in order to tour eight or ten cities, including Edinburgh or Glasgow, Cardiff and Belfast, in much bigger theatres. The tours played to 80 or 90 per cent capacity in some cities. In others, such as Manchester, Nottingham, Coventry and Aberdeen, audiences were surprisingly moderate, only about 50 per cent. Bournemouth showed total indifference with houses no more than a third full. Yet it was never a case of substituting understudies for the provinces: the full cast seen at the Old Vic was the cast that toured. It needed longer exposure than this to build a national audience.

At the Old Vic, the National played to 200,000 paying customers, per year. In 1966–7, with the help of the Queen's Theatre, it managed 355 performances, 100 more than the previous year, and the total audience of 287,000 represented an average of 92 per cent of capacity per night. Television productions were being made of *Much Ado About Nothing* and *A Flea in her Ear*. All this was being managed on a budget of £650,000, half of which was earned at the box office and half provided by grants, increased that year to cover an accumulated deficit of £250,000. The actors were hard-worked, although the number of new productions a year was only six. The National had certainly not played safe by relying on star names. Apart from Michael Redgrave, who played a season, there had been only a few brief guest appearances – O'Toole, Edith Evans and Miles Malleson were the most notable. People began to wonder where were Richardson, Gielgud and others. Olivier himself had been sparing with his performances: three leading roles and two minor, if showy parts. In 1967 he undertook (again at Tynan's suggestion) a surprising but shrewdly-chosen new role: Captain Edgar in Strindberg's *The Dance of Death*.

It was certainly the ugliest part he had ever set himself. Physically his Captain was a Prussian with close-cropped hair and moustache, and a choleric red complexion, which grew redder when he had a fit. His character was as unyielding as the kepi he had strapped on over his chin, which jutted aggressively above the tightly-buttoned carapace of his uniform. Strindberg puts arrogance, pomposity and a military coarseness into this failed artillery officer of fifty-six, sometimes coming out in bluff barrack-room humour. But most often he inspires terror and hatred in his wife, herself a failed actress. Yet the more they protest their mutual hatred, the more grimly they hold on to one another. There is a complex bond between them – Olivier put it at '10 per cent love and 90 per cent hate' – and when death does overtake the Captain in the midst of his mean-spirited triumph, Alice, his wife, says brokenly, 'You may laugh – I must have loved that man.' Until that moment Geraldine McEwan, usually the mocking *provocateuse* of comedy, had turned herself into a bitchy, slit-eyed Fury of a wife, delivering her insults with a mirthless smile in a throaty voice. It is a bleak play, and it received a sombre, careful production from Glen Byam Shaw in which Olivier's cruel, malevolent brute left an unforgettable imprint on the memory, not only for his rages but for his sudden, clumsy little mazurka of satanic glee – a dance of deathly mockery.

Many shrewd judges have pronounced it Olivier's finest performance at the National. Robert Stephens, who played the wife's would-be lover, 'mainly in order to be able to watch him construct a great performance', remembered an instance of Olivier's self-criticism and readiness to take advice. Perhaps the Captain's most memorable rage breaks out when he is alone in his own sitting-room having just learned that he is to be disgraced for stealing. He goes to a cupboard, takes out the bottles and throws them out of the window; he tears up his wife's letters, kicks her piano, sees her portrait above it, loads his service revolver and puts six bullets into it. 'He kept saying the scene wasn't right, he didn't feel happy with it,' said Stephens. 'I suggested that if he split it up, the pauses could be made more terrifying than the actions. He took notice of this. He walked slowly to his desk, took out the pistol, and paused. The audience thought he might be going to shoot himself. He terrified them. He toyed with the idea of an ugly make-up, but in the end, when he asked me into his dressing-room to see it, all he had done was to take some tooth-black and paint the marks of decay on his teeth. That was real ugliness.'

Geraldine McEwan was surprised to be offered a part so much outside her previous range. 'He said to me, "You can play comedy and that means you can play anything". Although it is a harrowing play, we both enjoyed ourselves to a surprising degree. We would sit there racked with emotion as the first act curtain fell and yet we would reach the dressing-rooms in fits of laughter.' Curiously enough, Captain Edgar seems not to have caused Olivier the nervous strain of other parts. 'You could see him enjoying himself,' said Robert Stephens. 'He said playing Edgar was easy because it was him.' But then he had once said that of Archie Rice. Olivier, who never stopped acting, could never decide which was the real him.

In 1966, in a church hall on the Fringe of the Edinburgh Festival, the Oxford Theatre Group had presented a very fraught production of a play by an unknown writer entitled *Rosencrantz and Guildenstern are Dead*. The director had left and the stage-manager was trying to keep the show together when the author, a dark, thin, smiling young man of twenty-eight, showed up, took over rehearsals and, after several sleepless nights, got the play open on schedule. The *Observer* critic, Ronald Bryden, wrote the following Sunday: 'It's the most brilliant debut by a young playwright since John Arden's.' On reaching home, Tom Stoppard, the young Czech-born playwright in question, found a telegram from Kenneth Tynan demanding to read the play. This was odd because the script had already been sent to him, and to several other managements that had rejected it. The RSC had taken a year's option but had not produced it. Stoppard was eking out a hack's living writing the diary of an imaginary Arab student in London for broadcasting on the BBC's Arabic Service.

Tynan, now alerted, bought the play and it was performed the following spring as the National Theatre's first venture with an untried new author. It was also a bold departure in play-writing: to use another play (*Hamlet*), which the audience could be assumed to know, as the setting for an alternative view of the action. Rosencrantz and Guildenstern, Elsinore's obliging nonentities, were promoted to the leading roles without being given any more to do than Shakespeare allotted them. They pass their time waiting in the wings, like the two tramps who wait for Godot, to be pitchforked into the violent events that are taking place, incomprehensibly to them, off-stage. Ingenious as this is, it could easily have remained nothing more than ingenious, as some reviewers thought. But it is not by chance that Rosencrantz and Guildenstern pass their time playing games of chance in which chance seems to have stopped operating. The coins they toss come down heads eighty-five times in a row. Is their summons to Elsinore, are their deaths (which they can see coming) a matter of chance or of a prescribed fate? The play can be read as a comment on the predestined fate of characters in plays and as a metaphor for life, in which all human beings find themselves summoned to an Elsinore not of their choosing, and to a death which they cannot avoid. When Rosencrantz and Guildenstern (played by John Stride and Edward Petherbridge) were snuffed out, their resignation was curiously moving.

Tynan's enthusiasm for the witty text was not shared by Olivier, but seldom has a new play by an unknown author been received with such acclaim. The audience exploded, exhilarated by the undeniable smell of discovery, as well as success, as the curtain fell. Tom Stoppard was not there to experience it. 'The play had been on for about five minutes when an elderly man just in front of me said to his neighbour, "I do wish they'd get on with it." My nerve broke. I went to the pub and never came back to the theatre.'

Most of the next morning's notices hailed Stoppard as 'a stunning new playwright' and I declared that the National had pulled off 'its biggest gamble to date – a winner at 66 to 1'. Harold Hobson on the following Sunday called it 'the most important event in the British professional theatre for nine years'. Nine? It was nine years since he had made his celebrated lone discovery of Harold Pinter. The play stayed in the National repertoire for the next four years. It was the first NT production to transfer to Broadway. It was also produced throughout Western Europe and in Japan. Asked in a New York television interview, 'What's it about?' Stoppard replied, 'It's about to make me very rich.' It was. In the next ten years, his agent Kenneth Ewing calculated, it had made him £300,000. The text alone sold 600,000 copies and duly became a set book for English examinations. Stoppard would not go into tax exile. 'Can you become a Swiss subject and go on living in England?' he asked me wryly.

The state of the company by the summer of 1967 could not have been stronger or livelier or more versatile. This was demonstrated during rehearsals of the next production. *The Three Sisters* was strongly cast – Joan Plowright as Masha, Robert Stephens as Vershinin – and Laurence Olivier was directing it himself. A good *Three Sisters* is not a rare achievement on the English stage but this proved to be outstandingly good, ranking not far behind the National's *Uncle Vanya*. And yet, only two weeks into rehearsals, Olivier was told he had cancer of the prostate and had to enter hospital at once to be treated by a new form of radiotherapy. He told Robert Stephens to take over the production and promised to come out of hospital every Friday evening to see a run-through and give notes. This is what happened. Anthony Hopkins took over his role in *The Dance of Death*. ('How was Hopkins?' he would ask visitors. 'Not better than me?') Derek Jacobi took over Tattle in *Love for Love*. *Three Sisters* opened to general admiration, as though he had been present throughout. He left hospital the day afterwards, considerably weakened by the treatment but, as it proved, cured of cancer.

When he looked back at his company towards the end of his life, Olivier reflected: 'They were a company in the true sense of the word. Any one of my team, at any time, could have taken the helm and steered a play into safe harbour. I might have been the father figure but I wasn't so in the Victorian sense of the word: my company did speak and were heard. Look at some of the unknown names of my company and how many are known now . . . I was able to pass to them what had been passed to me.'

The 'unknown' names of those early days would have included Colin Blakely, Graham Crowden, Frank Finlay, Michael Gambon, Edward Hardwicke, Anthony Hopkins, Derek Jacobi, Robert Lang, Jane Lapotaire, Ian McKellen, Edward Petherbridge, Ronald Pickup, Louise Purnell, Lynn Redgrave, Robert Stephens, John Stride, Billie Whitelaw and Michael York. While those began to make their mark, actors already established, such as Joan Plowright, Maggie Smith, Geraldine McEwan and Albert Finney, were extending their range and adding to their stature in leading roles. 'The Old Vic was Mecca to actors,' said Joan Plowright. 'It was an actors' theatre, run by the man they saw as leader of their profession. Every young actor in the country wanted to be there. There was a tremendous sense of dedication, which you do not find now that the theatre is only one of the three media that actors move between.'

By the fourth year the acting strength was eighty-eight. Letters of application poured in and it fell to Michael Hallifax as executive company manager to schedule auditions and oversee casting – but Olivier always gave the final word. 'Sir Laurence never dropped being an actor-manager with his finger in every pie. Every actor who joined the company did the final audition for him. A lot of people came in as walk-ons and understudies who hadn't yet passed the Olivier test. But once he decided somebody had got something, he pushed them as hard as he could. Almost all casting was done within the company. I would go to his office with a visiting director like Zeffirelli and Sir Laurence would say "You ought to try X or Y – I can tell you they're going to be good." And he saw to it that he got his way.' Zeffirelli confirmed this – Olivier suggested Finney for Don Pedro in his *Much Ado*. Despite his film stardom as Tom Jones, he was to earn his passage with the company in this minor role. Michael York was given the part of a waiter. Olivier told Zeffirelli that he was going to let him 'simmer' for a while – that was National Theatre policy. Ian McKellen auditioned for Olivier and Zeffirelli, was given Claudio in *Much Ado* and had his heavy doll-like make-up applied by Zeffirelli himself, sitting on his lap. 'You enter and make all the audience fall right in love with you, caro,' he was told. 'A fat chance of that, I thought,' said McKellen, 'with Finlay, Jacobi and Stephens in all my scenes, let alone Michael York as the glamorous coffee-waiter.' Michael Gambon, having carried his spears, began to get a few small parts. 'After two or three years I went to the guv'nor and asked him if I could have some better ones. He said no. He advised me to go off and get some rep experience. He suggested Birmingham, where he had started. A year after I'd walked on as a messenger in his *Othello*, I was playing the name part and he sent me a good luck telegram. My fellow actors didn't believe it was genuine.'

Those who stayed and were promoted realized that they were the envy of their generation, especially if they got the Olivier accolade of a three-year contract – even though the basic salary could be only £12 a week plus performance fees. 'He was very picky about awarding those,' said Hallifax. According to Robert Lang, 'There were less than a dozen of us on that basis. It might have been only a third of commercial rates, but you had continuity. A lot of good actors outside, who were trying to get in, must have been very annoyed. For those who were inside, it was glorious.'

29

There was a strong family atmosphere in the early days. Olivier, who had three young children, insisted that he and everyone else had a holiday in August, so for three weeks the Old Vic played host to provincial or foreign theatre companies. He knew the names of the least of his actors (though he sometimes needed prompting) and often their children's names. He would ask, 'Have we had any babies lately?' He played Santa Claus at the staff children's Christmas party so realistically that the children were overawed. He prided himself on knowing as much as the stage-hands and fly-men about setting the stage and the jargon they employed. On Saturday afternoons he would watch the football on the television in the crew room. 'As associate director I had to tell people who had problems to come and see him,' said Robert Stephens. 'He was very visible, not only on stage or in the rehearsal room, but in the wardrobe, the wig department, the canteen, where he lunched off an apple, cheese and champagne.' 'He was very paternal and human as a leader,' said Gambon; 'he was also a mine of information about the craft of acting.' He was famous for his advice on how to tackle a tragic part – 'Go for the laughs'. 'I never trust actors who work on emotion; it's out of your control,' was another piece of advice. Olivier said more than once that his goal at the National was to raise the audience's appreciation of acting as an art, 'so that people will come not merely to see the play but to see acting for acting's sake'.

3

1967–70: Battles over Churchill and a Phallus

The question of what a national theatre should be like is a subject on which conflicting views are often violent and irreconcilable. It is wiser not to be dogmatic. So far this book has set out to examine what, in practice, Britain's National Theatre put on when it first opened its doors. Admittedly, only the best of it has been highlighted. Half of the twenty-six productions of the first four seasons were classics, comprising three Shakespeare plays, four other English classics and six foreign ones. Seven new plays (five English and two foreign) and six revivals of twentieth-century plays (four English, two foreign) complemented the classics.

When Harley Granville-Barker published his revised plans for a national theatre in 1930, the categories of play he foresaw being presented were Shakespeare, non-Shakespearean English classics, English plays written in the last fifty years, foreign play revivals, and new plays. These expectations had been fulfilled, though still on a modest scale – Granville-Barker was visualizing two auditoria providing forty or more productions a year. Within the limits of a single theatre and a grant hardly bigger than Granville-Barker had estimated thirty years before, the National Theatre had provided a balanced programme. And its attendances averaged over 90 per cent.

In the early days, Tynan had declared simply, 'Our aim is the best of everything.' But, of course, with only six or seven productions a year, it would be a very long time before the theatre could hope to cover the best of *everything*, 'the whole spectrum of world drama' (another of Tynan's phrases) on the list of 400 best plays in Western literature which he had compiled for guidance. As he pointed out in a lecture, there are two kinds of repertory theatre of distinction. One is the kind founded by a great director or playwright who deliberately creates a style, perhaps a revolutionary one, for his own purpose, such as Molière's Comédie-

Française, Brecht's Berliner Ensemble, Stanislavsky's Moscow Art Theatre, Peter Brook's Bouffes du Nord. The other kind is a theatre which aims to present the widest possible selection of good plays from all periods and countries, as did the National Theatre at the Old Vic. 'House style', such as Brecht dictated, a phrase which was much talked of at Stratford-upon-Avon at that time, was never mentioned at the Old Vic.

But this eclectic policy was not by any means generally agreed among the National Theatre's directorate. William Gaskill, for example, was a purist for whom Tynan was an object of suspicion – 'obsessed by people of external brilliance and not much else,' he wrote in his memoirs. Gaskill, like John Dexter, was totally opposed to engaging star actors or directors *ad hoc*. Introducing a star, like Albert Finney, could upset the spirit of the ensemble. In his eyes, so could the importing of Zeffirelli and Jacques Charon to direct in a foreign style. Gaskill at first had seen the newly hatched National as an opportunity to create 'the socialist ensemble of my dreams', a sort of Englischer Ensemble, hoping for a British Brecht. He was disappointed. He mounted *Mother Courage* in a production slavishly modelled on the Ensemble's, but it was impossible to recreate the same experience with an *ad hoc* group of English actors trying Brecht for the first time. His great breakthrough was *The Recruiting Officer*, which he restored to a comedy of realistic behaviour in the realistic social setting of a town like Shrewsbury, where George Farquhar had actually gone as a recruiting officer. Gaskill acknowledged how exciting the company was, but concluded that it could not be an ensemble in the Brechtian sense of having a common political purpose. After two years Gaskill went back to attempt to create one at the Royal Court, where he succeeded George Devine on his retirement in ill health.

Two years after Gaskill, Dexter, too, departed amidst one of the rows for which he was celebrated. It centred on his long-cherished ambition to direct an all-male *As You Like It*, preferably with boy actors taking the women's roles, as in Elizabethan times. There were plans to do the play to pop music and Paul McCartney was asked to write some. But Olivier, not surprisingly, lost confidence in the enterprise in which Dexter planned that the love scenes should be 'like Genet – Orlando does believe Rosalind is a boy when he makes a pass at her'. What he wanted and what Olivier was prepared to have were miles apart. The production was postponed and Dexter left. 'I was very angry because I put a lot of work into it,' he said. He was also fed up with working for only £60 a week.

His departure left Olivier bearing the whole burden of direction, with only Tynan to turn to for advice. Although Olivier was not a man to be pushed around, he would defer to the opinions of Dexter, Gaskill and Tynan – if they outweighed his own over the choice of plays. Now he was left alone with Tynan at the very moment when the latter was becoming obsessed with a play called *Soldiers*, by Rolf Hochhuth. It was a play that dominated the headlines of 1967 in a way that plays many times as accomplished have seldom managed to do. Looking back over more than twenty years, one cannot quite believe the fuss. Who cares about *Soldiers* now? When it was revived at last, twenty three years later, how many people had even heard of it? The whole saga of the dispute over *Soldiers* between Olivier and Tynan on one hand and Chandos and his National Theatre Board on the other occupies a substantial twenty-page appendix in Olivier's *Confessions of an Actor*. It consists of letters, memos, submissions to the Board and letters to *The Times* in heated or anguished prose. The dispute raised some important principles and had harmful long-term effects on the National Theatre.

Soldiers is set in 1943. Its chief characters are Churchill, his scientific adviser Lord Cherwell, who recommends saturation bombing of civilian cities, including the Hamburg firestorm and the obliteration of Dresden, and Bishop Bell of Chichester, one of the few public opponents of this policy, who spoke out against it on moral grounds in the House of Lords. The last act of the play is mainly occupied by their debate of the moral issue. So the theme of the play is the necessity in war to sanction indiscriminate destruction, which the author Hochhuth endorses. He is behind Churchill, even if later historians show that 'area bombing' did not achieve the promised objectives. The secondary plot, which illustrated the same theme, is the death of General Sikorski, head of the Polish government in exile, when his aircraft crashed into the sea on take-off from Gibraltar on 4 July 1943, killing everyone except the pilot. The play suggests that this was deliberate sabotage by the British secret service to which Churchill turned a blind eye because having Sikorski as his ally was gravely complicating the good relations he needed with Stalin. Again, the play suggested that Churchill would have been justified in condoning this 'assassination' in order to help win the war.

But, of course, in 1967 when Churchill had been dead for two years and when his war leadership was just beginning to be questioned, such actions were not going to be generally condoned. So was the sabotage a fact? Hochhuth claimed to have evidence, indeed proof, given him by unnamed British secret servicemen, to protect whom it had been locked away in a Swiss bank, not to be opened for fifty years; but surviving witnesses, including the pilot, rejected the allegation of sabotage. There was also the very doubtful matter of motive: was not Sikorski more valuable to Churchill living than dead, whatever his quarrels with

Stalin? Nevertheless it was on this shaky foundation for the far-fetched allegation against Churchill that Tynan persuaded Olivier to go into battle. Why did they do so, especially for the sake of a play that was far too long (the text weighed six pounds) and grievously lacking in dramatic tension?

The key to the motives of both men is surely to be found in the note Tynan sent Olivier about it before the Board had considered the play. 'I'm worried,' he wrote, 'that we are losing our lead, that we are no longer making the running, that what the NT does has become a matter of public acceptance rather than public excitement.' He went on to instance the activities of the rival RSC. Its 'Theatre of Cruelty' season in 1964 had presented the *Marat-Sade*; in October 1966, Peter Brook's anti-Vietnam War montage, *US*, which used the imagery of Buddhist monks burning themselves to death, had assaulted the audience's sympathies. A group of actors, representing the mutilated and blinded by wearing paper bags tied over their heads, climbed down from the stage and advanced up the aisles moaning piteously for help. A searchlight was turned on the stalls audience to show their reactions. Would they help – whatever 'help' meant in the case of actors who were being paid to moan at them? At the end of it Brook's cast were instructed to remain on the stage in silent contemplation. They stared at us. We looked back, baffled rather than contemplative, at them. After a considerable waiting period, Tynan's voice was heard clearly from the stalls: 'Are we keeping you? Or are you keeping us?' Nevertheless, this was the sixties, this was a time when theatre audiences expected to have their emotions assailed. Tynan's unease was that this involvement in public controversy was passing the National Theatre (and him) by. It was all very well to do the classics superbly. But the new plays it presented had been non-controversial and non-political. Above his desk Tynan kept a minatory notice which urged: 'Rouse Tempers, Goad and Lacerate, Raise Whirlwinds!' It is not hard to see how this creed now affected his judgement over *Soldiers*. 'Hochhuth is the test of our willingness to take a central position in the limelight of public affairs,' he urged Olivier. 'If the play goes on under our banner, we shall be a genuinely national theatre and, even as the stink-bombs fly, I shall be very proud of us.' Olivier accepted this special pleading and may well have regretted it as the stink-bombs flew and Tynan fulfilled his longing for public notoriety.

Lord Chandos, Chairman of the National Theatre Board, had, as Oliver Lyttleton, been a close friend of Churchill and a member of his war cabinet. He was an arch-Tory and he was not prepared to have the conventional wisdom about Churchill's conduct of the war questioned. Neither did he like Ken Tynan. Chandos, like his mother Edith

Lyttleton before him, had campaigned for most of his life for the establishment of a national theatre, so he must be presumed to have appreciated drama and what makes a subject for drama. Olivier did not like him. He represented the Establishment which one side of Olivier deplored, although a bit of him was a little anxious to join it. 'There can hardly have been two men with less in common than Chandos and myself, save for the intensity of enthusiasm we shared for the erection of a national theatre,' wrote Olivier.

The two men were now on a collision course, as Tynan was perfectly well aware. 'It seems likely that if the play is presented by the National Theatre, Lord Chandos will resign,' he told Olivier. But it was his own resignation that he had to consider when on 24 April 1967, the nine members of the Board united behind Lord Chandos in declaring that the play 'grossly maligned' Churchill and Cherwell and was 'unsuitable for production at the National Theatre'. To this, at Olivier's request, a sentence was added to say that Olivier was 'unhappy' at the decision. It was thereby made publicly plain that the National Theatre Board could and did overrule its Director on his choice of plays. It had happened once before in 1965, when Wedekind's *Spring Awakening*, about the traumas of adolescence, had been banned from production by the Board (after being passed by the Lord Chamberlain) because it contained a scene suggesting group masturbation.

One cannot help concluding that Olivier had been manipulated by Tynan into treating the staging of *Soldiers* as a test-case of a principle of which the play was a bad instance. However high-minded, it was not an effective play in theatrical terms, as Olivier in an unguarded moment admitted to his wife. ('I don't like the bloody thing – but if you think I'm frightened of doing new stuff, you'll despise me, won't you?') Had he had Dexter or Gaskill to advise him ('It was a dreadful play that didn't deserve to be put on at the National or anywhere else,' wrote Gaskill), he might well have trusted his theatrical instincts. Also the play muddied its major theme, the ethics of area bombing, by the unsustainable allegation that Churchill had Sikorski murdered. This in turn muddied the purity of Olivier's argument that as Director he should be free to select plays without interference from the Board. Would not the Board be justified in preventing the Director from bringing a national institution into disrepute by presenting phoney history based on an invention masquerading as fact? Lastly, Tynan appears to have misled both Olivier and the Board by claiming that a number of distinguished historians, to whom he had put the Hochhuth thesis about Sikorski's death as a possibility, had pronounced an 'open verdict'. One of those consulted, Hugh Trevor-Roper, wrote to Chandos to say that he rejected the Sikorski theory as absurd and believed any reputable historian would do so. How could this be described as an 'open verdict'? Chandos was convinced that Tynan was deliberately lying to them all.

The aftermath of the *Soldiers* dispute was a nightmare of accusation and counter-accusation and letters to *The Times*. It developed into a personal vendetta between Chandos and Olivier over Tynan. Chandos publicly invited Tynan to resign. Olivier for his part stuck loyally by his literary manager. 'Were Ken Tynan to be got rid of I should be extremely unhappy and most unlikely to find a replacement who could in any way compare to him in the way of theatrical brains,' he wrote to Chandos. Thanks to Olivier's defence, Tynan stayed – on condition he stopped making public attacks on the Board. According to his widow and biographer Kathleen Tynan, 'Chandos would go purple in the face, shouting at Olivier "Get rid of him!" ' 'He is a man completely lacking in probity and loyalty and is unscrupulous and untruthful,' Chandos wrote to Olivier. 'This man is the man whom we are to keep, temporarily, at your request.'

Olivier's problem was that the Director's relationship with the Board had never been precisely defined. 'My choice when I joined the National Theatre was cloudy but simple,' Olivier wrote to *The Times* at the height of the row. 'Do we have a National Theatre with a *faute de mieux* ambivalent contract between its Director and the Board or do we not have a National Theatre at all? I decided to plump for the former with the apparent recent results.' At the beginning of his tenure he had actually asked the Board to appoint a drama sub-committee, which duly met, to help him choose a balanced repertory. After the Board vetoed *Spring Awakening*, there was a plan that any future difference of opinion about plays should be settled between Olivier and Chandos personally. This did not happen when the *Soldiers* dispute arose. One of the people who came out in defence of Olivier's right to complete artistic freedom was, not surprisingly, the head of the Royal Shakespeare Company, Peter Hall, who wrote to *The Times*: 'Theatre Companies have never been run by committees and never will be.'

But there is no denying that a national theatre is in a unique position among theatres. Its public visibility and prestige make its main house a difficult place in which to exercise the sort of completely untrammelled freedom of subject and treatment that a small experimental theatre (perhaps including the Cottesloe) enjoys without question. It is not a matter of logic but of the audience's reasonable expectations. Tynan claimed that the Director can always be sacked if he loses the confidence of the Board and should be given complete freedom of action until he does so. But that supposes that such a director could be trusted as absolute dictator, beyond the reach of advice or restraint. That is not the way we run the country, so why should it be the way to run the National Theatre? If a National Theatre Board is worth having at all – Tynan argued that it was not necessary – then surely one of its functions is to be consulted in advance about controversial plays planned for the repertoire, not so that it can ban them but in order to encourage debate and second thoughts if necessary. There will always be plays which it is not wise for a national theatre to present and *Soldiers* was certainly one of them.

In the year following the controversy, 1968, the Lord Chamberlain's censorship of plays was abolished and *Soldiers* was presented commercially at the New Theatre by Michael White in consort with Tynan and the director Clifford Williams. It had already been premièred in Berlin in 1967 before an audience which contained no fewer than five hundred theatre critics, many of whom called it 'boring' and 'dead'. When it opened in London in 1968 it received more respectful notices as a play that debated an important issue, but ran only for three months. Public indifference, after all, was its fate. The Czech pilot of Sikorski's plane sued the producers for libel (and would presumably have sued the National had it done the play). He was awarded very large damages. 'I took the play off not because of the libel action but because it wasn't getting audiences,' said Michael White. 'It wasn't a good enough play. It's one I wish I'd never done.' Tynan, too, reflected after the event that it had 'probably changed nothing'. There he was wrong. It had changed his standing at the National Theatre so much for the worse that ultimately he was demoted. It had irretrievably damaged the relationship between Olivier and his Chairman, Chandos. A 'small, painful little war that lasted three years' (Olivier's description) ensued. Relations deteriorated steadily until Chandos was asked to go. It must equally have undermined Olivier's faith in Tynan's advice.

Soldiers caused cracks in the ice but they took some time to open. The company made a highly-acclaimed tour of Canada that year, led by Olivier, recovered enough to appear in all three plays presented. Meanwhile, with him safely out of the country, the all-male *As You Like It* was unveiled to the public, now directed by Clifford Williams. It aroused immense publicity and curiosity. The papers were full of pictures of the actors being fitted for their female costumes. Ronald Pickup, fast emerging as a new leading actor, played Rosalind to Jeremy Brett's Orlando, with Charles Kay as his confidante Celia, Richard Kaye as Phoebe and Anthony Hopkins as a brawny, blonde Audrey. After a few nervous giggles, the audience accepted the transvestism with surprising phlegm. Camp was resolutely avoided. There were no false breasts, falsetto voices or high-heeled mincing walks. The designer, Ralph Koltai, had removed the Forest of Arden to a dream world of white light, perspex geometrical shapes, panels patterned like frost crystals and trees represented by hollow plastic tubing, and the costumes were black and white plastic. It was a stylistic forest which induced a dreamlike state in which it did not seem unduly far-fetched to be watching a man playing a girl pretending to be a boy pretending to be a girl. (The love scenes were sexless rather than ambivalent.) 'If it's all a dream, then an abstract design is acceptable as a forest. And because it wasn't real, it made it possible to accept that the men were really women,' said Koltai. 'As You Didn't Know You Liked It' did good business. But what was the point of it all? Why were male actors playing women's roles in the middle of the twentieth century?

After a disappointing National debut in Molière's *Tartuffe*, Gielgud returned in 1968 to play *Oedipus* in a legendary production by Peter Brook. It was perhaps the bravest thing he ever undertook. He had never before risked an appearance in an avant-garde production, and Seneca's scarcely-performed version of the story had been turned into that with a vengeance. Brook demanded ten weeks' rehearsal, an unprecedented luxury even at the National, giving the company physically demanding exercises for voice and body. They were drilled in groaning and screaming, and practised Maori chants; there were exercises in which they were told to imitate snakes and hiss. Gielgud was one of the actors least likely to enjoy this way of working. Gielgud and Brook had done famous productions of *Measure for Measure* and *The Tempest* together at Stratford in the fifties, so Brook must have known quite well that Gielgud was the least 'physical' of actors – 'the best actor in England from the neck up', in Tynan's phrase. Brook described their first day's rehearsal, sitting in a circle while each actor tried a physical exercise: 'When John's turn came, there was a moment of tension. What would he do? The older actors hoped he would refuse. John knew that after the confident young actors, he could only appear ridiculous. But he plunged in. He tried, he tried humbly, clumsily, with all he could bring. It was no longer the star, a superior being . . . In a matter of seconds, his relation with the group was transformed . . . From that moment he was held in true admiration and respect.' But how necessary was it to put this elderly and none-too-confident star into this humiliating position? It may be wondered how much it really achieved. Gielgud's own memory of it was that the preparation was 'agony and misery and I really resented it in some sort of way, except that I love Peter Brook . . . I made a bit of a fool of myself which increased their respect for me but not mine for myself'. He added, 'We never quite knew what Peter was driving at.'

The text, rewritten by the poet Ted Hughes, was a sound picture laden with images of plague, death and cruelty on a symphonic scale.

This was accompanied in the choruses by those vocal explorations of sounds of horror and terror made in rehearsal. The actors droned, hissed, panted, gasped, beat out tattoos with their hands, and gave sudden rhythmic laughs as a counterpoint to a narrative underscored with *musique concrète*. It was variously described as a voodoo session, an oratorio or a barbaric Mass. It began as the audience was filing in. Members of the chorus were discovered already clinging to the pillars of the stalls and dress circle, hissing and droning naturalistically all round the auditorium.

The play began on a golden set with a large metal cube revolving slowly centre-stage, containing the riddle of plague-stricken Thebes. The cast were uniformly clad in dark brown suits and black textured sweaters. The myth was told by actors whirling round, writhing on the floor, and, in the case of Jocasta (Irene Worth), impaling herself upon a golden spike through the womb. The blinding of Oedipus was achieved without a drop of stage blood. Gielgud simply placed two black patches on his eyes, opened his mouth in a soundless scream like a Francis Bacon portrait and, striking the stage with his staff as he attempted to move off, cried out 'Lead me!' Up to this point the audience was appropriately horrified and benumbed.

Brook's plan had been to follow the violent climax of the tragedy with a sudden switch to song and dance – catharsis followed immediately by bathos, such as the ancient Greek dramatists employed. The actors were to reappear in the auditorium dancing in the aisles to a jazzed-up version of the national anthem. When Olivier heard of this 'childishly insolent' plan, he hit the roof and demanded that Brook should reconsider following a dazzling production with an 'incomprehensibly infantile lark'. Brook agreed to cut out the national anthem if Olivier would promise to cut out playing it at any other performance at the theatre. He would think of something else and on the night of the dress rehearsal Olivier found out what it was. As the play ended a carriage was drawn on bearing a shrouded column. After Oedipus had been led off by the chorus, its leader returned and tore off the shroud. What stood revealed was a six-foot, burnished golden phallus round which the chorus, now gaily caparisoned, danced to the accompaniment of a Dixieland jazz band playing 'Yes, We Have no Bananas'. After that, Gielgud recalled, Olivier and Brook 'had a terrible quarrel in my dressing-room and I left in exhaustion about two o'clock in the morning. The next night when I came back, there was a crack in the full-length mirror on the door right from top to bottom. I was told that one of them had thrown an ashtray at the other. I don't know which one it was.'

Nothing was thrown at the mirror. Frank Dunlop, who had recently

39

joined as associate director, was present and reported, 'It was the slamming of the door that cracked it. Larry was hysterical about the phallus. It was going to be a scandal. he never forgave me for taking sides with Peter Brook.' The following day, Olivier gave in over the phallus, outnumbered three to one by Brook, Dunlop and Tynan. 'I felt weak; I was weak; and weakly I gave in . . . I knew I should remember it as the punch that started my undoing,' he wrote in his memoirs, more in self-accusation than in anger with Brook's intransigence.

In the event the golden phallus did not add appreciably to the play's effectiveness. If anything it distracted from the fine performances Gielgud and Worth had given. The audience did not understand the point that Greek and Roman tragedy were often defused by a satyr play or communal celebration afterwards. They did not join in the dancing. On the first night, in the silence that greeted the unveiling of the golden member, Coral Browne's unmistakable voice was heard to observe to her companion: 'No one we know, is it, dear?' And thereafter, on Oedipus nights, the traffic in Waterloo Road came to a standstill as the phallus, too big to be accommodated backstage, was duly wheeled round the front of the theatre from the scenery store in the annexe. It proved to be the last appearance of Peter Brook and Gielgud at the National Theatre under Olivier. Peter Hall was to invite both of them back. But Brook by then was too committed to his own company in Paris to accept.

After 1967, the *annus mirabilis*, there was no way to go but downhill and this way the theatre went, gradually at first but with increasing momentum. In the following years, average attendances slipped from a record 97 per cent to 92 per cent, then to 89 per cent, then 83 per cent, and, at their worst, to 79 per cent in 1971–2, by which time there was a deficit on the books of £140,000. Something seemed to have leaked away from the organization. Leading actors drifted away – Albert Finney, Colin Blakely, Frank Finlay, and Lynn Redgrave, soon to be followed by Maggie Smith and Robert Stephens – partly because of film offers, partly because the salaries at the National were so low. The original directorship was now no more, and Tynan was soon to take extended leave of absence in which he put on *Soldiers*, followed by his long-planned 'erotic entertainment', *Oh! Calcutta!* The gap in the directing team was partly filled late in 1967 by the arrival of Frank Dunlop, who had made a reputation with a company he called 'Pop Theatre' at the Edinburgh Festival. His condition for taking on the dogsbody job of administrative director was that he would be allowed to start a young people's theatre. This was assented to because nobody seriously supposed he would succeed. Dunlop did some straightforward but

40

effective productions. One was Brecht's version of *Edward II* after (a long way after) Marlowe, and now retranslated into English. Somerset Maugham's 1919 comedy, *Home and Beauty*, in which the fluffy Geraldine McEwan found herself with two husbands owing to an error in the wartime casualty lists, turned out to be a reliable audience-puller, often revived. He followed this with a spectacular adaptation of Webster's *The White Devil*, brilliantly designed by Piero Gherardi, the Oscar-winning film designer, a bloodbath that only just kept the excess of horror and villainy this side of laughter.

It was in the selection of new plays that the National had lost its touch. An inexplicable attempt to turn John Lennon's books of verbal absurdities, amusing only on the page, into a play called *In his Own Write* made for a confused and unsatisfactory evening. An Italian woman novelist's play, *The Advertisement*, required Joan Plowright to play a boringly garrulous and self-pitying woman at extreme length. An over-ambitious play about the Indian Mutiny, by Charles Wood, obscurely entitled *H* (for Havelock, the general who put it down), attempted to squeeze a teeming canvas into brief episodic scenes, and an elaborate toy theatre setting. An experimental season at the small Jeanetta Cochrane Theatre commissioned plays by women novelists in the hope of discovering new dramatic talent but without notable success. A complex play on the life and disputable significance of Che Guevara by John Spurling was not the stuff of which hits are made. These followed each other in succession inside a year with depressing effect, amid revivals which did not reach the previous standards of excellence. Only Shaw's rarely-staged *Back to Methuselah*, finely directed by Clifford Williams with brilliant space-age settings by Ralph Koltai, was worthy of National status.

Olivier had warned Robert Stephens that the good days would not last. 'They never do,' he observed. 'They didn't last at the Old Vic for Ralph Richardson and me.' Just as a bad patch looked like becoming permanent, the curtain went up on an arrestingly good new play, *The National Health*. Its author, Peter Nichols, had made a striking stage debut with a dark comedy about a family's attempts to cope with a spastic child (based on personal experience), *A Day in the Death of Joe Egg*. His new play, set in a hospital ward where the gravely ill are moved steadily nearer to the door as their turn to die approaches, was also based on personal experience (Nichols had been in four hospitals with a collapsed lung). 'I think hospitals are hilarious as well as sad,' he said – and exemplified this in the character of the porter, played by the impish newcomer Jim Dale, whose comic guide to the facts of death in hospital laughed off one's squeamishness. Nichols exposed the forced cheerfulness with which death is rendered unmentionable to those whose time is up, while others are pulled back from it to a helpless and meaningless form of survival. Olivier, who had suffered much hospital care, disliked the play and prophesied disaster, but the newly arrived director, Michael Blakemore (who had already directed Nichols's work at Glasgow Citizens' Theatre), stood up to him and the play proved a much-needed hit which brought the National back into the contemporary world.

Work began on the building of the new South Bank theatre on 3 November 1969, and it was expected to be completed by 1973. In order to gear up the company to running more than one auditorium, the Cambridge Theatre with its large auditorium seating 1,270 was taken in June 1970, for the rest of the year. Meanwhile Frank Dunlop's energetic lobbying for a youth theatre had borne fruit with Olivier and the Board: the company had made a surplus of over £30,000 on its operations, and, with the Arts Council putting up another £30,000, this was used to provide the Young Vic Theatre. 'It meant waiving the rules about the use of grant money, and we owed it to Jennie Lee and Roy Jenkins, the Chancellor, that it went through,' said Dunlop. Jennie (Baroness) Lee attributed the swift agreement of the Government to Olivier's personal charisma. 'He came to see us to plead for a junior Vic. Great actors can be concerned only for themselves, but here was Laurence Olivier pleading for the talented young to be able to perform without straight away being exposed to the full glare of a national theatre and professional critics.' She asked him to put his case on paper, sent it to the Treasury and to the Prime Minister, Harold Wilson, and received financial consent 'almost by return of post, entirely due to Laurence Olivier'.

A hundred yards or so down the Cut, on the corner of which the Old Vic Theatre stands, an open-stage auditorium fitted with wooden benches was built on a raft of concrete above the cellars of the bombed houses that stood there before. It stands behind an old-fashioned Waterloo butcher's shop, and the shop, with its nicely decorated white tiles, became the unusual foyer of the Young Vic, with a new coffee bar attached. It was opened on 12 August 1970, by Dame Sybil Thorndike, to serve as a young people's theatre but also as a studio for the company, from whose younger members all its early productions were cast. The opening production, *Scapino*, was a popularized version of Molière's *Les Fourberies de Scapin*. Former pop star Jim Dale hugely enjoyed the title role, thwacking left and right with a rubber sausage, and pulled in a new, young audience. *The Taming of the Shrew* sailed close to pantomime, full of cheeky Cockney interpolations. Not everything on the bill was knockabout comedy – there was *Waiting for Godot*, and

42

Oedipus by Sophocles in W. B. Yeats's translation. The theatre was welcomed as a breeze of fresh air. Within a year the Young Vic company was touring European festivals, winning plaudits and awards. One disadvantage of its success was that it robbed the main house of the services of Frank Dunlop who became its full-time director.

The major event of 1970 was the return of Olivier to the Old Vic stage to play Shylock for the first time in *The Merchant of Venice*. It was not planned to be an Olivier part. Joan Plowright was to play Portia and suggested as director Jonathan Miller, who had begun his directing career at Nottingham Playhouse. Olivier at first protested that he did not want to play it, but, Joan Plowright noticed, 'he was doing terrible things in the mirror while he was shaving, beginning to think of a face'.

Miller transposed the play from the sixteenth century, when Jews lived in ghettoes, to the late nineteenth century, when some were accepted members of mercantile society and lived like princes, or rather, like Rothschilds. In top hats, frock coats and striped trousers there was no outward difference marking out Jew from Gentile. Olivier's first thought was to exaggerate the Jewishness of his appearance, aiming at a ringleted, hooked-nosed, goatee-bearded echo of the film *Disraeli*. When he first put on his make-up, according to his memoirs, he was told by his director: 'You don't want everybody to talk of nothing but George Arliss and Disraeli, do you?' – and obediently scraped it all off. Miller's own account in *his* memoir suggests that it was a more gradual process. Olivier had invested in dentures costing several hundred pounds which completely altered the shape of his face, the slight protrusion of the upper lip, he thought, giving it a Semitic look. 'With the exception of the teeth, he gradually lost the other excrescences, partly because I suspect that he could see that the production could have made him appear as a ridiculous pantomime dame in the rather ordinary nineteenth century set.' In return, Miller suggested a piece of business on which Olivier seized memorably. On hearing the news that Antonio's ships have gone down, he executed an awkward little jig of triumph.

There was, however, a graver problem than what make-up to employ: the paralysing stage fright that had plagued him since October 1964, when it began in *Othello*. When he had taken the small role of the solicitor in *Home and Beauty* the year before (under the traditional actor's pseudonym 'Walter Plinge' in the programme) he had been unable to learn his lines. 'He had the script open on a music stand in the wings and was still trying to learn his lines when it was time to go on,' recalled Robert Stephens. This time he could not hide behind 'Walter Plinge' – Shylock was one of the 'Big Ones', as he called them. As the first night approached, his dread of making a fool of himself grew greater. He begged the other members of the cast at all costs not to look him in the eyes when they played a scene with him. But according to Joan Plowright, shortly before the first night curtain he was threatening to go out and get on the first bus that stopped outside the theatre. The first night passed off without catastrophe, and the strangled off-stage cry with which Olivier's Shylock ended the play, although it sounded like agony, may really have been one of relief. With the *Merchant* his fear began to lift after five and a half years. As to the production itself, nobody ever quite agreed how much of a success it was. The nineteenth-century setting, costumes and manners had the advantage of making the lines and the business relationships feel fresh and free of their 'school play' familiarity. But it was implausible that cool city gentlemen should spit such coarse anti-semitic hatred at a banker so useful to themselves, calling him cur, wretch, devil, and simply 'Jew'. The pound of flesh seemed even more far-fetched a penalty when the flesh in question was filling a stiffened shirtfront and businessman's striped trousers. Olivier, in later years, dismissed his performance as Shylock. But there was no denying the danger with which he invested a man whose fawning gentility and attempts at bonhomie proclaimed him an outsider. It was the sudden glimpse of the rage and hatred in his heart for the Christians ('vile, heartless, money-grubbing monsters', as Olivier described them) that made him suddenly terrifying.

The box office registered a surge of response both at the Old Vic and two months later when the company moved into the Cambridge Theatre. First, its repertoire was joined by a Restoration favourite, *The Beaux' Stratagem* by George Farquhar, once again clarified by William Gaskill, making a brief return to the company. With Maggie Smith and Robert Stephens in the leads (they had become husband and wife in private life), it shone like a cleaned masterpiece. They also took the leads in *Hedda Gabler* in a production directed by Ingmar Bergman. Olivier had seen Bergman's production from the Royal Dramatic Theatre, Stockholm, at the World Theatre Season and said, 'I want that in English in my theatre.' But he had not reckoned on the frustrations of dealing with Bergman, who refused to answer written or telephoned invitations. Later Olivier found out that he was in London – and presented himself uninvited at the door of his Savoy suite. Bergman agreed to come over for five days, all he could spare from filming, block the moves in the play and leave Olivier to take over rehearsals. On his arrival he showed the prickliness of his temperament. There was no one waiting to meet him at London Airport and by the time Frank Dunlop arrived he was already booking his flight back to Sweden. The hotel he was booked into was too noisy. Once more he declared that he was going back to Stockholm and threw a playscript at Dunlop with the words

'You direct it!' Transferred to a suite at the Dorchester, he consented to begin his initial rehearsals, with Olivier in attendance. On his departure, having blocked the play, Bergman confided in Robert Stephens, who was playing Løvborg, that it was best they rehearsed for the next four weeks without any director, as he feared Olivier would change his instructions. Bergman only returned for the last week of rehearsals.

The play was to open at the Cambridge Theatre, where the season had already begun with *The Merchant of Venice*. When the first dress rehearsal was called, it was found that, because the set of the *Merchant* was in place, the *Hedda Gabler* set, a bare, red cell-like chamber matching the violence of Hedda's moods, was pushed five feet further downstage than had been planned. Bergman's reaction was by now predictable: he immediately cancelled the dress rehearsal and the opening along with it. He was off back to Stockholm. When 'Lord Laurence' had finished his *Merchant of Venice* he, Bergman, would come back and they would do *Hedda Gabler* together. 'We were all seated in the stalls listening to him cancelling the production when Olivier, who had been sent for, walked onto the stage alone. Bergman pinned him there and gave him a terrific telling-off,' Stephens recalled. 'He said, "You have lied to me, you have taken away five feet from the depth of the stage so that I cannot light it. Never mind, I will come back when you have finished your *Merchant of Venice*." He made mincemeat of him. The result was that the *Merchant* scenery had to be taken down and packed into pantechnicons outside while the *Hedda Gabler* set went up. We had our dress rehearsal but Bergman never saw the opening night. He said he didn't need to – "I have given you *Hedda Gabler*. It is yours now" – and he went back to Stockholm for the last time.' Later on, in Sweden, he told Stephens: 'When I arrived in England there was no one to meet me! I am Ingmar Bergman. If I had invited Laurence Olivier to Sweden, not only would I have been at the airport to meet him but my entire company also.'

No doubt the uncertainty over whether the play would open at all enhanced the neurotic intensity which Maggie Smith invested in the part of Hedda. With a mirror as her constant companion in which to examine her white mask of a face, she paced and smoked and contemplated herself, shuddering with disgust. She suffocated with boredom in front of it and finally shot herself in front of it. Studied narcissism could go no further. Some found it a peerless performance, others a precious, over-studied one, in which respect it matched what was a very 'stagey and statuesque' production in which there was little resemblance to living human beings: rather it was like observing the life of the praying mantis under glass.

45

That June, however, it must have been with a sense of achievement, with a conviction that his theatre was once more climbing to the high ground of excellence and popularity, that Laurence Olivier succumbed to the invitation of a life peerage, the first ever offered to an actor. He had first been approached two years earlier and ducked. He gradually weakened beneath the further blandishments of Harold Wilson and Lord Goodman on the understanding among his colleagues that in the theatre he was not to be called 'Lord'. He would continue to be 'Sir Laurence' or 'Sir'. It did not take place for another year, but his maiden speech in the House of Lords shows so piquantly how Olivier responded to a role, off-stage as much as on, that it is worth quoting a little of it here. Mindful, no doubt, that he was following in the steps of Sir Henry Irving, first actor-knight, Baron Olivier of Brighton had donned the ermine and lavished on their lordships the sort of lines that Victorian actors relished. 'My lords,' he began, 'I have the honour to crave the indulgence of your Lordships' House. During the maiden speech which follows, I fear your Lordships may find grim cause to reflect upon the prescient genius of the introducer of this tenderest of courtesies and, if I fail to achieve it, then I must beg to suggest to your Lordships that it would be most contrary to the chivalry for which your Lordships' House is so famous to withold your gallantry and refuse to indulge a maiden of sixty-four.' What this preamble meant nobody quite knew but it afforded as many flourishes as Osric could have managed. He reached his peroration: 'I believe in the theatre; I believe in it as the first glamourizer of thought. I believe that in a great city, or even in a small city or a village, a great theatre is the outward and visible sign of an inward and spiritual culture.'

Not long after his ennoblement, in August 1970, when everything seemed set fair, Olivier was stricken with major thrombosis in the right leg. It meant the end of his appearances as Shylock or in the planned revival of *The Dance of Death*. It meant absence from the stage and the helm for months to come. It looked as though the great career had come to an end, for, as he said to the Press, 'I get too puffed to do an emotional scene or a long speech. In the theatre an actor needs that little something extra – adrenalin perhaps, or heart – and just for the moment, I haven't got it any more.' As a result, the National entered on the rockiest year of its existence so far.

4

1971: Year of Disasters

One of the immediate results of Olivier's thrombosis was the postponement of the project most dear to his heart, a production of *Guys and Dolls* with himself in the lead as Runyon's crap-shooting hero, Nathan Detroit. *Guys and Dolls* had been a Tynan suggestion, and Olivier, in his enthusiasm for what would be his first song-and-dance role since Archie Rice, had talked the Board into agreement. The director was to be Garson Kanin, best known for writing and directing the play and film *Born Yesterday*. Preparations started when Olivier told Geraldine McEwan that she was to play Adelaide. She replied that she had never been in a musical, never sung and never danced. 'You can learn,' he said. 'The thing you have got to get absolutely perfect is the accent.' After six months taking singing and dancing lessons, she was told that Sir Laurence wanted to rehearse 'Sue Me'. 'We sang this number together and, to my great surprise, he had already got his whole performance together. It was wonderful. He was going to be sensational! I could see now why he wanted to do it.' On the premiss that his company could do anything, Olivier was prepared to gamble on the costly production. He himself was inspired by the part of Nathan Detroit as by few others at that stage in his career, and that alone leaves one wondering what we missed.

In his absence through sickness, business at the Cambridge Theatre was down to 76 per cent and there was a series of lacklustre productions at the Old Vic, which left the company down £60,000 on the season. Olivier, although quite quickly out of hospital, was convalescing with his right leg much heavier than his left. He was more often absent than present from the office. Frank Dunlop was also absent from administration as the Young Vic had become his full-time concern. Olivier's solution was to suggest appointing his wife as his co-director. 'I had always helped behind the scenes as "the guv'nor's wife",' said Joan Plowright, who had only recently returned to the stage two years after child-bearing, 'so he had arrived at the idea that I could direct the company. It was absurd. I hadn't the training and I was bringing up a family of young children – his!' Lord Chandos, too, thought the idea absurd and this angered Olivier. Their relationship grew 'more sore and more sour'. By November 1970, Olivier had asked for a private meeting with Lord Goodman and Jennie Lee at which he said he could not go on working any longer with Chandos as chairman. They would have to find another director. He was persuaded to carry on with the promise that Sir Max Rayne, who had recently joined the Board, would in due course take over from Chandos.

The swiftness of the consequences took Olivier by surprise. After the next Board meeting, Oliver Chandos told him quietly, 'Well, it seems they've decided to get rid of me. I suppose I am getting on a bit – or something.' Olivier fought down his memories of the days when he would 'bring his face, flushed with fury, uncomfortably close to mine' and said with sincere sympathy, 'Oh Oliver, that must seem terribly ungrateful after all you have done to bring about the National Theatre.' Chandos was nearing eighty. He had an autocratic way of handling the Board (and, at times, the theatre) as if it was his personal fiefdom. But after his lifelong campaigning on behalf of a national theatre, his sudden dismissal did seem ungrateful. Olivier must have felt one of his frequent twinges of guilt as he watched Chandos walk away, unaware of the role he had played in having him removed. Chandos did not long outlive retirement, dying early in 1972.

Tynan, who had been away on leave of absence, had been demoted at Chandos's insistence from literary manager to one of two 'literary consultants', the other being Derek Granger. It had not lessened his uneven effect on the repertoire. One of his suggestions was that the National should mount a play by Fernando Arrabal, a leading name in the Theatre of Cruelty, and engage the young South American, Victor Garcia, as director. The play, *The Architect and the Emperor of Assyria*, concerned two survivors on a desert island after a plane crash who pass the time playing rather sinister fantasy games in which they assume the roles of murderer and victim, mother giving birth to child, cannibal and prey, and many more. Also on the stage was a curious object to find on a desert island, a shining yellow fork-lift truck. Before rehearsals began, Olivier approached the diminutive and frizzy-haired young director with a marked copy of the script. 'Cher maitre, there are a few things I would like to ask you about the play . . .' he began, when Garcia took the script from him and dropped it ceremonially into the wastepaper bin. 'Sir Laurence,' he said, 'I detest literature. I abominate the theatre. I have a horror of culture. I am interested only in *magic!*' The magic which he contrived with the noisy fork-lift truck and his two hard-pressed and near-naked actors Anthony Hopkins and Jim Dale did not charm many onlookers. 'Pompous triviality from a pretentious fake' was a typical comment from the notices.

It was not an auspicious way to begin 1971 and it was soon followed by another botched project, again much promoted by Tynan: Shakespeare's *Coriolanus* directed by two of Brecht's leading disciples from the Berliner Ensemble. Brecht virtually rewrote *Coriolanus* as a Marxist epic and the production of the resulting *Coriolan* in Berlin by Manfred Wekwerth and Joachim Tenschert was celebrated as a model for Brechtian performances. By some misunderstanding they thought they had been invited to the National to stage it again. In fact the National intended them to stage Shakespeare's play of the same name. Armed with the annotated prompt book of the Berlin production and photographs of every grouping, they set about trying to make Shakespeare's text fit Brecht's dramatized political lecture in twelve scenes. White billowing half-curtains divided scene from scene, behind which the scenery was noisily trundled about while the play – and the audience – waited to get on with the story. The famous alienation effect was very considerable, resulting within one week of rehearsal in the departure of Christopher Plummer. Anthony Hopkins took his place as Coriolanus. The Brechtian production and Shakespeare's text never meshed. The result was written off as 'singularly incoherent'.

By now people were getting restive about the National's apparent unreliability. One of the first shots fired across its bows came from John Osborne, no admirer of subsidized theatre at the National or the RSC, although he owed his own career to their subsidized poor relation, the Royal Court. Writing in the *Evening Standard* in March 1971, he called the National's record 'poor to disastrous', and poured out a heartfelt contempt for Kenneth Tynan: 'He seems to attempt to be the archetypal Oxford clever dick . . . The theatre's use of glum gimmicks like plant hire machinery and golden genitals are to him a joke.' He summed up the National as 'a factious institution with all the pressures of the commercial theatre and an indecisive, uneasy policy'. Osborne's paw-swipes were unjust (even Tynan could not be held responsible for the gimmicks employed by visiting directors) but there was enough truth in the charges of indecision and clever-dickery for the rhetoric to carry a sting.

Frank Dunlop's last production for the Old, as opposed to Young Vic, *The Captain of Köpenick*, brought to the National Paul Scofield – not before time, as many of the reviews suggested. (He had originally been invited to play Coriolanus but turned it down.) Carl Zuckmayer's cartoon comedy on the theme of subservience to authority told the story of Wilhelm Voight, a victim of bureaucracy who is forever kept waiting for an official permit. One day he dons a Prussian officer's uniform and suddenly finds the town hall doors thrown open and the mayor and the bureaucracy grovelling before him. Based on a hoax which the real Voight pulled off in the Kaiser's Germany of 1910, it was written in 1931 just before the Nazi night descended, while Germans could still afford to laugh at officialdom. Scofield contributed a marvellously-detailed and universalized portrayal of Voight, with sagging shoulders, drooping eyelids and a rusty rasp of a voice, with which he replied to questions. 'Occupation?' barked an official. 'Waiting,' he replied with infinite weariness, sitting there with a bowler hat, a seedy moustache and an expression of battered caution. It underlined how rare the opportunities to see top-class acting at the National had been lately. 'Voight has been played by the greatest German actors, but Scofield is one of the best I have ever seen,' said Zuckmayer afterwards. Scofield had signed on for a year and the natural presumption was that Olivier's acting shoes were to be filled by this ideal-seeming successor. But that was not to be. Although a palpable hit, the play was given only thirty performances. Scofield soon departed after being given only one other part, in a Pirandello play, *The Rules of the Game*, which did not extend him.

Whereas you used to have to book months ahead to get seats for the National, now you could get into any performance on any night, except for the few appearances of Scofield in *The Captain of Köpenick* and the even rarer ones of Olivier as Shylock. The Old Vic was playing to around 80 per cent of capacity. Was a National Theatre that could not even sell 700 seats a night doing its job? demanded an article by myself, headlined 'Panned, Pampered and Half-Empty'. I blamed its slipping popularity on the eccentric choice of plays and the paucity of top-class acting. When Olivier had fallen ill, there seemed to be no one on the bridge to take the helm as the leading actor. Where were Richardson, Gielgud, Redgrave, Guinness? They had either not appeared at all or, like Scofield, had come only on a short visit. Surely we had the right to expect the best actors in plays that appealed to a wide public? What was the theatre's policy? A few days later, Olivier made a rather half-hearted rebuttal of the complaints to the *Daily Telegraph*, especially on the lack of star acting. 'In three years you always run out of stars. I have tried desperately to create an ensemble. We still have about 15 of our 35 original players,' he said. It was argued that leading actors could not afford to spend long periods at the National, where the maximum regular salaries amounted to about £5,000 a year.

Nevertheless it was not the modesty of the fees, nor star actors' greed for money, that had kept them from the National Theatre, where the public naturally expected to see them. It was a lack of invitations to do so. The invitations could only have come from Olivier, and therefore it can only have been him who kept them away. Why did he not tempt Redgrave or Richardson with parts which they would want to accept? Why not offer to appear with them, or with Gielgud, perhaps in one of those supporting roles like Tattle or Brazen which he had been happy to play for the sake of the company? Many members of the young ensemble which he had 'desperately tried to create' had left and had not been invited to return.

The causes of all this lay deep in Olivier's character. His competitiveness as an actor was obvious and it sometimes made him ungenerous towards his contemporaries and near-equals (although not to younger players). His feelings towards Gielgud were coloured by a grudge he bore over their one appearance together, alternating the parts of Romeo and Mercutio in the 1935 *Romeo and Juliet* at the New Theatre. 'He made a vastly bigger success than I did as Romeo,' he admitted, still brooding about it forty-five years later. They embodied two different approaches to acting, the aesthetic and the animal, the poetic and the awe-inspiring, but could they never be combined? In the great days at the New Theatre it was Olivier and Richardson who had set their styles off against each other so memorably, Olivier playing Shallow to Richardson's Falstaff, Richardson playing Richmond to Olivier's Richard III. Since 1946 people had waited hopefully to see them reunited on stage. Richardson, too, was one of those who waited in vain for such a call when the National Theatre company was founded and was bitterly hurt not to be included in it. The two men had spent their young days together at Birmingham Repertory Theatre. 'He's my oldest, dearest friend,' said Richardson one day in answer to my question why he never appeared at the National, 'but I suppose he just doesn't buy my acting.' This was obviously absurd, so I persisted: had he *never* been asked? 'Oh, I *was* asked,' said Sir Ralph, as if fractionally lifting a stone which he would sooner not look beneath. 'He did ask me at the beginning if I'd like to play some old *dukes*. I said that I'd played those old dukes before. I wanted something fresh. Perhaps he didn't have anything.' A similar mystery surrounded the non-appearance of Alec Guinness at the National Theatre. 'Well,' he once said to me, 'one has to be asked.' Had there never been an invitation? Well, yes, he *had* been sounded out about appearing in *The Merchant of Venice* some years before the recent production. And turned it down? The part, he explained gently, was Antonio. 'Of course . . . one didn't know who had it in mind to play Shylock.' Well, one knew now.

So Olivier remained unchallenged as the one and only megastar in the National Theatre firmament – to his disadvantage, as it now turned out. There was no one to take over the tiller, even had his nature allowed him

51

to hand it over. Frank Dunlop, who had administered the company for the past three years, refused to stay on when he was denied any official title or authority. 'I had been acting as the director's deputy. I asked for it to be made official. One needed visible authority. But Olivier found it very, very difficult to think of anybody running the place other than him. He made lists of possible successors but no one took them very seriously,' said Dunlop. 'He probably didn't intend anyone to. And he never suggested one of his associate directors.' Dunlop gave up administering the Old Vic for the Young Vic.

Olivier had settled the matter of his successor at Chichester in 1965 by offering the post to Sir John Clements 'over a gin and tonic'. He seems to have believed that the National could be passed on in much the same feudal manner. Clements was one of those he had in mind to succeed him. Among others to whom he suggested it were Richard Attenborough, then making his name as a film director, the actor-director David William, and Richard Burton, to whom the job was 'offered' over a number of drinks one night at Olivier's house in Brighton. Burton, who felt the need of a worthwhile job to do, responded eagerly and seems to have taken it as an official invitation. 'The following weekend he came to dinner and he started asking me if I would help him to run the theatre as I had helped Larry,' said Joan Plowright. 'I had to explain that the job was not in Larry's gift, it was a government appointment.'

By now the new chairman, Sir Max Rayne, and his finance committee were alarmed. The accumulated deficit of £60,000 was mounting steadily as the new season advanced. It was necessary to go begging to the Arts Council for supplementary grants, which would bring the total to above £400,000 for the first time. Economies were needed and the first was decided upon at a Board meeting in mid-June at which the new administrative director, Patrick Donnell, took Olivier's place, one of the duties he had assumed to take some weight off Olivier's shoulders during his convalescence. 'I was the one who put my foot down and said "We will not do *Guys and Dolls*",' he confessed. Donnell was faced with the inexorable fact that it was impossible to put on a large-scale musical in the small auditorium of the Old Vic at a profit. The run could not be made long enough to recoup the high costs. They would be gambling everything on a West End transfer to pay for the show. As Donnell put it, 'The get-out figure was impossibly high. And could we risk so much on such a fragile body as Olivier's?' The Board agreed with him. Olivier learned of the decision from board member Binkie Beaumont, who rang him up and said something that infuriated Olivier: 'I wouldn't have objected to the proposed musical had it been *Oklahoma!*' – which had been presented in London originally by Beaumont. But where was there a part for Laurence Olivier among these cheerful cowboys? One could hardly envisage him strolling on to sing 'Oh, What a Beautiful Mornin' ' – nor did he feel like singing it then.

In his memoirs Olivier describes the *Guys and Dolls* cancellation in trenchant terms as a body-blow to his will to continue. 'I felt drained of everything except a helpless exhaustion. I had lost my courage . . . If one finds that one's colleagues and friends are content to take actions that they must know are acts of treachery, then it is more than hard, and in my case impossible, to continue the grotesquely unequal struggle any further.' Treachery was his word for it. He was convinced that he had been betrayed – a frequent feeling with Olivier – by a Board which had already forbidden him to mount *Spring Awakening* and *Soldiers*. He had every reason to feel frustrated. He was indignant that his artistic judgement was being overruled on financial grounds.

The high risk involved could have been worth taking. *Guys and Dolls* was proved in due course (although in a much larger theatre) to be the biggest money-maker the National ever had. But who was going to say it was worth taking then? Not Sir Max Rayne, whose main concern was to eliminate the growing deficit by 'cutting our coat according to our cloth'. The show had already been designed, the cast had been coached in their accents, a Broadway musical specialist had been working on the dancing, and Geraldine McEwan had had her singing lessons. But Olivier had to tell his company the show was off, at which 'a great groan went up', according to Denis Quilley. That Monday night Olivier entered in his diary 'Gs and Ds cancelled after twice laid on – decided not stay much longer – 9th year'.

So it was with low spirits that Olivier embarked on the National's first really disastrous venture, the inaugurating of the New Theatre (later renamed the Albery) as its West End showcase. It meant doubling the size of the repertoire and of the company, in order to prepare to occupy its new building, which was in fact nowhere near ready for occupation. Why did nobody realize that? It was not as though it was being built on another planet; a short walk from the Old Vic brought you to the site. Better information about the woeful delays could surely have been obtained by the Board and an expensive error averted. John Dexter (who had just returned to the company) and Michael Blakemore, the new associate directors, thought the West End venture the biggest mistake the Board made. 'It was catastrophic,' said Dexter. To Michael Blakemore, it seemed a futile exercise. 'It was very difficult logistically. And, since we didn't have a date for moving into the South Bank, why try to run both theatres? It's better to run one theatre well.' There is no need to dwell on the productions presented, *The Rules of the Game*, not the best Pirandello, and *Amphitryon 38*, a pre-war piece of rather whimsical Giraudoux about the god Jupiter's philandering with a human spouse, Alcmena. An anarchistic celebration of William Blake by Adrian Mitchell, *Tyger*, was the excuse for crude satire and propaganda in favour of any and every anti-Establishment cause, set to pop music. The main thing to be said about them all was that they were not calculated to bring in West End audiences, as West End audiences markedly proved by staying away. *Tyger* was an embarrassing mess. A 'cranky panto' originally intended for the Young Vic, its simplistic send-ups of the Arts Council, MI5, and royalty, of Shakespeare in a stetson and Tennyson, Whitman and Browning in striped blazers and boaters might have worked in a club theatre revue, but did not sit worthily on the stage of a national theatre. It did little service to William Blake by representing him as an elderly forerunner of the hippies. Playwright and critic Frank Marcus wrote in the *Sunday Telegraph*: 'What is surprising, indeed incredible, is that the National Theatre should have lavished its huge resources of money and talent on this deplorable concoction.' It made the fourth consecutive dud show since *Coriolanus* three months earlier. 'Four flops in a row – now they'll have to get rid of me!' remarked Olivier in Tynan's hearing. Jonathan Miller's production of *Danton's Death* by Büchner, though a marked improvement, did not arrest the decline in audiences.

Sir Max Rayne took over officially as Chairman on 1 August, amid widespread portents that the theatre was well down the road to artistic and financial disaster. Soon afterwards, Olivier went to see him to offer his resignation. There are different ways of offering to resign. On Olivier's account of the interview, he was playing the humble courtier. 'I told him that if he felt that I had been there long enough, he would find me entirely co-operative and that I would help all I possibly could in the search for a successor.' But Sir Max (now Lord) Rayne's memory of the occasion throws a rather different light on the offer. 'What he said was, "I suppose you want my resignation?" I replied that of course all of us hoped he would lead the National Theatre company into the South Bank.' What Rayne did not say at that stage was that the Board had decided that in view of Olivier's illness and long absence convalescing it was necessary to 'identify a successor', as Rayne put it, by 'taking discreet soundings'. Among those sounded were Lord Goodman, who happened to be a personal friend of Rayne as well as Chairman of the Arts Council, and Binkie Beaumont. Both favoured Peter Hall as the only possible candidate. 'A lot of other people, who might have been regarded as candidates themselves, agreed that there was nobody other than Peter Hall who would fit the job', according to Rayne.

It was sometime in July that Hall himself had first been 'sounded out' about succeeding Olivier. In the foreword to his *Diaries*, Hall describes how soon after he had resigned from his job as co-director with Colin Davis of the Royal Opera at Covent Garden, 'I was asked by Lord Goodman to lunch at his flat to meet Sir Max Rayne, the new chairman of the National Theatre . . . At the lunch I was asked if I would consider succeeding Olivier. He had indicated, though vaguely I gathered, that he was thinking of stepping down . . .' Hall said that he would be happy to talk further only if Olivier was really determined to resign; and it was agreed that if there were to be conversations Olivier must be brought into them. At that moment, Olivier was saying he was going one day, and thinking of staying the next. Did Goodman and Rayne decide between them that the time had come to ease Olivier out, even if he did not really want to go? Did they prematurely indicate to Peter Hall that the job was his if he wanted it? Some people even asked, did Hall resign from Covent Garden because he had been tipped off that the offer was coming up? There is no reason to doubt that he was increasingly unhappy at Covent Garden, where he had already been working for a year, and realized that it was a mistake to carry on there. But any informed man of the theatre, looking at what was happening to the National, would wonder how long it would be before it looked for another director.

It is impossible to know whether Olivier wanted to go more than he wanted to stay, or vice versa. His personal resentment at the cancellation of his pet project *Guys and Dolls* knocked a good deal of gilt off the gingerbread. He was a wily and experienced actor-manager who knew quite well that no theatre company stays on top for ever and his had hit the inevitable dip in popularity. Was it best to get out now? There was his age – sixty-four that May – and his health, which had been undermined in the past four years by cancer, appendicitis and now thrombosis, with attacks of pneumonia thrown in. All this, and the fact that he had spent nine years on a comparatively modest income and had three growing children and their educations to provide for, must have weighed in favour of chucking up a job and its recent frustrations. But, for all that, Olivier's physical resilience was amazing. He had made a remarkable recovery, so much so that he was about to undertake one of the longest and most demanding roles of his career – James Tyrone in O'Neill's four-hour autobiographical tragedy, *Long Day's Journey into Night*. If he could play that, he was far from finished. His closest associates do not believe that he seriously contemplated throwing in the sponge. For one thing, he wanted his successor, if there was one, to be an actor. Olivier did not want to hand his company over to a director. In particular he did not want to hand it to Peter Hall, the former overlord of Stratford. There being no viable alternative, it seems he made up his mind to stay and plunged into the part of James Tyrone.

Long Day's Journey was the last throw at the New Theatre. It was announced that the National was to pull out of it as soon as possible. Obviously it had not run two theatres successfully. This caused another outbreak of National gloom in *The Times* and other papers. Tynan defended the National's recent record and denied that it was in crisis and that Olivier might be sacked. 'We had seven really great years and now we have had a bad year. I am only surprised that the slump didn't come sooner. Maybe we have made mistakes – put on the wrong play here, used the wrong director or actors there. But there is nothing wrong with the National that a couple of hits will not put right.' This was only part of the truth and he knew it. Privately he was complaining to Olivier about the weakness of the company, even suggesting that it should be cut back to fifteen actors.

Olivier was by now engaged in an heroic rescue operation. He had not wanted to play in *Long Day's Journey*: he didn't care for the play and he didn't like the part. 'I didn't want to play the role of an actor. I sensed that I would be very good in the role but something kept telling me not to . . . Why is it that the poor old Thespian is invariably portrayed as a drunk?' To give Tynan the credit as well as the blame he deserves, it was his persistent pressure that had helped to persuade Olivier to change his mind. There was also financial pressure. 'One set and five in the cast,' Olivier remarked. 'The great god money, and Ken, won.'

Those who saw it were profoundly grateful to the crisis at the National for forcing Olivier into giving what was probably his greatest performance in a modern stage role. It took time to win his enthusiastic participation even after he agreed to do it. The Australian director, Michael Blakemore, had been a junior actor playing supporting parts to his Titus Andronicus and Coriolanus at Stratford. 'It was very hard for a man like him to take me seriously as a director when he had known me as the young actor playing the Roman Captain. He was prickly and sceptical. He said it was "the woman's play". I told him the father's part was pretty good too. He virtually directed himself in the two-handed scenes, where he knew what he wanted to do. But in the four-handed scenes he was amenable to direction. In the second half of the rehearsal period he became quite different, very light-hearted, as actors playing tragedy often are. We knew we were on to something good.' Constance Cummings hauntingly played the pitiable morphine-addict mother, and Denis Quilley and Ronald Pickup as his two self-destructive sons, one a tormented drunkard, the other tubercular, gave the performances of their lives. The house was rapt for four hours.

Olivier later described the part of O'Neill's father, James, the wasted Irish-American actor, as 'one of the richest ever written'. He identified with the man's obsessive parsimony from personal experience. 'There are some things which, as James Tyrone found, one never forgets. When I first became an actor I lacked for food, I was hungry, out of work and terrified.' It was the multiplicity of layers in his portrayal that made it so spell-binding. James Tyrone, obsessively returning to pick the same sores over again, could easily become a bore but Olivier finally won sympathy for him as he veered from self-righteousness and self-justification to self-pity, self-disgust and finally to naked and moving vulnerability. Beginning with a monster, he ended with a painfully recognizable human being. It was remarked how well-integrated Olivier's performance was – strong without eclipsing everyone else's. He permitted himself one physically spectacular backward step into mid-air off the table, on which he had climbed stingily to remove lightbulbs from the chandelier. 'Michael Blakemore handled him brilliantly,' Denis Quilley recalled. 'He said that for the first three acts, Tyrone is a very good part but it's the fourth act that makes it great. So if some of the effects are not made in the first three acts, Act Four is still there waiting. Olivier took the point instantly. From that point it became a foursome, a string quartet.'

The reviews vied with one another in the relief with which they declared their renewed faith in the National Theatre: 'This is what the National Theatre exists to do and it does it superbly . . . A great relief to salute one production up to its best standard . . . the National once again finds the form that seemed lately to have deserted it . . . the National is itself again.' It was as though a revered elderly relative, after some unfortunate lapses on the bottle, was going straight once more. The queues for returns formed round the theatre and the box office did capacity business. 'After the first night, he came into the theatre next morning rubbing his thumb against his fingertips,' remembered Michael Blakemore. 'He looked at us and said "You can smell it . . . success!" ' It was the same smell in the same theatre that he had noted after the first night of *Richard III* twenty-seven years earlier, 'unmistakable – like seaweed'.

For weeks he had seen practically no one except the cast as he prepared himself for the long night's test of stamina. He had been, as always, meticulous over detail. He wore Tyrone's suit for three weeks before the opening. He took great pains to find the right watch-strap. He became obsessive about turning off light bulbs at home in Brighton. He had saved the company's prestige and finances. But, unknown to him, his own position at the head of it had already been promised to his arch-rival.

5

1972: 'Given the Boot – Again!'

Four actors, however brilliantly they play together, do not make a company any more than a string quartet amounts to an orchestra. By itself, *Long Day's Journey* did not prove that the National had recovered its all-round form. But the opening, only a month later, of Tom Stoppard's second play for the company, *Jumpers*, confirmed it. It was a highly original combination of dazzling dialogue and spectacularly swift scenic effects, carried out with impeccable precision and comic gusto, the sort of highbrow challenge that no commercial theatre would attempt. 'I don't think I would have written *Jumpers* if I hadn't known I could show it to the National, where they wouldn't recoil from a large play with acrobats,' said Stoppard. It brought into the company two fine new leading actors. Michael Hordern was brilliantly wayward in the part of the anguished moral philosophy don, George (Moore), whose erudite debate with himself on whether moral values are absolute or relative ('What, in short, is so good about *good*?') form the intellectual backbone of the piece. His is a serious inquiry counterpointed by hilarious diversions such as his accidental killing of his pet tortoise and hare which he keeps to demonstrate Zeno's paradoxes. The arrow from his bow which kills the hare, followed by the scrunch with which Pat, the adored tortoise, perishes beneath his owner's foot are perfectly prepared *coups de théâtre*. His wife Dotty is a disenchanted popular singer of songs about the moon, who is in mourning for its violation by the moon-landings. The body of a rival philosopher is hanging on a hook in her bedroom next door, where she also entertains the university vice-chancellor in her capacious four-poster. As Dotty, the other newcomer, Diana Rigg, was dottily delicious, an ornament to the stage and to Stoppard's wildly surreal plot involving a team of yellow-vested acrobats, or Jumpers. This required the utmost attention from an audience frequently struggling to keep up with the latest swerving delivery while helpless with laughter. Peter Wood, the

Restoration comedy specialist who thus began a long partnership with Stoppard, directed the piece with all the verve it needed to become airborne.

It could be said that *Jumpers* was the National's gymnastic riposte to the RSC's *Midsummer Night's Dream* directed by Peter Brook, which had opened towards the end of the 1970 season at Stratford and proceeded triumphantly via Broadway to the Aldwych in 1971–2, followed by a world tour, and became the most celebrated, most praised, most talked-about Shakespeare production in the world. This physically acrobatic production staged in a glaringly white circus ring in place of the fairy-haunted wood, blazed across the stage at the time when the National was at the ebb of its reputation. It was easy to jeer then that the title 'national' was being borne by the wrong theatre. The RSC's name was known world-wide while the National Theatre, it was said, meant no more abroad than the National Coal Board. The long-standing leaders of the Stratford company – Peggy Ashcroft, Judi Dench, Eric Porter, Ian Richardson, Donald Sinden, Brewster Mason – had stayed with it and were attracting newer arrivals such as Alan Howard and Emrys James. By contrast the National forces had been looking depleted. The deficit on the season (£80,000) had accumulated with the previous year's to make £140,000, equal to nearly half the Arts Council grant. As it pulled out of the unlucky New Theatre in 1972 the company was cut from 70 to 40.

After *Jumpers* had been praised so highly – 'To fail to enjoy it is not actually a criminal offence but it is a sad evidence of illiteracy,' wrote Harold Hobson – journalists wrote of the National regaining its confidence but made the sort of criticisms that were going to become familiar in the years to come. One of the economies had been to cut out touring. 'Provincial audiences grumble that while their taxes go to support the National, if they want to see one of its productions, they have to pay the fare to London on top of the expense of their tickets,' complained the *Birmingham Post*. Theatres, struggling along on small grants, resented the fact that the National could go cap in hand to the Arts Council and emerge with another £50,000 – much more than most of them received for a year's work. 'A bad patch' was the preferred euphemism for the past year or so, although Olivier said frankly, 'We had a great set-back, let's face it. We have to take risks, this is our job, but risks don't always come off. We were perhaps too ambitious. Now we have to be good boys. We are not really supposed to make money but here we are in the rat-race.'

With *Long Day's Journey* to his credit, following *The National Health*, Michael Blakemore's was the newly rising star among the directorate. His views were quoted alongside Olivier's. 'A safe diet of familiar

59

Shakespeare and Restoration plays would probably fill our stalls,' he said, 'but that is a deplorable way to run a theatre. Trouble always comes from adventurous choice.' All the directors agreed that the rivalry with the RSC was healthy. Said Tynan tartly, 'Our delight at their successes is slightly greater than our delight at their flops.' And Patrick Donnell, the administrator from the RSC who had joined the National, warned, 'If we become sick, there might be a move to push us both together in one company.'

According to Olivier's published memoirs, which are not always totally reliable about dates, it was on 2 February 1972, (the opening night of *Jumpers*) that he went to see Sir Max Rayne, his chairman, and said he was concerned about appointing a successor. 'I made it as clear as I could that the job was really beginning to get a bit thin on top for me now.' So begins the saga of the succession, which still arouses feelings to this day and which did considerable damage to the morale of the National Theatre company at that time and for long afterwards. Unknown to Olivier, the members of the inner Board had already considered the question of his successor and their choice was as good as made. Rayne had been taking his discreet soundings since the previous July, before he became Chairman. For most of that year Olivier's illness and convalescence had prevented him from attending Board meetings. Patrick Donnell acted as his go-between with the Chairman. The two men had been friends since Donnell administered the Shakespeare Memorial Theatre at Stratford in the fifties, when Olivier was appearing there. Rayne and his Board were not reassured by this arrangement. 'Everyone was agreed that we could not go on dealing with the director at arm's length, through an intermediary,' said Rayne. 'There was no doubt that the time had come to identify a successor.'

In this process, Olivier himself had not been helpful. His suggestions about possible successors had always been half-hearted. 'He was tired, he was spent, he was half resigned to going, but he would then get a second wind and wouldn't face the fact that he would have to retire,' said Donnell. 'Sometimes he would ask, "What do you think of the idea of so-and-so?" A lot of woolly ideas were floating around but people were afraid to talk to him about it. No one on the staff would come forward because of the awe of his persona.'

When Olivier again tried to solve the problem by suggesting that his wife, Joan Plowright, should take over, he thought of it on the same pattern as Brecht being succeeded by his widow, Helene Weigel. 'I told him he really mustn't be so silly. I wasn't Helene Weigel and it wasn't the Berliner Ensemble,' recalled Joan Plowright. 'I decided to leave the company and go to Chichester for the 1972 season, so that he could decide for himself. His reaction was to say, "If you go, I shall resign."

That made me feel that his heart wasn't in it any longer.' She secretly hoped that Olivier would resign, although she did not want to be instrumental in persuading him. She was thinking of what George Devine had said to her when she visited him on his death-bed: 'Don't let it do this to Larry.'

Olivier's latest suggestion was that the National should be run by a 'Regency Council', to consist of his wife, Tynan and the associate directors, while he took a back seat in some honorary capacity. Everyone could see that this was not a plan to give up power but to keep it at one remove – to perpetuate the situation that had existed for the past year. 'That was unacceptable to anybody,' said Rayne.

But why did the Board, or at least the Chairman, not tell Olivier plainly that they wanted Peter Hall as his successor? One reason given by Rayne was that Olivier's energies and time were so fully stretched with *Long Day's Journey*. 'I was very reluctant to discuss the question when he was involved in such a long, demanding part. I rather fobbed him off when he mentioned it. We arranged to have a chat after he had finished in the play.' Victor (later Lord) Mishcon, who chaired the Board in Rayne's absence, remembered it like this: 'I think Olivier took it for granted that he was actually going to choose his successor and that we would go to him merely to ask who it was to be. We felt that *we* had the duty to make the choice. While we were more than happy to have his advice we were not necessarily prepared to accept his nomination.' Another reason for reticence was that the negotiations with Peter Hall were not going smoothly, and it was by no means certain that he would accept the job. Although Hall had said that he would not discuss the appointment until Olivier was ready to participate, it did not stop him from discussing it with his old colleagues at the RSC, of which he was still an unpaid consultant director. At some point he asked his successor at the RSC, Trevor Nunn, down to his house on the Thames at Wallingford. The two men had been friends since 1966, the year of Nunn's first notable Stratford production, *The Revenger's Tragedy*. Both men shared the similar background of a Suffolk childhood, rising by scholarship to Cambridge and through university theatre into the profession and early success. Hall had got his chance to run the Stratford company at twenty-nine, Nunn at twenty-eight. Both shared a didactic manner which went down well with RSC actors and which had become part of the Stratford ethos.

'He took me for a walk and told me of the approach that had been made to him,' Trevor Nunn remembered. 'He was in a quandary. He didn't want to go back to the day-to-day running of a huge and complex organization. Covent Garden had not been right for him. But he didn't want to spend the rest of his life in films or the West End theatre.'

Shortly afterwards Nunn said he had the solution: Hall was to return to the RSC and they would run it jointly, enabling Hall to take off what time he needed to direct opera or films and TV. 'I think he was genuinely torn. He had begun to feel that if you are asked to run a national theatre, it is difficult to say no. It is as though destiny is working in your life.' Had he been angling for it all along? 'Not according to the evidence of my eyes and ears,' said Nunn. 'I believe he was genuinely unable to decide.'

Hall also consulted his new agent, Laurence Evans, Chairman of International Creative Management. Evans represented many of the top leading actors, including Olivier, for whom he had managed the New Theatre at the end of the war. 'Peter Hall asked me to lunch one day in mid-March at Prunier's and said "I have been offered the National and I don't know what to do. Should I take it?" He added that the offer was strictly in confidence and nobody must know of it, especially Laurence Olivier.' This put Evans, as agent for both men, into an impossible situation. He rang Binkie Beaumont. 'I told him what I knew and said that Laurence Olivier hadn't been told anything about it. It certainly came as a surprise to Binkie that I was aware of the manœuvring. He had two stock phrases. The first was "Fa-a-ancy" spread over three syllables, rather like Dame Edith Evans' "handbag". The other was, "I'm ama-a-azed". I forget which one he used. I said that I would wait for the rest of the week for someone to tell him, but if they did not, on the following Monday I was going to tell Larry myself.'

But for this there is no telling when the Board would have seen fit to tell Olivier. As it was, he did not have to wait until the following Monday. On Friday, 24 March, Rayne managed at last to make an appointment with the Oliviers, who had been in Italy. 'I told him we still wanted him to stay on and take the Company into the theatre on the South Bank but we felt we ought to appoint a successor and favoured Peter Hall. I added that we wouldn't want to do anything that didn't meet with his approval.' This, Rayne maintains, the choice of Hall appeared to do. 'On the face of it, he seemed happy about it. There was no visible sign of bitterness at that time. He accepted it with what seemed to be a good grace.' Or perhaps he was just acting? Olivier was asked not to tell his colleagues of the Board decision until negotiations with Hall had been completed. Hall and Olivier met on the following Monday, 27 March, for a four-hour discussion. 'He is clearly upset and his feelings are very ambiguous,' Hall noted afterwards. 'He wants to retire as director of the National and can't wait to get out of theatre. He also does *not* want to retire . . . Another part of him doesn't want me to be his successor. I am Royal Shakespeare not National. I have not been Larry's man, ever.'

Olivier began, not unnaturally, to brood on the unwelcome *fait accompli* that had been presented to him, the man who had brought the National Theatre into being. It owed more to him than any Board member like Rayne, who was a newcomer, or Goodman, a sort of latterday Cardinal Wolsey to successive prime ministers, and the prime fixer of many arts appointments. And yet he had not been taken into their confidence. On the contrary, while he almost single-handedly pulled the company out of its nose-dive by an heroic piece of acting, the Board had been negotiating behind his back with a rival whom he most pointedly had not recommended. He could not even tell his colleagues what was going on. He could not tell Tynan that Hall categorically refused to work with him. 'He was absolutely pole-axed by the news and by the secrecy, the way it was handled,' said Joan Plowright. 'Peter Hall had been discussing it with his Stratford colleagues but Larry was the last to know. He felt wounded, humiliated and furious at having been kept in the dark.'

There now followed two weeks of anxious secrecy, and then ten days of uproar. Both Olivier and Hall were terrified of the Press getting wind of the negotiations. Hall was determined to negotiate a very different contract from Olivier's. If he went to the National he wanted more power, *vis-à-vis* the Board, and a much higher salary. Olivier had been doing the job at an extremely modest salary of around £10,000 a year. He had supplemented it considerably by doing a number of film cameos and an American TV commercial for Polaroid, which he insisted should not be shown in Britain. Hall took a hardheaded meritocrat's approach to money. He did not accept the Establishment notion that one should work in the arts for the honour of it. 'I think that Rayne appreciates that bread is also needed' – by bread he had in mind something more like £20,000 – admittedly to run a much larger theatre. He also wanted the freedom to do outside work, which involved a good deal of finesse in the wording of the contract. He was horrified that Olivier's contract was worded so that the Board could appoint associate directors and advise on (and vet) plays. While this was being argued by Laurence Evans, Hall was worrying whether he should tell Trevor Nunn, who was still looking forward to welcoming him back to Stratford. Meanwhile, he was due to direct a musical, *Via Galactica* on Broadway.

He was in New York on Sunday, 9 April, when *The Observer* printed the brief Hall-to-succeed-Olivier story which had apparently been leaked to it by a member of the Board. 'Hall will probably take over when the new National Theatre building opens,' it read. Hall, pestered by telephone calls, admitted that discussions were going on. The floodgates opened the next morning with every paper giving the 'announcement expected shortly' the status of certain fact. Tynan and his wife were touring the châteaux of the Loire when he learned of the leak by telephone from his assistant. He telephoned Olivier and cut short his holiday. Michael Blakemore was also in France. John Dexter was in Hamburg, directing opera. 'Olivier telephoned me and said "Have you read *The Observer* this morning? I have been given the boot – *again*!" ' For Olivier, the situation had now taken on the semblance of a re-play of the sacking of himself, Ralph Richardson and John Burrell from managing the Old Vic in 1948. It confirmed what his old friend Richardson had prophesied would happen if the Old Vic turned into a national theatre. 'They're not going to stand for a couple of actors bossing the place any more. We shall be out, cocky.' Now they were not going to stand for an actor bossing the full-scale theatre on the South Bank. Olivier had been, as he saw it, twice rejected – because he was an actor.

Events now had to move fast. The effect of the leak on the company was to cause consternation and a spirit of loyal indignation, even though rumours that Hall would be the next director had been plentiful. But when? The rumour was the following December. Olivier called a meeting at the Old Vic next day, attended by sixty members of the company. He apologized for their having learned of the plans through the newspapers. He himself had only been told a fortnight earlier and then asked to keep the secret. He emphasized that nothing had yet been signed. He categorically stated that he would remain artistic director until the company was established on the South Bank and reassured them that their jobs were not in danger. The result of this unhappy and confusing fifteen-minute meeting was to increase the resentment in the company. Not only had they not been told, Olivier was not told either. They had all been snubbed. Duly leaked, by Tynan this time, this atmosphere resulted in reports headlined 'National Theatre Torn by Successor Crisis'.

The next afternoon, 12 April, the Board issued a statement that it was discussing an eventual successor as director 'in consultation with Laurence Olivier himself'. It ended: 'No decision regarding a successor has yet been reached. An announcement will be made in due course.' Considering that Hall's agent was at that moment finalizing a contract, that was a disingenuous statement if not, strictly speaking, untrue. 'National Theatre denies report that Olivier is to be replaced,' ran the misleading headline in *The Times*, which went on to quote Tynan: 'I and my colleagues feel that to take a decision of this magnitude without consulting the artistic executive was rather reckless behaviour.' Rayne, for his part, was reported as saying, 'As soon as there was anything to tell, Lord Olivier was told. There has been no lack of harmony between myself and him.' The following day he went further, reported by

Sydney Edwards, then arts reporter of the *Evening Standard*: 'There was never any difference of opinion and nothing was done without Lord Olivier's knowledge – there is nothing sinister about it at all. Peter Hall is a possibility but nothing is definite. Nobody's throat has been cut.' Until then no one had suggested that knives were out.

By now, Olivier had disappeared into the film studios to begin work on *Sleuth* with Michael Caine. Hall had just returned from New York to attend a meeting of the Board for the first time. Before it took place, an angry Tynan saw Rayne to insist that the Board should meet the artistic directorate to hear their views on the succession. He mentioned Blakemore's name. Rayne, he said, replied, 'Alas, I have never met Mr Blakemore.' But in private Tynan did not blame Rayne and Goodman for taking a necessary decision about the future so much as Olivier for refusing to nominate a possible successor from one of his own team. He saw it as 'passing a vote of no confidence in us all'. (He did not know that Olivier had at the last moment, according to his memoirs, proposed Tynan's own candidate, Blakemore.) Rayne invited Tynan and his colleagues to the next Board meeting the following week. By then further discussion would be pointless. That very day Hall settled the details of his contract.

At the end of the first week of the crisis, Hall went to Stratford to see Trevor Nunn and the RSC's general manager, David Brierley. On the Tuesday of that week he had entered in his diary, 'The truth is I don't know whether I want to go to the National Theatre or not.' By the Saturday, when he met Nunn, he practically knew he was going and that their dreams of teaming up were gone. Trevor Nunn remembered, 'We sat there talking and it got dark and nobody switched the lights on. We sensed that something momentous was happening in his life. I think he had gradually realized that back in Stratford he would be retracing his steps and that it wouldn't work. It had got pitch dark and it was very emotional. All one could see in the darkness were glistening eyes.' Hall called it 'one of the low points of my life. There were tears in everybody's eyes – very un-English.' Then a new variation of the idea of teaming up together made its appearance: they should amalgamate the two companies, to make one strong National Theatre! 'The suggestion came from Trevor and was eagerly supported by David. We became very excited and euphoric. All our problems seemed solved,' noted Hall. He left Stratford with the idea that skilful politicking could bring the amalgamation about two or three years hence – an idea that would certainly have surprised the National Theatre Board when it appointed him as its director-designate.

One of the few really substantial objections voiced to Peter Hall as director was that there was already one company created in his image, the RSC, and the National under him would make two. That Sunday, Hall was quoted as saying that that was 'one of the chief worries I had about the job'. No one else had yet heard of the possibility that we might end up with two companies that were dominions of a single empire, with Hall as its Caesar and Nunn as its Pompey.

The Sunday newspapers anticipated the confirmation of Hall in the job, in such terms that it was clear that the whole appointment saga had now become a drama of personality clashes and a public-relations disaster from the point of view of the theatre. Rumours of 'damaged feelings, conspiratorial silences and intrigue' were referred to. It was called 'The National Succession' and 'an insensitive and indecorous muddle'. Rayne maintained that Olivier had expressed unqualified pleasure at the surprise choice of Peter Hall, 'as he still does'. There was something here that did not add up.

The last act resembled farce to some participants and tragedy to others. On Tuesday 18 April, the Press was awaiting the announcement promised for that night, after the Board meeting in the huts at Aquinas St. Before Hall's arrival a deputation of Tynan, Blakemore and Dunlop (Dexter was still directing opera in Germany) were invited to say their say. Tynan proposed that associates like themselves should in future have the right to attend Board meetings and be consulted on decisions. He also asked for associate directors' jobs to be guaranteed for three years and proposed that Blakemore should be named Deputy Director to make it clear that he should stand in for Hall in his absence in the future. Blakemore recalled: 'Rayne gave us a hearing but he was adamant. He wasn't prepared to admit that the Board had acted in any way wrongly.' The Board certainly had the constitutional right to appoint a director without consulting anyone, including his predecessor. Whether it was psychologically wise to do so was a matter of judgement. The one concession from the Board was that the announcement would state that Peter Hall would be joining the theatre in 1973 to 'work with Olivier *and* the artistic executive and take over after the new building opened in 1974'. The complaints concluded, they left and drinks were served. By the time Hall was called in, 'the atmosphere was euphoric and crazy'. The Press release which had been passing between Rayne, Olivier and Hall all day was now further amended, by John Mortimer, to correct its English. The announcement ended with the recommendation that at the end of his term as Director, Olivier be made Life President of the National. It included the news that his name would be given to the main auditorium in the new building.

Hall departed for Vienna to direct a Pinter play, having told the *Daily Telegraph* that he would be joining the theatre as early as possible the following year 'as Olivier is very keen that I should. For the past month he has been most enthusiastic and eager about my appointment.' He also emphasized that the first approach to him by Lord Goodman came ten days *after* he had withdrawn from his Covent Garden appointment. 'I have never sought this job or played to get it.' At the same time he was quoted in the *Evening News*: 'A theatre company is the most political kind of organization – it's a political metaphor. If you're not prepared to engage in politicking, you shouldn't be in the theatre.'

Everyone felt bruised by the struggle. Despite the sops to his pride carefully included in the final Board announcement, Olivier probably received more comfort from his co-star at Pinewood, Michael Caine, who gently ridiculed him for having worked so long and at so much expense of spirit, when he could have been leading a much more comfortable life making films. Tynan, whose opposition campaign had come far too late to stand any chance of success, sent an uncharacteristically mollifying letter to Hall in Vienna saying, 'None of us had anything against you personally. So: Congratulations!' 'Perhaps,' pondered Hall in his diary, 'I will just write a charming letter back.' He didn't, though. When Tynan's proposals for the executive to be guaranteed three more years, etc., came up at a full Board meeting on 3 July, Hall made his feelings plain. 'I asked for it to be minuted that a condition of my accepting the job was that Tynan should go . . . I was fed up with everyone pussy-footing around the subject.' Two days later he looked into Tynan's office to tell him so.

The two men's differing accounts of their encounter are a fascinating guide to the role that self-esteem plays in the perception of such events – immediately, not in memory, for both men kept diaries. Hall described how Tynan told him he was thinking the time had come for him to move on – 'Before I could deliver my blow – I wonder who had warned him?' Tynan recorded Hall's extravagant, but he thought sincere, tribute to his part in creating the NT, going on to say, 'He hopes I don't envisage that I'm to be thrown out. Nevertheless, he's not entirely sure and wants my views on whether we shall get on, both being so good at politicking.' Tynan's response, according to Tynan, was to disabuse Hall of the thought that he had ever intended to stay on after the move. When Hall on his side said 'gently' that he didn't think they would get on, 'he hotly denied this'. Hall adds, 'I told him I thought it best to resolve matters now in case he should hear rumour . . . I am sorry about this situation. Ken will certainly be gone before I am fully involved with the National.' Tynan, on his side, describes how Hall outlined some of his plans for the new National and admitted to feeling a 'slight pang' that he would not be involved in the new policy. The sad thing about this personal incompatibility was that it did not extend to their views on theatre. 'They didn't like each other,' said Kathleen Tynan. 'Ken thought Peter Hall was ambitious, unctuous and power-crazy. But they agreed on a lot of matters to do with the theatre.'

The result of the non-consultation about the succession was to leave not only Tynan but Blakemore and Dexter and many of the actors in Olivier's company festering with indignation at the way he and they had been treated. 'Disgracefully,' according to Blakemore, 'the Board treated Olivier like an irresponsible fool.' 'They treated him shabbily, doing it behind his back and presenting him with a *fait accompli*,' said Denis Quilley. 'I know he felt betrayed – and my natural reaction was to side with him.' 'Shabby' was also the word used in more than one place in print and inevitably the resentment rubbed off, unfairly, on Olivier's successor, as if he had been party to a dishonourable backstage deal. After it was all over, Hall told the Oliviers that he bitterly regretted that he had not defied the secrecy enjoined on him when he was approached.

In retrospect one may wonder if there had been another reason for the Board's secrecy – to prevent an effective counter-attack being mounted by the Olivier directorate. 'If we had known it was coming we would have gone straight to the Press and made a stink,' claimed Dexter, 'but the people who had created the company were, as Tynan said, dismissed like a collection of hired hands.' If Olivier had fought the Board by making his feelings about his treatment public, he commanded such loyalty from his company and the public that the Board might have backed down. But Olivier had no workable alternative to offer, except to carry on himself. The only time he gave the faintest hint in public of his sense of being wronged came ten years later when he wrote in his memoirs, 'Why all the secrecy? Why the shoddy treatment?' His dedication to the idea of the National Theatre was too great to allow him to say anything then that could harm it in the eyes of the public, though he left his friends in no doubt of his feelings in private.

Meanwhile the recovery of the company's fortunes was continuing on the stage of the Old Vic, if not in the boardroom. Just before the succession crisis broke, one of the company's home-grown stars, Ronald Pickup, had impressed as Richard II in the first straightforward Shakespeare production (by David William) that the National had put on for years. He went on to play the hypocritical Joseph Surface in *The School for Scandal* with dazzlingly swift changes of manner between malice and sententiousness, positively capering behind the backs of those he was gulling. This production, by Jonathan Miller, stripped Sheridan of the usual velvet-and-lace tablemat glossiness and substituted the frowzy, down-at-heel, unkempt eighteenth-century world of

Hogarth. Amid grimy-looking furniture and scruffy, insolent servants, their employers were plain, tetchy, louche, tawdry and full of unattractive self-interest. The production was a sell-out and was succeeded by another in July, *The Front Page*.

Ben Hecht and Charles MacArthur's 1928 study of the Chicago newspaper world, whose cynical reporters are hanging around waiting for a man to be hanged, was a surprising choice for the National, being better known in its film versions. The Board were not in favour of doing Broadway hits. But Michael Blakemore, who had discovered that the play had never been performed in England, fought to do it. It was then suggested that he would have to cast American actors in the leads. Instead, Blakemore showed American period films to his cast, led by Denis Quilley as the star reporter, Hildy Johnson, and Alan MacNaughtan as his editor, who snarls memorably, 'Who the hell's gonna read the second paragraph?' 'The accents may not have been perfect Chicago,' said Quilley, 'but MacArthur's widow came to see it and praised it enormously.' The artfully designed mechanism of the plot climaxed in the astutely managed crash through the press-room skylight of the condemned man, which made the audience gasp. Blakemore kept his cast of blasphemous pressmen and the unrolling of the plot going at such an exhilarating clip from first to last that the production became the comedy counterpart to *Long Day's Journey* and as much of a hit.

It was ironic that the National, brought so low in esteem a year earlier, had by the summer of 1972 completely recovered from its doldrums. By then, no one would have seen any pressing need to find a new director or to change the directing team. A largely fresh company had been recruited, numbering among its regulars Gillian Barge, Anna Carteret, Paul Curran, Gawn Grainger, Maureen Lipman, Harry Lomax, Alan MacNaughtan, Louise Purnell, John Shrapnel, Jeanne Watts and Benjamin Whitrow. 'It was by then a very happy company, small, about 40 strong, with everyone working to absolute capacity,' Blakemore recalled. 'We had three resounding hits. The pattern of subsidized companies is always a series of waves and troughs. We had been through a trough. We had a wave coming up – it lasted for two marvellous years. If the Board had had more theatre people on it, they might have known that would happen.'

6

1973: An Old Vic Indian Summer

The bad news of 1972 arrived at the very end of it: the building on the South Bank would not be ready on 23 April 1974, after all. The earliest it could open was the spring of 1975. Olivier and Hall now had to contemplate two years running in harness together and neither of them welcomed the prospect. In January 1973, Olivier told Hall privately that he was not prepared to 'soldier on'; he would leave at the end of the year. The Board's over-hasty anxiety about his fitness to carry on resulted in his leaving two years earlier than he need have done. This, to put it mildly, was a pity. The company's run of success and high morale of 1972–3 did not survive his departure.

The Press was given the news in carefully edited form on 13 March: Hall would join as co-director with Olivier for six months from 1 April, and on 1 November would take over completely. Olivier would stay on to appear in two plays, then take a sabbatical. It was 'hoped' he would return for the opening of the South Bank theatre. Olivier offered the somewhat disingenuous explanation: 'The delays reduce the glory, the pride and the term of office of Peter Hall, who could lose two and a half years in waiting. I feel the cliff-hanging a bit of a strain.' There was no visible trace of reserve between the smiling Olivier and the beaming Hall. Tynan, on the other hand, looked sombre in a black shirt, possibly selected as a mourning gesture for the theatre that he, too, was leaving, while new directors of Hall's choice – Harold Pinter and John Schlesinger – were joining.

None of the reporters present guessed at the real story that was concealed under their noses: that Peter Hall was in the midst of manœuvres to merge his new theatre with his old one, the RSC. He had already floated the idea at Lord Goodman, who was enthusiastic, as he had been once before. He saw it as a way of economizing on management, directors, staff and overheads. The new chairman of the Arts Council, Lord Gibson, and the secretary-general, Sir Hugh

Willatt, did not favour such 'rationalization'. They pointed out that for ten years Hall had been arguing the need for the two theatres to have separate identities. Why now take the opposite view? Very surprisingly, Hall had managed to persuade Olivier, at least for a time, that the merger would be a good thing. He even signed merger proposals along with Hall and Trevor Nunn. But he soon smelled a rat when it became plain that such an organization would have Hall at the head of it and Nunn as his deputy. He saw it as a takeover of the National by the RSC. The RSC chairman, George Farmer, on the other hand, saw it as a takeover of the RSC by the National. Secret meetings were held at a farmhouse near Stratford and in the offices of (who else?) Lord Goodman. Draft budgets were drawn up and estimates made of the savings that would result from the amalgamation. Then, sensing opposition, Hall produced a modified scheme for an 'association' between the two companies, with himself and Trevor Nunn on the board of each. Goodman then advised Hall to leave any form of merger for three years, whereupon Hall took a course he had resorted to before – a leak to the Press to bring the debate out into the open. Fears were expressed that there would not be enough top-class actors, directors and designers – or money – to serve so many auditoria. That was the main argument in favour of merger. There was one main adverse reaction. State patronage, declared the *Evening Standard*, should not be in 'virtually monopolistic' hands. If there was not lively competition between the two major companies, there might be 'an incestuous decline'.

The situation was hardly clarified by a letter to *The Times* from Olivier recalling that he had most earnestly sought such a merger in 1960, when Stratford needed a London home and the National did not yet exist. That engagement had been broken off (he did not say that it was Peter Hall who broke it off), but 'comfort was found in the thought that friendly rivalry was a Good Thing'. Adding that the possibilities should not be dismissed in a day, he ended in Delphic vein: 'In this permissive age we don't have to get married – we might just live together for a while.' This last utterance begged the vital question – live together as one household and, if so, where and run by whom? Hall's original plan was that the RSC should give up the Aldwych Theatre as its London home and move into the Lyttleton auditorium on the South Bank. But the Barbican Theatre, which he had helped design, would be ready one day. When that happened, the RSC would move in to do continuous Shakespeare and there would be no Shakespeare on the South Bank. His later plan for an association envisaged that the RSC would provide all the Shakespeare productions on the South Bank and actors and directors would have a choice of working with either

71

organization. But how much RSC Shakespeare would there be? Hall imagined about six months of the year. Olivier thought it should be much less. Trevor Nunn was alarmed at the idea of the RSC doing nothing but Shakespeare. Hall then reflected that it was equally worrying if the National could not do any Shakespeare at all.

It all came to nothing because as soon as the realities of sharing a theatre or the repertoire were faced, enthusiasm waned speedily. They meant that either Hall or Nunn would have to give up directing Shakespeare while the other did nothing but, which did not suit the ambitions of either. A merged organization would also be gigantic and unwieldy and it soon ran into opposition from Hall's associate directors, from the Arts Council, and finally from Hall and Nunn themselves, who wrote a joint letter to the Council saying that they wished to maintain their independence. The engagement was again broken off. 'A great feeling of relief,' noted Hall. 'The merger now seems to me one of the silliest ideas I have ever been seduced by.' Looking back fifteen years later, he reflected: 'It seemed to us then that there were limited resources and if we pooled them, we would both be stronger. But I'm sure we were right to conclude that it wasn't a good idea. We now have two national theatres competing with each other. Most countries only have one.' According to Trevor Nunn, 'All the signals were that two national theatres were not going to be tolerated. If someone had wanted then to close down the RSC, this was a way of enabling it to continue.' It did not prove necessary then – but the threat is always liable to recur.

Meanwhile Olivier 'topped out' the new building on 2 May. He and Lord Cottesloe, Chairman of the South Bank Theatre Board, which was responsible for getting the building up, poured the last shovelfuls of cement on the roof while construction workers shouted 'Nice one, Larry!' The five hundred guests wandered round the shell beneath, wondering how long it would be before it was habitable. A furious Denys Lasdun was fighting a proposal for a 380-foot hotel tower on the site immediately behind the National, which would loom over it when viewed from the river. After an orchestrated pressure campaign and letters to *The Times* from leading architects, no more was heard of the hotel tower.

The Indian summer of Olivier's regime was continuing to yield memorable productions. *The Misanthrope* brought Molière to the National for the first time. The notorious difficulty of rendering his rhymed couplets into English without making them sound like lines in pantomime was overcome by the young poet and classicist, Tony Harrison. He gave Molière's characters – the misanthropic Alceste, his faithless love Celimene, and his foolish rival Oronte – a racy turn of contemporary speech. Alceste's outburst dismissing Oronte's lame sonnet to Celimene was typical:

> Jesus wept!
> It's bloody rubbish, rhythmically inept,
> Vacuous verbiage, wind, gas, guff,
> All lovesick amateurs churn out that stuff!

Alec McCowen, making his first, overdue appearance with the company, gave a virtuoso display of arrogance and disgust, wearily puckering his nose and closing his eyes with disdain for the insincere, scandal-mongering society, especially the flabby Oronte (Gawn Grainger). Diana Rigg reigned over her salon coiffed, jewelled and gowned as a Parisian society hostess and heartless *femme fatale* of the period. And the period? De Gaulle's France, circa 1966, as rich in self-conscious *chic* as the court of the Sun-King in Molière's time. The verse dropped in references to the Elysée Palace, the *Prix Goncourt*, André Malraux, *Le Figaro*, and Château Mouton Rothschild. John Dexter's fastidious direction and the glassy, *haute couture* salon and costumes created by Tanya Moiseiwitsch gave the audience that special lift which comes of realizing that you have enjoyed a foreign classic more than you ever imagined you could.

Dexter and McCowen went on directly to another memorable production, Peter Shaffer's *Equus*, in which the manner of the presentation was as vital as the matter presented. It turned into a theatrical triumph. The play is an examination of a true case of a boy who blinded a stableful of horses, an occurrence which Shaffer had learned of through a friend, James Mossman. The play explored the reasons for such behaviour in an arena of combat, a lighted ring surrounded by the audience, partly seated on stage, and by benches on which actors waited their turn to perform. Sculpted horses' heads made of leather and silver wire were strapped to the actors' perfectly visible heads and strutted metal platforms were lashed to their feet like hooves. Flicks of the head, exhalations of breath, the use of the neck, legs and stamping of the feet captured the equine essence so well that, thanks to the designer John Napier and the movement directed by Claude Chagrin, they were instantly accepted as striking visual symbols of the nobility of horses. The boy is gradually revealed, through the probing of the psychiatrist, to have created his own primitive religion in the form of Equus, a horse-god, and experienced the ecstasy of mystical union by riding naked. The psychiatrist has to rob him of the capacity for horse-worship, which he envies, to return him to 'normality'. Whether or not this was a convincing reason for the boy turning on his horses to blind them, it provided an overwhelming and erotic theatrical experience in Dexter's hands, with Alec McCowen as the doubt-tormented psychiatrist and Peter Firth as the anguished seventeen-year-old boy. It proved a very durable production, much revived at the National, transferred to the West End, produced around Europe, Australia, South Africa, Japan and the United States and winning every theatre award in New York, where the part of the psychiatrist was played by Anthony Hopkins and Richard Burton among others. But it was originally the riskiest possible enterprise. 'I didn't lie awake at night wondering if it was going to fail, because rehearsals were intoxicating and developed so much intensity,' said Dexter. But Shaffer reflected that only the National would have risked presenting it in the first place.

Equus wiped out the company's previous deficit, playing to standing room only on most nights. Olivier now began to plan his farewell appearances. He had just won an Emmy award for the television film of *Long Day's Journey Into Night*, networked in the US in March and shown throughout the British ITV network on Easter Sunday. For his next appearance Tynan suggested the Neapolitan playwright, Edouardo de Filippo, an institution in Italian theatre, whose company in Naples was practically an extended family to him. As director, Zeffirelli was asked to pay a return visit. He suggested *Saturday, Sunday, Monday*, which appealed to Olivier because of the part it offered to Joan Plowright. She was formidable as the Neapolitan mother presiding over a tightly-knit family from a stew-pot of real Italian *ragu*, simmering on stage and gently flavouring the atmosphere of the Old Vic with the essence of Naples. Olivier contented himself with the minor part of Grandfather, a retired gents' outfitter with a twitching moustache and a compulsion to re-shape other people's hats to his liking. No one could say it tested him very far, but with his usual attention to detail he appeared at rehearsal with a manual on Italian hand gestures and their meanings. 'I was less happy with his mock-Italian accent – soon everyone in the cast sounded like Scottish ice-cream sellers,' wrote Zeffirelli, who argued that they would not play Chekhov in funny Russian accents. Among themselves the cast referred to the play as 'Via Coronazione'. 'We underestimated it,' said Denis Quilley. 'When we got it on, we could see it was a warm-hearted comedy, not *Woman's Own* after all.' The histrionics of Italian family life went down well enough with English audiences for the production to transfer to the West End and de Filippo declared himself well satisfied, especially with the details of speech and gesture that Olivier had captured. It was in this eccentric part that he relinquished directorship of the National on 1 November.

He had moved out of his office into a smaller one down the passage, despite Hall's protest. He suggested that his swansong might have been *King Lear*, with Hall as his director, but then withdrew the idea. His wife had threatened, 'If you do anything as predictable as Lear, I don't think I shall speak to you again. Do something modern, for heaven's sake.' In the end he settled on a play Tynan had commissioned and had been trying to get him to read – *The Party* by Trevor Griffiths. John Dexter had dropped the script on Olivier's desk, saying, 'Read that – you won't like it.' Olivier was intrigued by the character of a veteran working-class Trotskyite, John Tagg. There were two things about it calculated to appeal to him: a twenty-minute monologue calling on young British revolutionaries to get their act together and the fact that it would be his first crack at a Glaswegian, a new challenge to his craftsmanship. Paul Curran, a native, schooled him in the niceties of the city's accent and speech-patterns. Distrustful of his memory, Olivier spent four months learning the lines.

At the first read-through in the huts, 'Down went the book. Up came the speech. I plunged. Twenty minutes later I had done it. Word bloody perfect,' Olivier wrote with justifiable pride. When he came to play it on stage, he added, 'I could feel the company willing me on. Twenty minutes is a long time, a very long time . . .' He insisted that Diana Boddington, the stage manager, time the speech each time. Sometimes he took eighteen minutes, occasionally as little as sixteen. Dexter, who was directing, marvelled at the completeness with which Olivier inhabited the character. 'He wasn't imitating Glasgow, he *was* a Glaswegian. He delivered the speech sitting down. He "did" nothing. He restricted his voice to this narrow range, with just one shout, and gave a most lucid exposition of Marxist theory, which I am pretty sure he did not understand, but made totally compelling.' Olivier did not look on it as an exposition of anything. 'I am grateful to Trevor Griffiths for giving me such an *animal* to fight with night after night.'

And so, on 21 March 1974, Olivier walked for the last time on to the stage on which he had played kings, heroes and villains since 1937, wearing a baggy suit and uttering the thoughts of a disenchanted Glasgow communist. He did not know it was his last performance on any stage, but had he known, he later claimed, he would have made the same choice of part. After the last performance there were two parties at the Old Vic. One was the official farewell and presentation given by the Board in the downstairs bar; the other was the cast party in the rehearsal room at the top of the building. Characteristically, Olivier soon excused himself from the first and joined the second, where he sang songs to Denis Quilley's accompaniment – 'I'm not sure he didn't do Archie Rice's "Why Should I Care?" ' said Dexter. 'Peter Hall looked in and, realizing it was really a family party, left very quickly.' On stage that night at curtainfall, Olivier had received his last Old Vic ovation and as he stood there acknowledging it, Peter Hall had walked on behind him to make a presentation. He himself described how Olivier turned and looked at him. 'For about a hundredth of a second I saw the natural reaction: "What are *you* doing here? Get off the bloody stage." ' Then the actor's mask took over and both men carried on with the leave-taking.

At the time he left it, Olivier's National Theatre at the Old Vic was regarded only as the swelling prologue to the imperial theme then rising in so-far unseen pomp and splendour on the South Bank. Tributes to his work at the Old Vic were somewhat less than generous, as if it were only a foretaste of the real thing. One is inclined to question that assumption now. The new triple-stage complex eclipsed the Old Vic in size, output and public awareness, but has it equalled it in quality, in standards of acting and production, in theatrical excitement? Those who remember both are apt to look back on the Old Vic years as a golden age, comparable in many ways to the golden age of the wartime Old Vic company of Olivier and Richardson. The opening of the new building was not, as younger theatregoers quite naturally assume, the real beginning of the National Theatre, after a practice knock-up in outmoded premises. Bigger buildings are not a guarantee of bigger achievements. In leaving an old theatre for a new one, the company may have lost something irreplaceable. It could, after all, have kept the Old Vic and supplemented it with a second house on a more modest scale.

By the end of Olivier's ten-year period as Director, his company had mounted some seventy productions. Of these, thirty were outstanding successes with the public, averaging audiences of over 90 per cent, and winning overwhelming critical approval. That is a high success rate by any standards. Nevertheless Olivier's record was criticized on various grounds: that it was a 'museum theatre', not adventurous enough in mounting modern plays; that it was a showcase for Olivier; that there were not enough other stars; that there was too little company identity; finally that its programme was not as interesting as the RSC's. Let us take these in order. Museum theatre: it was true that the National's major glories were its forty-two classical productions, which made up 60 per cent of the repertoire. But so were some of its new plays: the five from Peter Shaffer and Tom Stoppard were big audience successes. Over the ten years the National also gave the first London airing to plays by Samuel Beckett, Bertolt Brecht, Max Frisch, Arthur Miller, Eugene O'Neill, John Arden, Charles Wood, Peter Nichols and Trevor Griffiths. The strikingly original productions of *The Recruiting Officer* and *Love for Love*, *The Misanthrope* and the all-male *As You Like It* showed that there was no museum caretaker's approach to the classics.

As for the complaint that the theatre was a vehicle for Olivier, he had appeared in only nine of the seventy productions and taken over roles (usually minor) in four of them (usually briefly). He directed nine of them. So only one production in eight could be said to have been a showcase for the leading actor of his generation. Perhaps it was nearer the mark to say that he should have appeared more often – certainly it would have done the box office nothing but good. There was substance in the criticism that not enough other stars appeared, notably Gielgud and Richardson, for reasons that have been examined already. Company identity, so strong in the early years, had faltered as actors who had made their names with the National were lured away. But in the last three years another, near-permanent company had been built up, led by such artists as Michael Hordern, Alec McCowen, Diana Rigg, Denis Quilley and one of the original band, Frank Finlay. Comparisons with the RSC are difficult to make. The National included only nine Shakespeare plays in its list: its productions of *Othello*, *As You Like It* and *The Merchant of Venice* were at least on a par with any RSC production except Peter Brook's *Midsummer Night's Dream*. In the field of controversial plays it looked as though the RSC would always have the edge – after the banning of *Soldiers*. Neither could hope to compete with the Royal Court as a political forum. But 'national' had been shown not to mean 'nationalistic' under Olivier. The forty-two classics were evenly divided between English and foreign-language plays.

The criticisms, therefore, were not of much force. The virtues of Olivier's regime were those of a close-knit, actor-manager's company with what he called 'the hot breath of unity'. His boast – 'There is nothing that this company cannot reach' – was made good over a wide range of targets, Shakespeare and Strindberg, Farquhar and Feydeau. Russian, American, French and Italian plays were all sure-footedly staged within the last two years as well as an English repertoire that spanned Shakespeare, Sheridan and Stoppard. True, the company had not shone equally in Greek tragedy, Brecht or French classics other than *The Misanthrope*. Its few experimental productions – other than the amazing Peter Brook *Oedipus* – were its weakest point. But for versatility combined with high-level performance it had not been bettered in recent theatrical history. As for standards of acting, especially in productions which included Olivier, to quote Peter Shaffer's comment, 'it is hard to accept today's foothills when one has seen the Alps'. The dips in the company's standards all coincided with Olivier's serious illnesses and incapacity.

Olivier proved himself perhaps surprisingly permissive towards those around him. William Gaskill, from a very different theatrical tradition, asked him to improvise at rehearsals of *The Recruiting Officer*

– 'I think he hated it but he didn't show it. Larry was a very jokey person to work with.' Michael Blakemore was impressed with Olivier's tolerance in matters of taste. 'He often elected to put on a production that he personally disliked intensely, such as *Oedipus*, for which he gave Peter Brook ten weeks' rehearsal, or my production of *The National Health*, in which four-letter words were spoken for the first time on the National Theatre stage. He didn't like it but he went along with it.' Frank Dunlop pointed to the international standard of judgement Olivier exercised. 'He allowed me to go abroad for the right designer, such as Piero Gherardi, for *The White Devil*, or the Berliner Ensemble's Karl von Appen for *The Captain of Köpernick*. He allowed you to take risks.' His international outlook undoubtedly owed much to Kenneth Tynan, whose influence was sometimes for the better, sometimes for the worse, but who by no means deserved his curt dismissal from the scene, with not even the offer of severance pay (he was by now a sick man) until Olivier took up his cause.

Olivier ran his theatre like the old-style professional he was. He liked, for example, to have the box office returns for the night taken round to his dressing-room in the interval, where he would examine them at Lilian Baylis's large desk. Roger Lobb, than a box office assistant, later its manager, often performed this task. 'He was very good at counting the house when he was on stage. He would know within a small margin how many seats were empty.' His control extended to small details. Harry Henderson, an old soldier of the Indian Army, had been the housekeeper at the Old Vic for years before the National moved in. 'There were window boxes along the front of the theatre and he would expect me to repaint them to match the colour of the posters.' He and Olivier struck up a friendship through weightlifting. Harry kept a 'gym' in the theatre basement for the use of the actors, and Olivier, a fitness fanatic like his housekeeper, used it regularly for work-outs. There were seigneurial courtesies: an actor taking over a lead invariably found a half-bottle of champagne sent to his dressing-room with a hand-written note from Sir Laurence. But it had not always been so. Alex McCowen, who had worked in Olivier's company at the St James's Theatre in the 1950s, remembered, 'In those days it was Vivien Leigh who knew everyone's name and birthday, while he stayed in the background. The change from the remote figure he was then to the jolly and gregarious boss at the National was remarkable. He would drop in at your dressing-room and discuss the sort of make-up you were using. While he was rehearsing with Zeffirelli, he stopped me in a corridor and said confidentially, "The man wants me to do business before I've learnt my lines! How can you work like that?" On another occasion he called me to his dressing-room after rehearsals. I wondered what I had done so heinous that it had to be corrected in private. "Dear boy," he said, "do show me how you tie that green neckerchief of yours so that it stays in place. Mine always slips down." ' There are many such memories among members of his company of what Jonathan Miller felicitously called, 'a little touch of Larry in the night'.

He was essentially running a company for actors. After the opening of *Love for Love*, which received ecstatic reviews, Olivier turned to its director Peter Wood with genuine surprise and said: 'But *you've* got quite good notices!' 'As a theatre,' said Wood, 'it was about actors' performances, not about directors' productions.' Derek Jacobi saw it as a golden period. 'He called us his "children" and we grew up with the company, being gradually given responsibility. He was a friend, almost a father, for whom we felt respect and fear and love.' Olivier later claimed that 'My company did speak and were heard,' but many of them did not dare to. 'A lot of people were too frightened or in awe to approach him,' said Diana Boddington, who had been his stage-manager since the days of *Richard III*. He was not in the giving vein every day. He could be vain, prone to tantrums, coy and exacting of others' agreement. 'His favourite word was "Yes",' said Robert Stephens. 'If you said "No", as I sometimes did, he could hold it against you.' There was a gulf between 'Sir' and his company, and his brief to Michael Hallifax, who became executive company manager, was to bridge it. 'He said, "I want them to feel we care about them because we do." One result of the fact that we always cast within the company if possible was that there was a very small turnover – it was quite unusual if as many as six actors came and went in a year.'

There is no doubt that Olivier always intended to lead his company into the new building on the South Bank which had been designed with a great deal of advice from him. 'He used to say that we would march across the threshold together and then he would say good-bye,' according to Hallifax. But Olivier's own accounts of his feelings on leaving before he could do so veered violently between relief and resentment. 'I am really quite happy to go,' he said when he made the announcement. 'I am dreading the depression that is bound to come with retirement but a few sneaking advantages are beginning to show their dainty little heads.' For years no comment escaped him publicly about the manner of his going, whatever his private feelings of betrayal. He would not go near the new theatre, except for the royal opening night when, he confided, he felt like a ghost. He fell into the habit of deprecating his achievements at the National: 'I wasn't satisfied or happy with my work there.' Ten years after leaving he allowed a rare glimpse of his true feelings: 'I was always dreaming of marching my little troupe up the road but that wasn't for me. I was hoping to feel a glow of satisfaction but I was so tired out, I was just glad to let it go.' In fact, when he left he appeared to be in excellent form, looking much younger than a man of sixty-five who had carried his burdens. 'Isn't he *handsome*?' said a woman journalist at the press conference at which he announced his departure. It was after his departure that he was to fall ill so seriously that even he wondered if he would pull through. It looked like a classic case of the body collapsing because of a spiritual blow. Much later, when he came to write – or rather to dictate to Gawn Grainger, the actor who had become his confidant – the essays published under the title *On Acting* in 1986, he felt able to do himself justice at last: 'I was proud of my position as director of the National Theatre and always will be. I'm certain that the work we did there was a great credit to the British theatre as a whole. I am convinced that, pound for pound, for a while we were the best troupe of players in the world.' It was many years before people appreciated this – indeed the real consciousness of his achievement at the National as its creator and the establisher of its standards only became general after 11 July 1989, when he died and it seemed as if the whole country stopped involuntarily in the middle of whatever it was doing to absorb the knowledge that we would not look upon his like as an actor again. In the interval between his departure and his death he attended the new theatre as an anonymous member of the audience but said nothing, not even on the night when he was its star at his 80th birthday celebrations. It was a self-denying ordinance that he kept to strictly to the end. (Hearing of the preparations for this book he wrote to me, 'I hope you will forgive me but I feel that I have said and written all I wish to on that subject.') So there was a general forgetfulness, followed by ignorance among those who were too young to have seen him at the National, of what he did there. It began to be dispelled by the torrents of tribute that his death released. On the night of the day he died, the National's flags flew at half-mast and its lighted sign-board bore the single legend: 'Laurence Olivier 1907–1989'. Inside, audiences stood and were asked by Edward Petherbridge not only to remember him but to applaud – in case he is listening tonight'. Some of us asked ourselves whether the National on its grander scale had often equalled, let alone surpassed, the thrill that, at his best, he gave it.

7

A Building Out Of Its Time

When Denys Lasdun was selected to design the National Theatre in November 1963, he was the fifth architect to be appointed to the task. His predecessors had planned national theatres on a variety of sites. For the triangular piece of land opposite the Victoria and Albert Museum purchased in 1938, Sir Edwin Lutyens was persuaded to draw up plans, without fee. The site, now occupied by Sir Hugh Casson's Ismaili temple, was too small and although it was the right place for a museum, it was hardly right for the theatre. When war broke out, the National Theatre Committee offered the site on loan to the Government, which put an emergency water tank on it for fire-fighting. In exchange for the South Kensington site, the London County Council proposed that the theatre should be sited midway between Charing Cross and Waterloo bridges. Lutyens set about a second design, containing two auditoria behind a colonnaded façade along the river frontage. The plans went on view in 1942, the year Lutyens died. He was succeeded by Sir Hubert Worthington, formerly one of his assistants, who designed a traditional classical temple with portico. It became irrelevant when the LCC moved the site downstream to abut Waterloo Bridge, where the Queen Elizabeth Hall was later to stand. In 1946 a new architect was appointed, the Australian Brian O'Rorke, best known for his interiors for the liners of the Orient line. His building was to counter poise the new Royal Festival Hall, which was opened in 1951. In the same year the Queen (later the Queen Mother) laid the theatre's foundation stone. This was the theatre towards which the 1949 National Theatre Act had promised £1 million. Nevertheless, in 1953 it was refused planning permission. Its relationship to the Festival Hall was deemed unsatisfactory. The site was moved again, upstream of the Charing Cross bridge this time, to stand alongside County Hall. O'Rorke prepared new plans, which were approved in principle, but it was becoming clear that the projected cost had doubled and by now there were doubts in government circles whether it should be built there or, indeed, built at all. In March 1961, the Chancellor, Selwyn Lloyd, dropped his bombshell; we were not to have a national theatre after all. The money, or some of it, would go to regional theatres. The LCC countered by offering to pay more than half the estimated cost, the product of a penny rate, £1.3 million, if the Government put up its promised £1 million. The Government was at last shamed into agreeing. But it was stipulated that the new scheme should include an opera house (for the Sadler's Wells company) as well as a theatre.

At this point Lord Cottesloe entered the scene. Born John Fremantle, he had rowed for Eton and Cambridge and shot for England at Bisley, become a civil engineer and sat on the London County Council after the war, before succeeding as the fourth Baron Cottesloe. In 1960 he was made Chairman of the Arts Council and it was presumably in this capacity that Selwyn Lloyd now sent for him to ask whether a theatre and opera house could be built for the money available, namely £2.3 million. 'I said it looked a reasonable proposition,' Lord Cottesloe recalled, 'by which I meant that it was enough to make a good start on the O'Rorke design. So a South Bank Theatre and Opera House Board was appointed, with myself as chairman, to get it built. We finally went to tender on a rather different figure – £7.5 million.' But that was for a very different design.

Once again a new architect was to be chosen. The newly appointed board shrank from the marathon task of interviewing all architects who might apply. Instead a group of five assessors was asked to select a short-list of 20 from some 120 applicants. They were then invited to discuss proposals for two auditoria, a main house which was adaptable both as an amphitheatre and as a proscenium arch theatre, and a small experimental theatre. They were interviewed over three days by a committee chaired by the Festival Hall architect, Sir Robert Matthew. They came to the unanimous decision that Denys Lasdun was their man. Cottesloe recalled: 'The committee was particularly impressed when he said he knew nothing about designing theatres and would have to sit down and learn what was needed from our committee.' That was one shrewd stroke of Lasdun's. Olivier remembered another: unlike the groups of partners from other well-known practices, Lasdun arrived entirely alone. 'Very theatrical. Just him and nobody else. That was immensely effective and, as he knew perfectly well, quite touching. During the interview he put his finger on it very cleverly. He said, "Surely the most important aspect of what we are talking about is the spiritual one." Oh, my dear! We all fell for that.' Lasdun himself remembered telling them, 'If you want me as your architect you will have to work very hard with me. When you

82

have nothing more to tell me, only then will I want to be left alone to design the building.'

The man who walked off with one of the plum architectural commissions of the age as far as London was concerned was forty-nine, with a comparatively small architectural practice. He was nowhere near as famous as Sir Basil Spence, for example, who told the committee that he was much too busy to design a theatre – for which one must be profoundly grateful. Lasdun was of the generation that revered the Modern Movement in its youth, but he later modified his admiration for the dogmas of Le Corbusier. His best-known public buildings were the Royal College of Physicians in Regent's Park and the University of East Anglia. Both exemplified his fundamental belief that buildings should be at one with the surrounding landscape. He was in no way like the grey men of corporation architecture: his appearance had a flamboyant touch, which went with a choleric temperament – he can be very fierce in defence of his own buildings – and his pronouncements about his work often have a mystical, romantic ring. The National Theatre's Building Committee soon found that they were dealing with an artist, who listened patiently for two years while they discussed at monthly intervals the nature of theatre and the relationships possible between performers and audiences. But once they settled upon an agreed scheme, the time for consultation was over. As promised, he insisted on being left alone to get on with it, exercising complete autonomy, the artist's prerogative of knowing best. This was quite congenial to Lord Cottesloe and his board. 'I took the view that once you appoint an architect, you have to give him his head,' said that tolerant chairman, 'and we put no final limit to the cost. There was a firm government guarantee that it would be built and we assumed that the money would be forthcoming. We were only concerned with getting a building that would fulfil the requirements. We assumed that the government would find the money to build it and maintain it. The question of economizing on maintenance never arose.' This relaxed easy attitude, admirable from the point of view of the architect's freedom, was to have far-reaching consequences. The contrast between attitudes in the expansive sixties, when the design was being finalized, and in the cost-cutting late seventies and after, when the building was at last being put to use, could not have been starker.

Until 1966, Lasdun was working to the brief for an opera house and theatre complex on the bank of the Thames opposite Charing Cross, in front of the Shell Centre, and his first model for the twin buildings was unveiled in May 1965. The site itself was a better one than the ultimate position – more central and more imposing, although it suffered from the disadvantage of being dominated by the tower of the Shell complex designed by Sir Howard Robertson, one of the dullest missed opportunities of London's post-war riverside architecture. Lasdun's model overcame this by creating a theatrical townscape of twin buildings facing each other across a piazza, between tiers of stepped public terraces. The intricate geometry of these complementary buildings – most easily imagined as two pyramids of sandwiches each topped by the sugar-cube of a fly-tower – ingeniously brought the eye down from the Shell tower to river-bank level. The outdoor space between them would have provided a stage commanding a view across the river, from the Houses of Parliament to its left to the vista up to Trafalgar Square in front. It could have made a Trafalgar Square for the South Bank. But when the plan for a new opera house was axed in 1966 (by Lord Goodman, who had succeeded Cottesloe as Arts Council Chairman) this made nonsense of Lasdun's balanced scheme. And yet another site – the very last – was offered by the GLC on Prince's Meadow, then a derelict area immediately downstream of Waterloo Bridge. The site was not such an appropriate place for a grandstand, as it commanded a view mainly of Somerset House, the palace of income tax, which for all its baroque styling is a place bereft of human beings. Lasdun's outdoor terraces did not have the same function when they no longer formed part of an open-air piazza or forum between two buildings. They now hung like outside corridors from the sides of a single building, which began to resemble a liner with decks and a superstructure of fly-towers where bridge and funnels would be.

Cottesloe and his board had no choice in the matter of site – they had to take what was offered. But it is worth asking whether in fact the National was built in the wrong place, isolated on an untheatrical, unconvivial site on the wrong side of the river instead of in the heart of London's theatreland. The concert halls alongside it are the only concert halls in central London and created a new musical centre. But the Hayward Gallery and National Film Theatre alongside cannot be said to have gained in popularity by being so remote from other art galleries and cinemas. People hoped, by concentrating them all together, that an artistic quarter would be created which would gradually attract a surrounding environment of bars, cafés, restaurants, and other venues devoted to arts and crafts, such as sprang up round the Pompidou Centre in Paris. In more than twenty years nothing of the sort has happened. There is no *quartier* in the surrounding streets for the simple reason that there are no surrounding streets. The locality consists of bomb-sites, still mainly used as car and lorry parks. Beyond the theatre rises the shut face of the IBM building (designed by Lasdun). The hinterland is dominated by railway arches, the Waterloo Road intersections and its sinister pedestrian underpasses. It is a wasteland largely populated by down-and-outs, beggars and the homeless of 'cardboard city', which theatregoers leave as quickly as possible.

Neither the ambience nor the outer appearance of the theatre was Lasdun's first consideration; he was building from the inside out. The first two years of (surely very leisurely) talks were devoted to interior design. Ideas of staging were in flux in the sixties. The Building Committee which met monthly to debate the new theatre's require-ments was a constellation of theatre talent. Over the years it was attended by many men who had run theatres, Laurence Olivier and Norman Marshall (administrator of the Old Vic) as joint chairmen, George Devine of the Royal Court, Peter Hall, Stephen Arlen of the English National Opera and Michael Benthall, a later director of the Old Vic. Among others present at various times were directors Peter Brook, John Dexter, Frank Dunlop, Michael Elliott, William Gaskill and Michel St Denis. Designers were represented by Sean Kenny, Jocelyn Herbert and Tanya Moiseiwitsch, lighting technicians by Richard Pilbrow and actors by Robert Stephens. The main question under discussion, said Lasdun, was 'What is the nature of the theatre to be?' Lasdun visited the open stage theatres that Tyrone Guthrie had had designed at Stratford, Ontario, and Minneapolis. He was learning about the dichotomy of theatrical opinion between open or thrust stages, favoured by Peter Hall, Peter Brook and Michel St Denis, and the majority of the committee, who wanted a stage capable of being turned into a proscenium. Peter Hall went so far as to call the proscenium stage 'an historical hiccup' from 1700 until the present day, when theatre was reverting, in his view, to the older tradition of open staging. He wanted there to be only one main open-stage theatre plus a studio. Olivier had mixed feelings after his experience working on the wide-open, unfocused open stage at Chichester. 'I always felt that the open stage boys have gone back in time. Shakespeare had that sort of theatre. I suppose that the actors evolved the proscenium. The chap playing Richard III said, "Let's go back a bit further, then I'll only have to look in one direction when making an aside." And the comedian said, "It's awful to get a laugh from this side and not the other because they can't see the face I'm pulling." And bit by bit they went back and the proscenium was evolved. It arrived soon after Shakespeare's time and I always rather laughingly supposed that it must have seemed a tremendous improvement in their minds or they wouldn't have done it. Now we see the open stage as a great step forward. It is – and it isn't.'

Lasdun ruled out the all-purpose adaptable stage as impractical if it was to be of any size. In that case, Olivier insisted, there would also have to be a proscenium theatre, partly in order to accommodate visiting companies whose work could only be presented that way and because there were many plays that really did not work properly on open stages. It was the open stage auditorium that took the time. Before long Lasdun's office was heaped with discarded models. 'Really what you are asking for is a room with a stage in the corner,' he said one day – and drew it. From this germ the Olivier auditorium was evolved. There was much argument about the position of the 'point of command' – a zone from which the actor can see the entire audience within the 120 degree angle of his vision and the entire audience can see both of his eyes. If the audience seating is fanned out too widely, this point can only be found near the very back of the stage. To command the audience from no more than fifteen feet from the front row, the fanning out of the seating must not exceed 130 degrees. But contact between actor and audience also depends on distance and the steepness of the rake of the auditorium. Lasdun's final design divided the 1,160 seats into, it was claimed, 660 stalls and 500 balcony seats, none of them more than 75 feet from the stage. The circle is stepped back above and behind the last stalls row, with a concrete tier-front that was to cause acoustical problems later. The side sections of the stalls seating are raised in two 'wings', like the arms of an armchair. The rake of the seating is fairly steep, so that almost everyone is looking down on the stage, which itself is a mere half-metre high – and was originally designed to be even lower. The theatre is often inaccurately compared to the much bigger classical Greek theatre at Epidaurus, where the stage, or *orchestra*, is at ground level and the seating capacity is 15,000 people, who enfold three-quarters of it. The Olivier looks like a small lecture theatre compared to the stadium of Epidaurus. Even so, from the back rows of the circle its stage can look an awfully long way away.

On 12 October 1966, Lasdun's final plan was adopted by the South Bank Board with the recommendation of the Building Committee and with the following encomium from Olivier: 'This auditorium and stage answers everything we have ever asked for in terms of an "open" solution. It has perfect sight-lines; an acting area of the right size; the possibility of having enthusiastic members of the audience close to the stage (this refers to the front four rows of low-priced seats). It has a marvellous atmosphere. I particularly like the raised banks of seating at the sides. All members of the Committee are immensely happy with this concept.' Whatever criticisms might be made of the auditorium in future operation, they should be laid at the Building Committee's door, not Lasdun's. It was clear that he had been meticulous in carrying out their wishes. If it was wrong, it was this wealth of theatrical expertise that got it wrong.

After so much time had been lavished on the Olivier theatre, the

1963: Sir Laurence Olivier, the actor-manager, becomes the National's first
director (photo: Angus McBean).

1939: Sir Edwin Lutyens shows Bernard Shaw his plans for a National Theatre in South Kensington (photo: Hulton-Deutsch Collection).

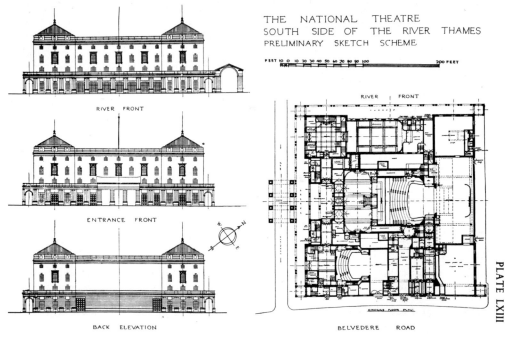

RIVER FRONT

ENTRANCE FRONT

BACK ELEVATION

THE NATIONAL THEATRE
SOUTH SIDE OF THE RIVER THAMES
PRELIMINARY SKETCH SCHEME

FEET 10 0 10 20 30 40 50 60 70 80 90 100   200 FEET

RIVER FRONT

GROUND FLOOR PLAN

BELVEDERE ROAD

PLATE LXIII

1944: Lutyen's design for the first riverside site between Hungerford Bridge and Waterloo Bridge (copyright: British Architectural Library).

1963: Joan Plowright as Sonya in Laurence Olivier's production of *Uncle Vanya* which transferred from Chichester to the Old Vic with Max Adrian (photo: Angus McBean).

1963: Sean Kenny's sketch of his sweeping ramp for the *Hamlet* production; as a result of its weight the revolve often had to be pushed round by hand (reproduced by kind permission of the Sean Kenny Estate).

1964: Edith Evans, whose faulty memory upset Coward's production of *Hay Fever*, as Judith Bliss, with Derek Jacobi and Louise Purnell (photo: Angus McBean).

1966: Laurence Olivier as Tattle in *Love for Love* taking his nocturnal walk along the wall beneath the bedroom window, between two spectacular leaps (photo: Zoe Dominic).

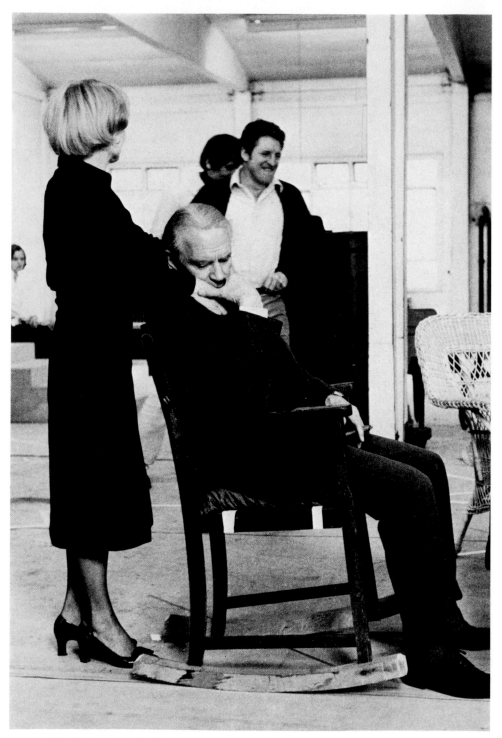

1971: Rehearsing in 'the huts' for *Long Day's Journey Into Night*. Constance Cummings, Laurence Olivier, Denis Quilley and Ronald Pickup (photo: Zoe Dominic).

1972: *Jumpers*. The problems of philosophy with an errant wife in the next room are demonstrated by Michael Hordern in Stoppard's metaphysical comedy (photo: Donald Cooper).

1975: John Gielgud and Ralph Richardson breaking new ground as the duo of writers in the chamber music of Harold Pinter's *No Man's Land* (photo: Donald Cooper).

Lyttleton, according to Olivier's memory, took 'about a week'. No doubt he exaggerated, but Lasdun's own description of it makes it sound an elementary matter: 'There are plays where actor and audience confront each other. The characteristic of confrontation is very straightforward. You need a rectangle and the audience, frankly, just facing. That is the essence of the Lyttleton theatre.' It is also the reason, most probably, why the Lyttleton is the least favourite stage at the National of the actors, directors, designers and, in many cases, playgoers, who use it.

Simple head-on confrontation is a pretty simplistic view of the evolution of proscenium theatres, on which nineteenth-century architects like Phipps and Matcham expended so much ingenuity. Interiors of a variety of shapes, capacities and atmospheres had been created, some vast and as highly decorated as wedding cakes, others as intimate and elegant as drawing-rooms. Not one of them was a confrontational rectangle, but a combination of curves, ellipses or horseshoes that made a great difference not only to visibility and audibility but to the quality of the audience's shared experience focused on the now denigrated proscenium. There is no mistaking a traditional type of theatre auditorium for a cinema; but that is the impression given by Lasdun's long, slightly curved rows of *fauteuils* without any dividing aisle and by the fact that the circle is positioned so that you cannot see the stalls from it and vice versa. There are no side boxes, no arch, no visible proscenium – nothing more than an opening of unusual width, approximately 45 feet. (The width can be narrowed to a minimum of 30 feet but this is hardly ever done; it would leave most people sitting at either end of the front rows without a view of the stage.)

So much for confrontation as a desirable form of theatre design. It works in cinemas because screens have no depth of recession, but it does not help plays if they look like a wide-screen experience in the cinema. One of the chief attractions of theatregoing as distinct from cinemagoing is the sensation of sharing the live experience with several hundred other people who can be magnetized, turned into one by the power of the performers. The shape of an auditorium is a powerful factor in focusing this reaction. Victorian and Edwardian theatres with their side boxes and often steeply curved seating plans were designed to promote intimacy not only with the stage but between sections of the audience. This art was lost in the thirties in such theatres as the notorious Shakespeare Memorial (now the Royal Shakespeare) Theatre at Stratford-upon-Avon. The Lyttleton, like most theatres of the fifties and sixties, could never be accused of intimacy. Nobody seems to have even aimed at it, despite the great intimacy they had been used to at the Old Vic. Why didn't they keep that as the National's proscenium theatre? It badly needed repair but could have been refurbished for a great deal less than the cost of adding the Lyttleton to the plans. Other national theatres operate in two separate buildings, but no doubt the utopian vision of three theatres under one roof with all their ancillary departments swept everyone along in those days.

The third auditorium had the most chequered career of all. It was originally envisaged as a private space for studio experiment and at one stage as a 'TV studio' where performances could be recorded. Then it was dropped at the end of the 1960s as one of the economies to keep the cost within the £7.5 million budget. But in 1972 the government of the day (Conservative) authorized the spending of another £2 million, most of which was to meet inflation. Lord Eccles, the minister responsible, said that he could not believe that the Board would want to use any of the money to reinstate a third auditorium. At this point Peter Hall, as director-designate, made an impassioned plea for a third stage. The space for the auditorium could not be taken away, because it occupied an area behind the backstage of the Olivier theatre integral to the building, but it was to be sealed off as a bricked-in void. He campaigned for it to be finished to rehearsal room standards, so that it was capable of being licensed for public performance. A sum of £50,000 was found from a 'housing the arts' fund to pay for seating and upper galleries. Hall claimed that once the other theatres were open the studio would cost nothing to run. By November 1973 it was being seen differently: 'The concept of the studio in the new building was totally demolished. It is now to be thought of as our third theatre – the Cottesloe Theatre,' he noted at the time. 'If there's one thing I want on my tombstone, it is that I saved the Cottesloe,' he told me at the end of his directorship.

The task of suggesting how the cheapest possible theatre could be fitted into the void was given to Iain Mackintosh. Mackintosh had worked at the tiny Georgian Theatre in Richmond, Yorkshire, and was a notable expert on the history of theatre building in this country. To the open and proscenium stages he now added the idea of a courtyard theatre whose rectangular auditorium was surrounded on three sides with tiers of narrow galleries, like those surrounding the inn yards that once served for open-air performances. The seating below would not be fixed but flexible and could be rearranged on several patterns. According to the varied seating arrangements, the theatre could hold from 200 to 400 people. Its interior was to be in the barest style, no more than a box finished in matt black paint, with the lighting bridges overhead clearly visible. Its overall dimensions are 66 feet by 56 feet, which is not, in fact, small; it is bigger than Garrick's theatre was at Drury Lane. Mackintosh wrote that his scheme aimed at offering those who used it 'enough, but no more, than is essential to experiment'. It was the last part of the building to be finished, in 1977.

Building work had been ceremonially begun in 1969 by Jennie Lee, who added a shovelful of cement to the first pouring of the concrete which was to be such a symbol of the National. She had declared, 'If we can't build a splendid theatre with £7,500,000, we all ought to jump in the Thames.' It would not be long before that sum proved inadequate. In 1973 it was increased by £2 million. By 1974 inflation was playing such havoc with the estimates that a new National Theatre Bill was passed removing the limit on the building cost altogether. By then the main phase of construction was finished and the building had been topped out on 2 May 1973, by Lords Cottesloe and Olivier. There was nothing underneath the roof as yet. Equipping the stages was to prove a saga of mishaps and disappointments, which added greatly to the delay in getting the building into operation. The problems arose from the need to provide quick and frequent changeovers for a heavy repertoire programme. Richard Pilbrow, the foremost lighting designer in the country, and his firm, Theatre Projects, were appointed consultants, and he and a number of technical experts visited theatres in Europe which had similar repertory output. It is necessary to look ahead, breaking the chronology of the rest of this history, in order to follow the technical problems through.

The biggest headache was the Olivier's open stage, supported by only small side and back stages on which scenery could be kept in readiness. Some sets could be rolled in on wheeled trucks, but large pieces of scenery had to be flown in and might have to be set at any angle. This required spot-line flying from 150 electric hoists, controlled by computer. The system had to be capable of placing a piece of three-dimensional scenery at any spot with precision, safety and silence and it was to be a very long time before the snags were ironed out of it – until 1981, in fact, when it was first fully used. 'The power- flying system in the Olivier is probably the best in the world,' claims Richard Pilbrow, 'but it took so long to commission and execute because, as with an aircraft, everything must have a fail-safe back-up system.' Even so, it did not seem enough. Pilbrow and his engineer colleague, Richard Brett, visiting the Burgtheater in Vienna, had seen a drum revolve with built-in elevators that could bring up or take down whole scene-settings to the level of the workshops below. The turntable was split into two semi-circular halves, each of which was an elevator. Using the two halves alternately, one setting could be in use at stage level while the other half was being set far beneath. Then the new scene could be raised into view, while the old one was spun round to the back of the stage and dropped out of sight. Whole scenes could be changed, or changed back to an earlier scene, at will.

There was one unforeseen difficulty: the drum had to be of vast proportions. The Olivier stage is level with the third floor of the building but the drum and its driving machinery went into a circular socket that extended sixty feet beneath the stage. It meant excavating an awe-inspiring hole in the ground and there was some doubt whether the Thames could be kept out of it. Then this new machinery, unknown in this country, had to be built. German firms had the experience to build it, but this was a national theatre and British tenders were much cheaper. The firm of Mole-Richardson set to work to construct the revolve, with a diameter of thirty-five feet, in a field near Thetford and there it remained under giant tarpaulins until the building was ready to take it. When it was installed, it was found that more wheels were needed to revolve its great weight smoothly. Safety factors raised more problems; to operate it, three television monitors were needed to keep danger areas under observation. In common with all the stage machinery, it could only be worked on after the actors had left the stage every night, for months that turned into years.

The upshot was that the drum revolve did not work until 1978 and then only as a scenery hoist between workshops and stage in between shows. It was not used during a performance, except purely as a normal revolve, until 1988, twelve years after the theatre opened. This was hardly an economic return on an investment of £500,000 – possibly half as much again if the cost of all the modifications and delays were added. Pilbrow, who got the blame for it, admitted contritely, 'I have had it on my conscience ever since the theatre opened. We went over the top. For years I doubted whether I would ever again recommend such a complex piece of machinery, which cost such an awful lot of money. Now, having seen it work to its full extent, I'm not so sure.' The consultants' brief was to install stage machinery that would keep backstage crewing to a minimum. If it had all worked, it could have saved its cost in wages. Unfortunately, none of the stage machinery worked until long after it had become the battleground of bitter backstage labour disputes.

No conventional London theatres have adequate facilities backstage for rehearsal. Rehearsals are held all over London in an odd assortment of church halls and working men's clubs under unhelpful conditions. The National was intended to change all that with its two stage-sized rehearsal rooms and several subsidiary ones, workshops for building and painting scenery and a paint-frame capable of taking a 104-foot-wide canvas for the Olivier stage. The scenic workshops, property workshop and armoury (the only other theatre to have one is the Royal Opera House) lie behind the stages, served by their own internal road and concealed by the blank, prison-like brick wall that greets visitors who arrive from the direction of Waterloo. The dressing-room block is built round a hollow light-well in the centre of the building. There are sixty-six dressing-rooms on three floors, with the wardrobe and wig department above them. Together with the staff canteen and the actors' green room, all this takes up a great deal of space, and was finished to very utilitarian standards. There are labyrinthine passageways of such uniformity that most newcomers to the building spend several days of disorientation.

Arriving audiences expect to endure being squashed mercilessly in the front of the house of most theatres. The National was expressly designed to end the fight to reach the box office, the cloakroom, the toilets or the bars. The front of house areas were laid out on a generous, one might say reckless, scale with foyers, staircases, galleries, bars and buffets flowing out of one another as if built as exhibition space, rather than as a corridor from the street to the auditorium. Exhibition was Lasdun's intention. He described the spaces as 'a fourth theatre' – 'all the public areas, foyers and terraces, are in themselves a theatre with the city as a backdrop,' he wrote in his romantic vein. The outside terraces were now lined up with Waterloo Bridge and stepped down in stages towards the river embankment. 'These strata are available to the public just to mill around in,' he explained in a television programme broadcast at the time the building opened. 'The front of house of the main theatres is really a viewing platform for the whole of the City of London.' Such cantilevered terraces could only be constructed of reinforced concrete, which was continued inside the walls to form the partitions of the foyers as well as the walls of each auditorium. It was textured by leaving the imprint upon it of the rough-grained planking in which the concrete was poured and set. The roughness was exaggerated by the choice of wooden planks of different thickness, producing unevenness in the texture of the concrete walls. Sensing the resistance that was widely felt to so much bare concrete, Lasdun defended it in advance partly on grounds of cost – they couldn't afford stone facing – but mainly for its sculptural qualities and its decorative character: 'Concrete can be a very beautiful material if it is used in the way that its own nature intends it to be used. It's going to weather, it's going to streak, and the streaks will have white patches that I think will be beautiful. I want the concrete to weather so that lichen grows on it and it becomes part of the riverscape, as though it's an extension of the river banks. A bit romantic, but that's what it will look like in fifteen years' time.' He was just as uncompromising about the concrete interior. Nothing was to mar its austerity – there is hardly a wood surface in the building and not so much as a bucket of plaster had to be poured. 'People have to use the concrete reality of the building, not tarted up in any way – just space, walls and light,' Lasdun declared. 'The ornaments are people, moving around in space, beautifully lit and carpeted.' It was a curious justification. All public buildings are 'decorated' by the people who resort there (the Royal Opera House, for example), but that does not make all forms of interior decoration superfluous.

No one could dispute that the building had consistency and a kind of harsh purity, whose antecedents could be traced back through the Modern Movement to Le Corbusier. Lasdun himself now calls it a 'classical' building, using the word in what some would see as a surprising and special sense. 'Classicism respects human scale, proportion, rhythm, repose, tactile qualities. I am a classical architect and it is a classical building, a serious building, an austere building, not at all frivolous. It's modern, it's sculptural, it's not in any style except one's own. Pure form, nakedly displayed, to quote the poet, Arthur Hugh Clough, is a very good description of this theatre, as far as I'm concerned.'

Upstream of Waterloo Bridge, more concrete forms are nakedly displayed: the Queen Elizabeth Hall and Hayward Gallery, also textured by the grain-marks of the wooden shuttering in which it is poured. The South Bank (except for the stone-faced Royal Festival Hall) has encased the arts in concrete, like a row of multi-storey art parks. One could well wish that, having waited a hundred years for the dream of a national theatre to become reality, we had waited a few years more until the concrete vogue had passed. By the time the theatre opened, in 1976, it had. Steel and glass, highly glazed stone or brick, anything but concrete, was the choice for subsequent public or major buildings. With the change in material, out went the heavy moulded style that only concrete made possible. With the passing of more years, its weathering quality, even its durability, became suspect. The National opened with the handicap of being cast in the fashion of yesterday.

There were some rumblings of doubt in 1976, though they were not universal. Some writers in the Press were reminded of 'the forbidding presence of a gun emplacement' (*Sunday Times*) or 'a cumbersome Dreadnought, dubiously relevant to the 20th Century' (*New Statesman*). Professional critics of the *Architectural Review*, which devoted a whole issue to the building, were not confident: 'It is unlikely, as a landmark, to inspire immediate affection; it is a smoulderer, not a fizzer,' summed up the critic Mark Girouard. Colin Amery was more forthright: 'Architecture in the past was much less doctrinaire, and a national building of this calibre would have celebrated more than the rigorous purity of one architectural ethic. Our successors may be mystified by our enthronement of concrete as a thing of beauty and the almost total banishment of colour.' As the years passed and virtually no more concrete public buildings were put up, doubts hardened into hostility, even detestation. By 1988, the Prince of Wales in his television programme 'A Vision of Britain' paused on his trip down the river Thames to reflect, 'The National Theatre seems like a clever way of building a nuclear power station in the middle of London without anyone objecting. I try very hard to appreciate this sort of architecture but I can't.' In his general scourging of the dogmas of the Modernists, he was voicing the reactions of a great many of his fellow-laymen, as the sales of his best-selling book on the same subject proved. The *Architectural Review* had been there before him, twelve years earlier: 'The National Theatre is big, forceful and made of concrete, when the prevalent ethos is for the petite, anonymous and vernacular. It has its roots in the international Modern Movement but there has been a general loss of faith in this tradition.' Will that faith ever return?

In a second television programme intended to answer the Prince of Wales, Lasdun, significantly, did not spend time defending the outside of his building. He complained that 'People today are obsessed with the outside, the outside style. The real evaluation of a building is the apprehension of space inside it . . . Certainly concrete is out of fashion at the moment but you have to understand the pluses and minuses that you get by using that material. I wanted to express form, surface and space in one material and the only material in which that could be done was concrete. Nobody seemed to object to the concrete inside the building, in fact they often stroke it.' Caressing rough concrete is not an activity that leaps to the eye when one visits the theatre on normal occasions – it may take place when Sir Denys is looking – but it was interesting that his defence concentrated entirely on the internal qualities.

The building has always been far better liked inside than out. The front of house, the foyers, bars, buffet and circulation spaces, Lasdun's 'fourth theatre', provide generous spaces on multiple levels connected by concrete stairwells. The only concession to softening the concrete walls and ceilings is the carpeting, in a pattern of purple and grey which in the mass looks silvery – a very restrained use of colour. The buffets and bars are open all day and the seating provided is ample for the few dozen patrons who use the place out of theatre hours. It is nothing like enough, of course, for the pre-curtain hour when theatregoers can be seen sitting on the floor – which was the architect's intention. The Lyttleton foyer has atmosphere, though it is a curious atmosphere, being neither that of a normal theatre nor of a hotel foyer, which it in some ways resembles. Its character is inward-looking, dark and almost

93

secretive, surprising in a building which occupies what the architect once described as 'probably the most beautiful site in London'. The view out of the ground floor windows is heavily restricted by the bulk of the outside terraces which overhang them. There is nowhere inside the building from which the sweep down-river to St Paul's can actually be seen. This is even true of the upstairs foyers to the Olivier Theatre. These are better lit and the large 'cathedral window' on the corner of the building offers a wide view of Waterloo Bridge – but not of St Paul's. Even the excellent restaurant has only one window whose view of the river can be enjoyed from only a handful of tables. Overcast in daylight, overhung by the oppressive grid of the concrete coffered ceilings, the foyers are spotlit from above at night as if the scene were the battlements of Elsinore. Splashes of overhead light are separated by large pools of near-darkness, so that theatregoers who have just arrived can be seen peering into the gloom to try to spot their waiting companions or, in the interval, edging into the spotlit patches in order to consult their programmes.

Although one set of unobtrusive entrance doors serves both theatres, there is no other connection whatever between the Olivier and Lyttleton foyers. It is a remote chance indeed that anyone attending one of these theatres will set eyes on anyone attending the other. Yet from the first floor upwards they are only yards apart and theatre staff with pass keys can move between them with ease along a hidden passageway. It appears that the Building Committee briefed the architect to keep the two audiences entirely separate. Possibly they felt that 2,000 people arriving at the same time could create confusion (although more than that number arrive nightly at the Theatre Royal, Drury Lane, Covent Garden or the Coliseum). The result is that there is no common foyer or reception hall of which anyone could say '*This* is the National'. It is a building that lacks a heart. Those who entered via the outdoor terrace by the first-floor level doorway leading to the Olivier staircase used to be greeted by a notice inviting them to patronize the Lyttleton terrace café. To reach this place, which is visible on almost the same level, it is necessary to go downstairs, cross the foyer and climb two flights of stairs to get back almost to where you are already standing. 'A lot of walking – but worth it!' ran this encouraging notice. A lot of walking – but why? It would have been a simple matter to make some internal connections.

It is not an easy building to find one's way about and the signposting is discreet to the point of illegibility at any distance. Many a patron has to peer anxiously at the graphic symbol on the door before daring to enter one of the toilets. This is a symbol of Lasdun's determination that nothing should clutter the bareness of the interiors and surfaces.

Seating, apart from the buffet areas, is confined to the sidelines, with the result that young people frequently sit on the floor. This has been praised as a sign of the building's internal charm; it is merely a sign of inadequate seating. There is no such thing as a piece of decorative sculpture or applied art permanently installed anywhere in the building, unless you count the plaques unveiled by the Queen or the famous movable foundation stone which finally came to rest embedded in a foyer wall.

The contrast between the National and the Royal Festival Hall, the neighbouring shrines of drama and music, could not be more marked. Both provide similar spaces for similar purposes, but one is an open building, the other a closed one. The Festival Hall's wide expanses of glass and its open balcony welcome the river with open arms, so that you are conscious of it and of the light reflected from it all through the front half of the building. The interior finishes are light and vari-coloured, whether or not you like their fifties taste, so the building itself is light in atmosphere. The odd thing is that the fifties Festival Hall makes the sixties National Theatre seem close, heavy, and darkly labyrinthine by comparison – qualities well suited to Ibsen or Strindberg but hardly to the drama as a whole. Finally there is a clear contrast between the two exteriors. The older one looks clean and the newer one looks dirty; the temple of music could be called light-hearted and festive in appearance, whereas the temple of drama is an austere and forbidding citadel This is partly a matter of cost. The Festival of Britain spirit, which produced the Festival Hall, did not stint the architects of the London County Council when it came to finishing the building in Portland stone. It may also be a matter of cleaning. Concrete gets dirty and no high-pressure jet hosing has been done on the National since it went up, because no money was available for it in the first fifteen years at least. How much of the staining is due to dirt can only be surmised. Lasdun's prophecy, that the special mixture of white sand combined with the concrete employed would develop white streaks as it weathered, is still waiting to be fulfilled. The building, as a result, looks depressingly shabby in anything but strong sunlight or floodlighting.

Although the Royal Festival Hall announced its name in bold lettering on its façade, the National Theatre remained anonymous for several years. The electronic signboard that signals its business and attractions to those crossing the river was installed in the teeth of Lasdun's passionate disapproval. 'It is a building that announces its presence. I don't approve of having the name on it,' he declared. 'You don't announce "St Paul's" or "The British Museum" on the outside.' He lost that battle but still makes it plain that he would have the sign removed if he could. It is a point that illustrates the difference between his approach and theatre tradition. The essence of theatre is the billboard, the 'marquee', the names in lights. They would seem inappropriate only to someone who was making an architectural statement rather than a theatrical one. Lasdun does not hesitate to compare his building to St Paul's in another respect. 'St Paul's wasn't liked by the time it was finished,' he points out. Changes in fashion overtook the reputation of Wren, just as they did that of Barry by the time the Houses of Parliament were completed. Hawksmoor's churches and Street's Law Courts were heartily disliked in their turn. Buildings that endure changes of fashion may come to transcend it. However hard it is now to find someone to say a good word for the National Theatre as architecture, Denys Lasdun is content to wait for posterity's verdict.

8

1974–5: Bring on the Knights and Dames

Binkie Beaumont, the leading impresario in the theatre of the fifties, said of Peter Hall: 'He thinks there are forty-eight hours in the day for him to do ten jobs in.' According to Lord Mishcon, Beaumont's advice to his fellow board members on the choice of Peter Hall as their director was: 'You're taking on a brilliant but difficult man and an empire-builder, but he'll undoubtedly measure up to the job.' 'He said we would have to try to control him as best we could but that he was almost uncontrollable as many people with a touch of genius are,' said Mishcon, 'so it proved.' A look at Hall's record during his eight years at the head of the Royal Shakespeare Company would have shown that his outstanding characteristic is his love of gambling. His career had taken off with a gamble, a production in 1955 of a new play from France, *Waiting for Godot*, by an author few had then heard of, Samuel Beckett, to plug a sudden gap in the repertoire of the little Arts Theatre where he was Director, lately down from Cambridge. Hall saw its potential for a breakthrough. If he was mistaken he, at twenty-four, had little to lose. "Theatre is about risks," he would often say.

By the age of twenty-eight, when he was offered the artistic direction of what was still the Shakespeare Memorial Theatre, he had ambitious plans to institute there the country's first permanent national company on long-term contracts and was determined to obtain for it, and for himself, a West End showcase. How could this be paid for? He persuaded the chairman of the theatre's governors, the brewer Sir Fordham Flower, to let him stake all the accumulated reserves (£140,000) on making the bid, then set about making loud demands for a subsidy to enable it to continue. Energetic and well-orchestrated publicity portrayed the RSC as a plucky outsider fighting for survival against a national theatre (which did not yet exist). Given a small subsidy, he expanded further, playing in three theatres to 700,000 people and demanding a larger subsidy. Unremitting expansion accompanied by maximum outcry was a technique that he had found very serviceable. He was to employ it at the National. It suited his gambler's nerve to live coolly on the verge of bankruptcy. Even in the tightest of spots, he rarely economized. He resigned, exhausted, in 1967, bequeathing his successor, Trevor Nunn, an accumulated deficit, with no reserves left to draw on. This was eclipsed in memory by the excitement of his initial achievement in creating a company of audacious temper and contemporary identity, with a different approach to staging Shakespeare.

He was an ideal hero-figure for the sixties, with the fashionable, almost obligatory working-class background and a glamorous first wife, Leslie Caron. His childhood had been spent at the single-track railway station of Barnham in Suffolk, where his father had been station master. At fourteen he had visited the Memorial Theatre at Stratford and vowed, 'One day, I'll run that.' This ambition, achieved through scholarships and taking chances young, made him a media star, bearded in his young days like an Elizabethan gallant, buccaneering but cheerfully calm in the stormy crises that seemed to be his incessant companions. His ready smile and ready flow of quotable remarks, his combination of accessibility and candour, were very attractive to journalists. He clearly enjoyed exhibiting his high profile, while exploiting it to make propaganda for his theatre's cause. But beneath the bonhomie he was, and remains, an ungregarious man. He prefers to avoid social gatherings and close personal contacts. But he smiles just as blandly when engaged in a confrontation or after reading an adverse notice as when things are going his way.

At Stratford he had the reputation of enjoying power and being ruthless in his manipulation of it. It is impossible to run a theatre without conflict. Actors tend naturally to make the director the scapegoat for their disappointments but Peter Hall attacted more than the usual share of disaffection, as well as affection from those with whom he worked well. Unlike Olivier, he did not enjoy the trust that actors award to a fellow-actor. He professed to love actors but, except on professional terms, he kept apart from them. As an insatiable workaholic, he crammed his seventeen-hour days with administration and committee meetings, which he seemed to enjoy. He was adept at persuading others to agree to what he wanted. Unlike many gamblers, he did not believe in luck. 'You make your own luck,' was his oft-repeated maxim. He also had an Achilles heel. He found it nearly impossible to say No to any invitation to work – play directing, opera directing, musical directing, television presenting, even a small part in a film. Within months of accepting the National directorship in 1972, he was attempting them all. 'You can't do everything,' he wrote in his diary shortly before he joined the theatre. 'I wish I could stop trying.' But he didn't really want to stop trying.

At that point he needed the National. Since leaving the RSC his career had lost momentum. His brilliant early years were fading into memory. He had made a mistake in choosing Covent Garden. The films he had so far made had been only moderately successful. And late in 1972, his standing on Broadway as a musical director 'bombed' along with the show, the space-age *Via Galactica*, which closed inside a week. Although he had once sworn never to direct a big theatre organization again, he badly needed to be back inside one. He reassured himself in his diary, 'I have to run theatres. I have an ability for that which I have proved to myself.' In a euphoric newspaper interview on his appointment, he declared: 'For me it's like being reborn. Having been round the course once, I am being allowed to go round again. When you're 28, you think it is much easier than it is.' Founding the RSC, he was to say, had been like leading a revolution with everyone running along behind cheering, whereas opening the National on the South Bank was like the unremitting slog of trench warfare.

The first issue that Peter Hall raised was his power relative to that of the Board. Under Olivier's contract, the Board had the final say in artistic as well as financial matters (as over *Soldiers* and *Guys and Dolls*). Hall was not going to accept this, nor the power of the Board to appoint associate directors without his prior approval. Fortunately Rayne saw eye to eye with him on a director's need for artistic independence. 'I took the view that when you appoint a managing director, you have got to give him freedom of action. If you don't like what he does, you don't keep him on. The Board agreed with me that we would not intervene in any artistic matter except over an issue of blasphemy, obscenity or *lèse majesté*.' Hall saw this rather differently. At his first meeting with the Board, he records, 'I told them that if I wanted to do a play I regarded as controversial, I would warn them about it and discuss it with them and if they wanted they could, of course, read it. I appreciated that they had the right to overrule my decision and stop me doing such a play. But I wanted them to understand that if they did it twice, I should resign.' This was accepted – though with 'much head-shaking and table-banging'. This agreement depended for its effectiveness, of course, on how conscientiously the Director took the Board into his confidence about the plays he wanted to present. As will be seen, the Board did not know what it was in for when it came to presenting *The Romans in Britain*, the play which caused the most brouhaha of his regime. The threat, 'Overrule me twice at your peril', was rhetoric.

The other respect in which Hall differed markedly from Olivier was over his salary. He was no subscriber to the Establishment convention that public service, especially in the arts, should be undertaken for the honour (or Honours) rather than profit. All that was anathema to one of the new meritocrats, who insisted on full commercial returns on their labours. Unlike comparable posts in the public service, the National Theatre Director's salary was not publicly disclosed. In fact, Hall took the job at approximately £18,000, to which were added the same perks as Olivier had enjoyed – a London flat (rented by the company) and a car. Olivier had served as Director at about half that salary and claimed he had never had a rise. But he had been free to supplement it by playing small roles in eight films, some of them highly paid, and in his last year he made *Sleuth* with Michael Caine, presumably for all it was worth. When National Theatre productions were filmed commercially, such as *Othello* and *Long Day's Journey into Night*, he drew his going rate. But for all that, he had suffered a considerable loss of potential earnings, which he now proceeded to remedy by narrating the lucrative television series, *The World at War*, and making his American Polaroid commercial worth a million dollars.

For Peter Hall's asking price, the Board might have expected to get his exclusive services. Nothing could have been further from his intention. A form of words that permitted him to undertake outside work was found and he quickly availed himself of it. In 1973 he directed two operas at Glyndebourne, directed one film and acted in one, in Germany. In 1974 he made another film. In 1975 he took on the job of presenting a television arts programme, *Aquarius*, despite the efforts of friends and colleagues to dissuade him. Inevitably this led to criticisms in the Press and in Parliament. People wondered why he needed to take on another major job, for which he was said to be paid another £18,000 a year, instead of putting all his energies into his theatre. At the same period he and his family were photographed for *Vogue* as the *soigné* occupants of a penthouse flat in the new Cromwell Tower at the Barbican. To occupy the 37th and 38th floor (plus roof garden) of one of these dismal towers was then thought the height of *chic* (the fact that it was a company flat was not mentioned). Then followed an advertisement for wallpaper, in which celebrities were photographed in their homes, widely published in the newspapers. 'Very Peter Hall, Very Sanderson' was the legend to a picture of him checking a score at his Broadwood fortepiano. The ad was pinned up, sometimes with, sometimes without comment, on backstage noticeboards in many theatres where shoestring productions and low pay were the facts of life. Hall finally admitted to his diary that these money-making ventures were a mistake.

These trivial personal details began to attract more odium than they deserved as 1974 wore into 1975. The country was by then in the grip of an oil crisis, of runaway inflation (20 per cent) and of a general loss of confidence. Theatres all over the country were faced with cutbacks or possible closure. The RSC, near insolvency, had been reduced to only three new productions at Stratford in 1974. The South Bank building would cost £1 million a year to service when it was at last ready for occupation, and the National's Arts Council grant, which had already leapt from £345,000 in 1972–3 to £1.5 million in 1975–6, had to be increased by another million. This meant that its share of the drama budget for all subsidized theatres in the country would rise from an eighth to a quarter. Meanwhile Fringe companies, now numbering over sixty, were campaigning for £1 million between them to enable them to pay their actors the Equity minimum. None of this endeared the National to the other theatres. Its salary scale, increased from a beggarly £18 minimum a week to a niggardly £25 (plus performance fees), left others far behind. Backstage rates were rather better; there was a £30 minimum for the assistant stage manager level. Other managements feared that the National would cream off not only their best actors but their best technicians. For leading actors the top salary levels were from £200 a week to nearly £500 for 'knights and dames' (including stars who were not so honoured). The ratio between top and bottom salaries, previously five to one, now exceeded ten to one, although star performers, who could expect a percentage of a commercial theatre box office, were still making quite a sacrifice at the National pay-rate. But it was much more than its nearest rival, the RSC, could hope to pay. Under Olivier, star names were seldom employed. But Peter Hall had already announced his invitations to John Gielgud, Ralph Richardson and Peggy Ashcroft to appear with the company on a continuing basis.

There had already been accusations of poaching because of the recruitment, at increased salaries, of John Goodwin from the RSC, as head of press and publicity, of Peter Stevens, from the Haymarket, Leicester, as general administrator, and of Gillian Diamond, from the Royal Court, as head of casting. All these currents converged in a letter to *The Times* on 15 October 1974, signed by the artistic director of the English Stage Company, Oscar Lewenstein, and thirteen directors of other subsidized theatres, about their anxiety that the National would drain the available resources of talent and finance. 'We can attest that the National has been busy for some time already endeavouring to attract technicians with offers of salaries far in excess of anything these theatres can afford to pay.' The signatories included Lindsay Anderson (Royal Court), Frank Dunlop (the Young Vic), Michael Elliott (the 69 Theatre Company in Manchester), Joan Littlewood of Theatre Workshop and Richard Eyre, director of Nottingham Playhouse, who was to becoming director of the National fourteen years later. They represented an influential body of opinion. Regional theatre representatives on the Arts Council Drama Panel had given Hall a rough ride at his first meeting with them in July 1973. 'Repeatedly I was asked: Why should you have such wonderful rehearsal conditions? Why should you have so much money? What did I mean by standards of excellence? What was excellence? Whose excellence? Recording this, Hall added morosely, 'Truly I have joined the Establishment.' The Have-Nots were not likely to sit back and admire the lavish plans of the most sleek and powerful of the Haves.

The then secretary of the Arts Council, Sir Hugh Willatt, recalled its Drama Panel's hostility: 'They believed that the National's demands would be met at their expense. As it turned out, I don't think they were. Peter Hall claimed that the National was helping to raise the general level of grants. Up to a point it did.' Sir Roy Shaw, who succeeded Willatt in 1975, found that the Hall-phobia was still as strong. 'In the regions, especially, there was a lot of envy about of Peter Hall's position. Here we had the most prestigious theatre in the country, with a lot of money and the capacity to draw the best actors, and people didn't like it. In fact they hated it! There were to be many accusations of extravagance at the National. So far as I can remember, we never found them to be justified.' It was not just repertory and fringe theatres who were sniping; the West End theatre managers feared for their business. They already had the competition of the Royal Shakespeare Company at the Aldwych Theatre in their midst. Now they were faced with what promised to be a star-studded rival attraction on the other side of Waterloo Bridge. They didn't like the prospect. Sir Donald Albery, Chairman of the Theatres National Committee, was a fanatical opponent. There were back-bench MPs in Parliament ready to voice these fears in the debate in November 1974 on the bill which removed the financial ceiling on the grant to the theatre. Norman St John-Stevas referred to 'gnawing rats, gnats and gadflies' and to 'the sheer theatrical bitchiness which is being directed at the National Theatre Board'.

Peter Hall did not enjoy exchanging the status of media idol for that of media butt. 'Who wants the National Theatre at this point?' he asked himself gloomily and answered, 'Not the Government, nor the Arts Council, nor the profession, nor the media in a time of austerity and increasing puritanism. So who does want us? Just us, I'm afraid.' A few days later he was wondering whether it was worth working at such pressure and 'putting up with all the shit about the National Theatre'. Later he was to look back on it all and say, 'I have always enjoyed a good scrap.' But at the time John Goodwin, the theatre's skilled propagandist and one of his few real confidants, recognized the symptoms of paranoia and warned him that he had better learn to be philosophical about being attacked as part of the disliked Establishment. Hall admitted that he was as 'raw as burnt skin'. According to Goodwin, 'There was deep fear throughout the profession both of the National and of him. We were very strung up and sensitive about the unrest in the profession, about having to fill three theatres, and spending such a lot of public money. I found the attacks bracing. They made us define why we were there, why we were as big as we were, how we could justify the money it cost. Every time we were attacked I encouraged Peter to hit back with a reply. The theatre thrives on controversy and in Peter Hall we had someone who was very good at it, but he found the attacks hurtful.'

To make matters worse, the company was having a bad year artistically. In 1974, Olivier's parting production, Priestley's *Eden End*, made little impact. The newly arrived directors, Harold Pinter and Bill Bryden, had no great success, while Jonathan Miller and Michael Blakemore got critical pastings for productions of plays that did not seem of National calibre. Far the most interesting production of 1974 was a new play, *Comedians* by Trevor Griffiths, given by the visiting Nottingham Playhouse company under its director Richard Eyre. The National had just done Griffiths's *The Party*. Why had it not taken up this impressive, off-beat work – an evening class for would-be comedians that turns sour – which included a remarkable virtuoso performance from an unknown Jonathan Pryce? There was nothing as attention-worthy in the home repertoire. *Spring Awakening*, which had been forbidden by Lord Chandos's board, was now performed under the new non-interference policy, and seemed outdated.

The only Shakespeare of the season was Peter Hall's first National production, *The Tempest*. For many this was the most disappointing event of the season. Both Olivier and Guinness had declined Hall's suggestion that they should play Prospero. Hall then asked Gielgud, already a memorable, almost definitive Prospero, whose recording of the famous speeches was fondly familiar to many. 'He is perhaps too gentle and too nice,' Hall noted, 'but I think I can push him into a harsher area of reality.' Why, some would be inclined to ask, should he be pushed? What Hall called his 'singing' was suppressed. Afraid, perhaps, of being thought old-fashioned, Gielgud accepted direction with which he was obviously out of sympathy. He admitted later, 'With Peter Brook's production I tried to convey in the last act that Prospero is really Shakespeare, who goes almost up to heaven at the end and resumes his kingdom, whereas Peter Hall thought he was a tired old man who did not want the kingdom back at all.' The production was encumbered with costly and elaborate masque effects, too big for the scale of the Old Vic but no doubt planned with the Olivier stage in mind. But by the time that was ready this *Tempest* had passed. The notices were with few exceptions dismissive. *Guardian* critic Michael Billington rated it as one of the four worst Shakespeare productions that he had seen. Instead of proving that he was the right choice as conductor of the costliest theatre ensemble in the land, Hall's debut set him back psychologically. His diary becomes soul-searching at this point: 'How can I ever run the National Theatre and at the same time direct plays, without going mad? The problems are nothing like as vast as they will be on the South Bank and yet I am at breaking point: very near the abyss, which is all too familiar from Stratford days.' In his Stratford days he had two breakdowns, one before *The Wars of the Roses*, which opened without him, and the second before his last unhappy production of *Macbeth* in 1967. Overwork had undone him then, yet he was now filming *The Homecoming*, editing his film of *Akenfield*, directing *The Marriage of Figaro* at Glyndebourne and considering directing a new film, while engaged on preparing *The Tempest*.

Olivier's departure (he gave his last performance on 21 March 1974) together with other changes in personnel had sapped company morale. The directors who had served him and willingly accepted the dominance of Olivier, were less willing to extend that towards Hall, their contemporary. The virtual expulsion of Tynan at the end of 1973 was a portent. Who was to go next? It turned out to be John Dexter, who removed himself to join the Metropolitan Opera House, New York, but made it plain that he would not have stayed anyway and warned Hall that the company were unhappy and lost and their loyalty was slipping. 'I smiled blandly through it all and told him I was going to stay and had a lot of stamina,' Hall commented. 'I told him that this company was dependent on leadership,' Dexter recalled. 'Unless he spent more time in the canteen and with the rude mechanicals, oiling the wheels, there would be muttering in the corridors.' The muttering was already apparent, above all to Joan Plowright, who was the recipient of it while she was playing in *Eden End*. 'I became the listening post for the complaints of the entire staff. They would tell me that "the old guv'nor" would never have done this or allowed that. So I decided to leave.' There were edgy meetings of the associate directors at one of which Olivier himself, making a rare appearance, complained that the company never saw their boss nowadays. 'He pointed out that I was the boss, I must be seen to be the boss, and I must do some bossing,' noted Hall. 'He thought I should give up my plans of directing *Happy Days*, *John Gabriel Borkman* and *Tamburlaine* and concentrate for the next year on being the leader.' Again he smiled through the complaints but admitted to himself that there was some truth in them.

At this time a gulf was also opening between Hall and Jonathan Miller, who was due to direct *The Importance of Being Earnest*. His unorthodox suggestion that it be done with an all-male cast met with stiff resistance from Hall and most of the associates. Miller was offended that his admired touring production of *Measure for Measure*, done on a shoestring and set in Freud's Vienna, had been given no showing in the main theatre. He thought Hall had dismissed it because it cost a mere £500 to stage and contained no star names. (Hall called it 'the best production of Miller's that I have seen' in his diary but was fundamentally out of sympathy with doing Shakespeare out of period.) The two men were uneasy with one another, not only artistically but personally. Both had great ambitions as directors of classical drama and opera but had very different approaches, which put them on an ego-collision course. The long delay in moving into the new building meant that several productions planned for the move now had to be abandoned. Whether by accident or design, the cancelled shows included all of Miller's. His response was to go to Greenwich Theatre and put on a trio of original, inexpensive productions of *Hamlet*, *Ghosts* and *The Seagull*. He had already left in spirit, and in February 1975 he officially resigned, to the evident relief of Hall, who could hardly have done more to ensure his departure. Miller gladly shook the dust of Hall's organization from his feet and became one of its most virulent critics. To him it was now the antithesis of the small-scale, united, convivial company with which he liked to work. In his book, *Subsequent Performances*, he explained his embittered departure with the words, 'I came up against a form of executive ambition on the part of Peter Hall which I found totally impossible.' In conversation and interviews he went a good deal further: 'Why did we get on so badly? I found him uncultivated, uncivilised, spectacularly middlebrow, a paranoid who didn't like people saying what they thought.' One of the theatre's enduring feuds had been born, in the course of which Miller called Hall 'an intellectual mountebank' and the National in its new home 'a mixture of Gatwick airport and Brent Cross shopping centre'. Hall, for his part, made unflattering references to Miller's 'concept' productions, such a his Mafia-style *Rigoletto* – 'I should not like anyone to think that *that* is *Rigoletto*.'

The last survivor of Olivier's team was Michael Blakemore, who was to remain for one year longer. Clearly, since he had been a suggested alternative to Hall as director, there was some difficulty in their relationship. Blakemore, like Dexter, felt that associate directors had too little say in the decisions that were taken, although they sat on what was called the Planning Committee. He had watched the acting company which he had helped to build up during Olivier's very successful last two years gradually disintegrate. (Hall had cast only one member of that company in *The Tempest* – Denis Quilley.) The Olivier tradition of cross-casting and promoting regular players was being abandoned, and by 1975 he felt that the knights and dames were taking over. Following Gielgud's Prospero was Ralph Richardson's *John Gabriel Borkman*, supported by Dames Peggy Ashcroft and Wendy Hiller as his twin sisters, a heavy insurance against failure. It was Hall's first venture into Ibsen (which he had also adapted with the Norwegian scholar Inge-Stina Ewbank). Ashcroft and Hiller lent distinction to the long uphill work of Ibsen's exposition, to the creaking accompaniment of the old man's boots, pacing the floorboards upstairs. Richardson, coiffed, as someone said, like Toscanini, lent his own wild-eyed touches of madness to the disgraced banker and finally met his death with a low, surprised sound. It was, Gielgud said aptly, 'as if a bird had flown out of his heart'. Peggy Ashcroft, who had led Peter Hall's first company at Stratford in 1960, had at first disapproved of his 'desertion' to the National. Now she lent her authority and virtuosity to his production of *Happy Days*, which was rehearsed for three weeks in the presence of Samuel Beckett. Like a composer teaching a musician a fiendishly difficult solo, he gave punctilious notes on the smallest gestures that Winnie makes in turning out her amazing handbag. 'All true grace is economical,' he said. Buried up to the waist, then to the neck, in earth, she dominated the stage by sound and facial expression alone. Ashcroft's spirit of lightness and courage in the face of gradual extinction demonstrated that great actors, like great musical per-formers, with age advance to make new discoveries.

The same phenomenon was reaffirmed when Richardson and Gielgud were reunited in Harold Pinter's *No Man's Land*. This was the first fruit of the commissions Hall gave to six playwrights to provide new plays for the opening season on the South Bank. Pinter's play was ready long before the theatre was and he naturally wanted to see it performed. The two writers, Hirst and Spooner, one sleek with success, the other crumpled with failure, suited the contrasted temperaments of Richardson and Gielgud perfectly, although at first it was not certain which of them would play which. When he first sent him the play, Hall suggested that Gielgud would want to play the successful Hirst. 'I said no, no, I want to play Spooner, much better for me.' Nobody had yet seen the Gielgud who inhabited Spooner, the garrulous self-styled poet with dyed yellowish hair, sandals and drooping cigarette, who had a propensity for lurking on Hampstead Heath and 'peeping'. People were astonished by his unexpected Bohemian seediness. Richardson, abrupt and monosyllabic in the manner of a heavy drinker, also astonished with his sudden falls, flat upon the stage. The two veteran showmen, allowing their personalities to flower extravagantly, became the talk of the time. Hall, director of four previous Pinter plays at the RSC, adeptly obtained precision effects of timing and silence. Whatever doubts there were about the underlying meaning of the play, there were none about its being an hypnotic production which all too soon departed to Wyndham's and commercial success.

The National had recovered its prestige, mainly, it must be said, by buying in star power. Of course, it was appropriate that actors of the highest calibre should appear on its stage – all of these were greatly overdue – and these were plays in which the star parts were all. So, instead of leading a company, four or five leading actors virtually took over its stage for themselves. Another group of distinguished players were imported for John Schlesinger's production of *Heartbreak House* – Eileen Atkins, Kate Nelligan and Anna Massey, with long-absent Colin Blakeley as Shotover. Diana Rigg was brought back for Tony Harrison's version of Racine's *Phèdre*, relocated in British India as *Phaedra Britannica*. A seasoned Irish cast was led by Stephen Rea as *The Playboy of the Western World*, under the young Scottish director Bill Bryden. It may well have been time for new blood, but there was soon very little of the old blood left to be seen. Ben Travers's *Plunder* brought back Frank Finlay as Freddy the playboy jewel thief, with Dinsdale Landen as D'Arcy, his dude accomplice. The playwright, nearing ninety, had the unusual satisfaction of living long enough to witness his own return to fashion (he had a new farce in the commercial theatre simultaneously). *Plunder*, with twenty-seven in the cast and four sets rich in period detail, was, as Herbert Kretzmer pointed out in his notice, 'the kind of production quite beyond the resources of any commercial management in Britain today'. It was hugely popular and was Michael Blakemore's last production for the National for many years to come.

Blakemore chose a meeting of the associate directors to deliver a totally unexpected diatribe on their powerlessness to affect policy under Peter Hall. He questioned the wisdom of abandoning the close-knit company of the past in favour of a loose and varied collection of actors, some of them paid vastly more than the rest. He objected to Hall's outside activities. But above all he raised the ticklish question of directors' earnings on National Theatre productions that transferred to commercial theatres. This was a direct challenge to Hall, who was receiving 4 per cent of the box office from the only transfer, *No Man's Land* at Wyndham's. Its 200 performances there earned £232,000 for the National, which acted as its own producer. The interests of the theatre, the author and the director did not coincide. Plays staged in the repertoire at the National earned far less for their authors than a straight run in the West End would do, so established playwrights would want a commercial transfer if possible. Pinter had made it a condition of the National presenting his play that after forty performances it would transfer. Authors have every right to secure the maximum exposure for their work. Actors with enough pulling power to receive a percentage of the box office, like Richardson and Gielgud, were certainly entitled to draw it. But what of the position of the director or designer, if in fulltime employment of the theatre? Did they have an equal right to the highest commercial rate of reward – particularly in a case where the director's share reduced the profit for the theatre which he ran? The meeting lasted until after midnight. 'It got out of hand,' according to Michael Birkett, then Hall's deputy director, who was in the chair, 'It was made into something dramatic and it shouldn't have been.' Hall was incensed by the discussion ('I had the greatest difficulty in controlling myself'). At a further meeting three days later, the associates were told by Hall that they could question all matters of policy and give their views on them, 'but that I reserved the right, having taken the consensus view, to overrule them.' He insisted that ultimately the decisions had to be his, although to overrule his colleagues would be a very foolish thing for him to do. The decision on a director's remuneration on transfer was also, presumably, his. It was a question that would return in the future to cause more controversy, next time in public. Outwardly, things remained as they had been. But Blakemore, feeling that his position was now untenable, resigned soon afterwards. It was the end of the old regime. There had already been a clear-out of the Old Vic administrators, Patrick Donnell and Anthony Easterbrook. Now there was no director nor anyone in a senior position left from the previous team.

Blakemore was another serious loss. As a senior director with a record of successful productions he could have provided continuity and the nucleus of a National tradition. That was not what Hall desired, as he made plain in an interview at the end of his term 12 years later: 'One of the greatest mistakes I made in my career when I came to the National Theatre was that in the interests of continuity I kept Jonathan Miller and Michael Blakemore. They both, I think understandably, deeply resented me. They thought I was the man from the other side, from the RSC, and they'd both wanted the job themselves, I'm sure, and were from Day One extremely unhappy. If I did say, well, I'm in the chair and this is what we're going to do, they regarded that as intolerable . . . It would have been much more intolerable if the cabinet hadn't existed at all and I'd just said, oh hullo, good morning, you're doing that play.' The old actor-manager dictatorship worked with a smaller company, given that Olivier was careful to be open to persuasion by a selection of other views. When he had only Tynan to consult, errors became serious. Whether a much larger organization – and the National is the largest theatre ever known in this country – can be run by cabinet government is still unresolved. Hall admitted frankly that he wanted the associate directors as a body to argue with and to be criticized by – but not, presumably, to tell him there was anything he could not do. Even Charles I might have found common ground with him there. He believed, like many others, that theatres must finally be autocratically run. There is no logical reason why their overall policy cannot be settled by committee or cabinet. But, as this period at the National showed, those who disagree in cabinet are not likely to last long. 'I have not got rid of anybody – they got rid of themselves,' said Hall – but it is a nice distinction. Olivier's team left because they felt they had no option.

When, if ever, was the building going to be ready? The main contractor, Sir Robert McAlpine and Sons, had had to adjust to many changes of plan. Parts of the design had been scrapped as economies, then reinstated, with complicated side-effects. There were less acceptable reasons for delay. When building began in late 1969 there was still a building boom and it was difficult to supply enough labour. By 1974 the boom had collapsed and some contractors saw the virtue of the job lasting rather longer. Bad labour relations on the building sites were traditional, especially on the South Bank. On at least one occasion a major cable was found severed. The equipping of the stages with complex machinery, for which six months was originally allowed, could not be completed in the time. When Lord Rayne asked for specifications of the interior finishes, materials and colour schemes, faces round the South Bank board table were blank; nobody had asked for such things before. 'Lasdun was left with almost complete powers over what was done. The seats and seat materials had already been ordered and nobody knew what they were like,' he said. The seats in the Lyttelton were changed at a late stage from green to brown upholstery. Rayne, together with Lord Goodman and Sir Joseph Lockwood, head of EMI, formed a sub-committee to chase up delays which became known as Rayne's Ginger Group. The crisis came to a head in October 1974. The official opening had been fixed for Shakespeare's birthday, 23 April 1975. The build-up of eight productions and their casts was well advanced. In October no contractor could promise to finish his job by the following May. Hall had to break the bleak news to his company that their contracts would not be renewed when they ran out. The Queen's invitation had hurriedly been put off. Gradually the possible date of opening receded through 1975 until it reached the spring of 1976. At the same time inflation had taken off, leaving the contractors, who had undertaken the work at 1969 estimates, looking at a certain loss. They began withdrawing men to other work in order to survive. Whose fault it was is impossible to determine – it was a combination of factors: changed plans, labour difficulties, intractable problems with unfamiliar equipment and the British tradition of not completing contracts on time.

In early 1975 Hall took the decision to move in as soon as one auditorium, the straightforward Lyttleton, was in a playable condition. His foot-in-the-door policy was begun on 3 September, when an advance guard headed by Richard York moved into the offices, picnicking amid the raw concrete and hard-hat areas. The trek from the huts in Aquinas St began in NT vans. Departments were instructed to destroy old files and unnecessary paperwork rather than clutter up the new offices. Quantities of documents, some of which perhaps should now be forming a National Theatre archive, were disposed of in plastic bags. The past was largely left behind when it moved, as if the thirteen years at the Old Vic were of little historical importance. Office space in the new building, it turned out, was barely adequate. John Bury, the Head of Design, arrived to find no provision whatever had been made for a design department. The two floors of offices have been cramped from the moment they were occupied. There was inadequate accommodation for cleaning and security staff.

On 22 September Hall moved into his office with a view of the river that can be seen from few public windows in the building and pronounced it beautiful. The piecemeal plan for opening theatre by theatre was announced to the Press, the Lyttleton the following March, the Olivier in the summer. When rehearsals began in the Lyttleton in February, the electronic flying system was not working, nor looked likely to work, so it was abandoned. A manual system was hastily substituted. Rehearsals were fraught, amid drilling, hammering and the humming and growling of the air conditioning. At an acoustic test of the auditorium, Albert Finney, bearded to play Hamlet, reduced the invited audience to collapse by stepping into the spotlight and mouthing his speech of welcome silently. It seemed only too possible, after all the delays and difficulties, that no one in the place would be able to hear a thing.

9

1976: Moving in Stage by Stage

Albert Finney, the National's new star and natural leader, threw himself into the task of cheering up the company and the raw concrete with the ebullience that came naturally to him. 'I don't think we've met. What's your name? Mine's Albert,' was his greeting to cleaners, secretaries, technicians, bartenders, any strange face around the building. Finney was thirty-nine and ready for the National. In his twenties, after starring in *Saturday Night and Sunday Morning* and *Tom Jones* and playing the lead in John Osborne's *Luther*, at the very moment when he could have had any part he asked for, he disappeared into the blue of the South Pacific. For a year nobody knew where to find him, while like Gauguin he went back to nature on unknown Polynesian islands. But in due course he felt lost without an audience and got back on the boat. He had tried living in Great Gatsby style on his film earnings but that, too, had palled. He had devoted himself to the racecourse and now, rugged and restless, had come back to the National, where he had last appeared in 1966, to play Hamlet. He had reached maturity as an actor without tackling any of the really challenging classical hurdles and was anxious now to prove himself. 'You have to have a go at the big classics to see if you can do them,' he explained.

The *Hamlet* that was intended to open the new building had to open at the Old Vic instead and play there from December 1975 until the Lyttleton stage was ready in March 1976. Peter Hall's last Hamlet had been the gangling, sixties-style student prince of David Warner at Stratford. With Marlowe's *Tamburlaine the Great* to follow, both men were gambling for high stakes in their partnership. They had been talking about it for two years. Hall, looking back on his Stratford days, was appalled at the cavalier way he had then cut Shakespeare texts. Now he was determined to do the play uncut, playing for nearly four hours and sacrificing matinées. Rehearsals went smoothly, but this seemed to him suspicious. He felt he was losing his grip. He admitted to himself that he felt 'my usual deep-seated desire towards the end to have a crisis, to have things go wrong so that I can heroically make them right at the last minute'. It was an interesting admission.

Finney met his own crisis at a dress rehearsal on the stage of the Old Vic. Even while he was playing the scene with Hamlet's ghostly father, he learned afterwards, his own father (who had been a bookmaker in Salford) had died. Before he could go home for the funeral he had to get through three previews and the opening night, speaking such lines as 'My father, methinks I see my father . . . in my mind's eye, Horatio.' Looking back on the experience, Finney admitted, 'It was difficult to get the words out. Even after six months it was tough to get through it. I'm not saying it helped my performance.' Despite these trials the first night was thunderously received. The cast themselves applauded Finney, knowing better than the audience what it had cost him. The notices were profoundly split into two camps. The *Guardian*, *Daily Telegraph* and *Daily Mirror*, among those in favour, admired Finney's 'heroic', 'rough-hewn', 'sexy' prince, who rushed on stage threatening to commit hara-kiri with a dagger for the 'To be or not to be' soliloquy. The discontents, including *The Times*, *Sunday Times*, *Evening Standard*, *New York Times*, and the rarely critical trade paper, *The Stage*, found his extrovert approach 'insensitive', 'rasping like a buzz-saw', 'petulantly eccentric', 'monotonous' and 'a rant without emotion'. It was remarkable, said many, with such a Fury in pursuit of him, that Claudius survived so long. This was no more, you might think, than the usual dissatisfaction with all Hamlets, but the extremes of opinion betrayed the power of the performance to provoke. There were few complaints about the length of the text, because the production moved so fast. It set a fashion in the years that followed for playing Shakespeare as written.

After a week of previews in which the Lyttleton auditorium was tried out on five plays transferred from the Old Vic, *Hamlet* was given its official opening on 16 March 1976. The box office was sold out and the queue for tickets sold on the day began to form at 5 a.m. Princess Margaret attended and at curtain time Ralph Richardson fulfilled his ambition by firing a rocket from the roof. He explained genially that 'Ralph's Rocket' was to remind Londoners of the existence of the National Theatre by exploding in stars. 'The whole of London should stop to say "Hullo – Curtain up at the National".' He added as he walked away, 'I love fireworks. They're so unnecessary.' Alas, they are also costly and after a while Ralph's Rocket was confined to first nights, then dropped altogether when the GLC withdrew permission. (It was reinstated, on first nights only, in 1988.)

The Lyttleton theatre was given a pretty generous welcome, with a few reservations about the great width of the 45-foot-wide, 30-foot-high proscenium. Michael Billington in the *Guardian* thought *Hamlet* benefited from the stage's great width and depth on which one never noticed the proscenium arch. Irving Wardle in *The Times* likened it to the inside of an expensive camera, and anticipated seeing its proscenium open or contract like a lens – a hope that was to be frustrated by the need for it to be left almost fully open to enable people at the side to see. Robert Cushman in *The Observer* thought the plays, except for *Hamlet* and *Borkman*, were dwarfed by the stage. The auditorium reminded him of a large lecture hall ('You feel splayed and crushed'), while Milton Shulman in the *Evening Standard* likened it to a conference hall with such sharp acoustics that when Willie, in *Happy Days*, tapped his straw hat with his finger, it rang out 'like a pistol shot' (what would be the effect of coughing?). The exterior of the theatre was treated with respect. 'Not a cultural mausoleum, more like a superb piece of sculpture,' thought Billington. It was also compared to a 'glittering luxury liner' and 'a successful attempt to convert a monastery into a comfortable hotel', while the *Financial Times* talked of 'the utterly unashamed use of concrete' and positively rejoiced at the texture of the shuttering. The *Economist* approved of its cost, then quoted at £16 million ('It may well be a bargain'). It might even have thought it a bargain if it had known the final figure would be more than £20 million.

It was left to the unrepentant *New Statesman* to give the building anything like a stringent going-over. Its theatre critic, Benedict Nightingale, described arriving at the theatre from the direction of Waterloo. 'Just ahead you see what might be a prison, might be a warehouse or, given the lack of windows on its rectangular grey, might be a top-secret establishment for research into germ warfare.' He appealed for something to be done to transform the 'awful desolation' of the area into something alive and bustling. He feared it would dwindle into a cultural ghetto which came alive only at 7.15 p.m. The columnist Mervyn Jones described the foyers as like an airport lounge, programmes overpriced, lighting too dim to read them by, buffet menu disappointing. The paper's diarist, A. J. P. Taylor, the historian, found it too dark to read the signs, difficult to find the entrance and dangerous to try to get out. He left through a door marked 'Exit' only to find himself led up to the roof via a fire escape. The door behind him had shut and there was no turning back – 'I was lucky to escape alive.' The disabled, with justice, complained that access for them had been forgotten. As though it was the theatre's fault, one man sent in a pair of trousers which he claimed he had torn in the attempt to negotiate the unlighted steps down from Waterloo Bridge.

None of this was really serious, but one complaint above all was universal – the ticket voucher system, which had been unwisely introduced on the assumption that every seat in the house was as good as every other, thanks to perfect visibility and audibility throughout. The theatregoer was invited to choose between buying a numbered seat for £4.35 or a voucher for an unnumbered seat at £2.35, which would be exchanged on the night for any seat available. At this time £4.35 was a high price, above the going rate in the West End, so every night there were queues of people waiting to exchange their vouchers. It was a cumbersome, bewildering system that involved queueing twice and people hated it. Naturally the closest seats had already gone to those who had paid the higher price so the voucher-holder was the first to discover that if, officially, all seats were equal, some were more equal than others. Distance made a great difference to the degree of intimacy. Before the year was out, the system had been dropped.

'The National Theatre Is Yours' proclaimed the poster designed by Tom Phillips to coincide with the opening. The television documentary produced by London Weekend Television in August was called 'Your National Theatre'. It was as though people needed to be bludgeoned into believing it – or perhaps reminded that they were somehow collectively responsible (guilty?) for its being there and costing so much. The large fee LWT paid for exclusive rights to televise inside the building had not provided them with the climax they had reasonably expected: an actual opening of the heart and centre of the place, the Olivier auditorium. The opening date had been set for 15 July and cancelled – the twelfth successive deadline not to be met by the contractors. By July the company rehearsing *Tamburlaine*, who had been allowed into the theatre, were banished again and returned to their stifling rehearsal room; the theatre would not be ready for the amended opening date in August either. Actors who had been rehearsing since April were growing stale in a play that is repetitious anyway, battle after battle, massacre after massacre, triumph after triumph, 1,850 lines of it (longer than *Hamlet*) and few of them memorable, other than 'Is it not passing brave to be a king and ride in triumph through Persepolis?' In August when 'Your National Theatre' was transmitted, the theatre still wasn't properly theirs, let alone ours. They were performing al fresco on the terraces of the building, the only place where they could invite an audience that hot summer. 'I was a juvenile lead when I joined this production,' Finney amused the cast by saying. Hall was just as unhappy and frustrated as his actors: 'Rehearsing a play with no opening date is like protracted necking with no possibility of orgasm,' he complained to his diary.

He was growing paranoid again, but with justification. The loss of

114

box office revenue that the Olivier should have been earning was £100,000 a month. The cost of the building had been much commented on and there was still nothing really new to show for it. 'Your National Theatre' was bland enough television but the programme did contain a charged moment when Laurence Olivier admitted that the choice of Hall as his successor had never occurred to him. 'To me he was the friendly enemy – a friendly rival I should say.'

Hall was rattled to find newspapers accusing him of biting off more than he could chew. 'Is Peter Hall Stretching Too Far?' was the headline over an interview by Gaia Servadio in the *Evening Standard* which instanced the large number of National productions that he was directing, his television commitments, his unfinished film, his plans to direct opera at Glyndebourne, and suggested that his total earnings must be in the region of £50,000. She warned that 'the present policy may end in disaster for the National and his own downfall'. Others wondered how Hall had time to direct *Tamburlaine* when he had a full-time job on his hands getting the rest of the building open. According to John Heilpern, who was acting as his assistant on the production, 'Hall looked close to breaking point.' And then the stage hands walked out on strike, just when technical rehearsals were at last due to begin on the new stage. They refused to work in the Olivier theatre when already engaged on the Lyttleton productions next door. When ten men were suspended for refusing to work, the remainder, some sixty stage staff, walked out and began picketing the theatre. It closed for four nights of tension and confrontation. Audiences were given their money back and were handed leaflets by the pickets apologizing for their disappointment.

There are two versions of this seemingly unnecessary confrontation. What was at issue was a new agreement on the terms of backstage work in a new building which contained two theatres. The agreement at the Old Vic had given them high earnings in return for the extensive overtime needed to manage the constant changeovers of the repertory system, often late into the night. The set of that night's production had to be struck and then packed into pantechnicons (because of the shortage of storage space) followed by fitting up the set for the next night's play. If the work lasted beyond midnight it counted as an 'all-nighter' and was handsomely paid for. Over the years 'old Spanish customs' had grown up and been accepted by the management rather than fail to get the curtain up on time. Demarcation between the three backstage branches – stage-hands, properties and stage-electrics – was absolute. Strictly speaking, a stage-hand might not move a prop, even if no prop man was present and everyone would have to stop work until one came. The basic rate of £60 a week compared well with the rate for most actors and was far better than stage-management rates. With overtime it could well be doubled.

But the plan for the new theatre was to economize drastically on backstage costs and manning, thanks to the new scene-shifting machinery and computer controls, and the deployment of a flexible crew to cover two, and later three, theatres. What seems to have been overlooked is the natural reluctance of any workforce to give up earnings they have already gained. 'We told them they needn't spend all day and night in the theatre and sleep in a bunk,' said Peter Stevens, who had been made general administrator. 'We pointed out that they could go home at civilized hours and have weekends off. But they wanted the overtime earnings they had had at the Old Vic. Their attitude was that if the hours were to be halved, the rate should be doubled to compensate them.' The men pointed out that the new stage machinery that was to save so much labour did not work. The computerized flying system meant to function at the touch of a button had been abandoned in the Lyttleton, which was back on a manual system. To complicate matters, the National stage crews and prop men were at odds with the leaders of their union, NATTKE – they included several militant extremists out for trouble. Labour relations had been good at the Old Vic, although the management had paid a high price for it. Now the men faced a new management in an unfinished theatre full of unfamiliar machinery which seldom worked and which they did not trust. It was a classic situation for a showdown in labour relations.

Even so, there might not have been one had the men not had a charismatic leader to turn to in Kon Fredericks, an assistant master carpenter and chief NATTKE shop steward. He was no ordinary stagehand. He had been, among other things, an actor, had a feeling for stage design, and was articulate, persuasive – and likeable. Rebel leader was a part he was well cast in. 'Kon appears to me to be having his finest revolutionary hour. The former actor cuts a romantic figure on the barricades,' noted Peter Hall. Simon Relph, the theatre's technical administrator and negotiator, admitted, 'I liked Kon and didn't mind working with him. His problem was in controlling his own men.' Kon himself, the object of such mixed feelings, did not look back on the conflict purely in terms of money. 'We were well paid at the Old Vic but it was also rewarding in other ways. Everyone enjoyed working there. We were expected to leave our lovely old theatre to work in this mess, designed by well-meaning amateurs. The South Bank contained two highly technical theatres which were then more or less unworkable. And they wanted to give us less money. It was a very simple issue.'

The unofficial strike was settled by the management reinstating the strikers without penalty while a new agreement was worked out. 'We were all ready to resign because the Board had overruled us on how to deal with the situation,' said Relph. 'The Board wanted anything rather than a strike all over the newspapers.' Lord Mishcon was the Board member deputed to oversee the negotiations because of his skills and experience as a solicitor. Earlier in his career he had specialized in advising trade unions, including NATTKE. 'I wanted peace, not at any price, but keeping in mind that there was such loss of morale in the company that the strike had to be stopped,' he recalled. On the return to work Hall called a much- postponed dress rehearsal of *Tamburlaine*. 'It was the only time I ever saw Peter Hall lose his cool,' said Denis Quilley, who was playing Tamburlaine's rival emperor. 'We had at last been promised this rehearsal but we assembled to find it had been vetoed by the stagehands. He took his script, threw it on the ground, stamped on it and walked away.' Hall took a beating over this first involvement in a labour dispute at the National. He felt it his melancholy duty to give way to men whom his lieutenants wanted him to sack. Having given way, he had little to show for it except threats to work to rule and to refuse overtime. The final opening date for *Tamburlaine* had been set for 4 October but he began to feel there was a jinx on it. 'I hardly dared walk round the building. I was aware of everybody looking at me to see how I was taking adversity . . . I was irritable and flustered and I kept on having moments of absolute despair.'

It was not only the stage-hands who had complaints about the building. The actors found little to enthuse about backstage, which had been finished to the cheapest possible standards and looked it. The dressing-rooms were another source of complaint. Those that were shared between six or eight actors were split up by internal partitions for privacy, but actors preparing to act together do not particularly want privacy; they like to be able to talk face to face. Above all, they did not like the atmosphere, so different from backstage at traditional theatres. 'You walked into the canteen and there were 200 people you didn't know, many of them not actors at all. It was like going to work in a factory,' said Denis Quilley. Gawn Grainger, who, like Quilley, was one of the few who had been taken across from the Old Vic company, recalled, 'After the Vic it felt horrible. It lacked the smell of a theatre. It was all concrete and concrete doesn't smell right. The dressing-rooms were little concrete cells with cubicles, like tiny hotel rooms.' It was a dispirited company that wearily approached the opening night, after rehearsing for two weeks short of six months.

Before the performance Hall had made a desperate rallying call to the company. 'If you think we're in the shit, you're right,' he began, and counselled them to put two fingers in the air to the National's critics. 'Say to them, This is what we are, this is what we can do and to hell with you!' The backs-to-the-wall spirit paid off in energy and brought cheers from the audience for Finney as the crazed savage who lived up to the title of *Tamburlaine the Great*. Contrary to expectation the play got goodish notices. The auditorium got even better ones. The comfort of its seats was tested over four and a half hours and not found wanting. 'I was delighted with the sense of comfort and informality – almost intimacy,' declared Felix Barker in the *Evening News*. Benedict Nightingale called it 'the most exciting auditorium in the country, even though I sometimes wished Peter Hall had chosen to baptise it with something less overwhelming than the Pacific Ocean'.

Tamburlaine was not chosen for the theatre's royal opening on 25 October. Royalty is not expected to endure too long an entertainment, so the choice fell on a little-known piece by Goldoni, *Il Campiello*, a modest Venetian comedy whose production failed to excite anyone. Only previewed a couple of times before the royal gala, it seemed that inept planning had left the theatre with no other choice in its repertoire for an occasion which demanded something special. The Queen arrived in torrential rain to be greeted by a demonstration outside the theatre, representing the Fringe, holding placards that read 'Whose National Theatre?' It was an evening on which the play was definitely not the thing. The state trumpeters muffed the specially composed fanfare. Photographs taken in the auditorium showed the Queen and the recently ennobled Lord Rayne presiding over the festive occasion with stony expressions. Princess Margaret was luckier – she attended a revival of *Jumpers* in the Lyttleton.

On her arrival, Lord Cottesloe reminded the Queen of her joke when, years before, he had invited her to open the new building. 'You replied that you doubted whether by that time you would still be here. But here at long last we are, Ma'am.' 'I am as happy and relieved as you are that my gloomy predictions have proved unfounded,' said the Queen, adding pointedly, 'My family have taken part in many ceremonies connected with the National Theatre and not all of them have been at the site on which we now stand.' The much-moved foundation stone which her mother had said should be put on casters had come to rest in the foyer alongside the plaque she was about to unveil. 'I am glad to join in what must surely be universal rejoicing,' she added optimistically, making no reference to the damp demonstrators outside, 'that the much-needed and long-awaited National Theatre is now a reality.' Lord Cottesloe on behalf of his Board handed the building over to Lord Rayne and *his* Board. Mr Peter Hall, as he still was, called the idea of National Theatre, over 150 years, 'one of the most absurd and eccentric dreams of the English people'. He prophesied: 'The more energy and, dare one say it, the more money that is put into the work that is done here, the more energy will flow out into the rest of the theatre all over the country.'

The main source of energy flowing that evening was waiting to contribute his brief and only performance on the stage of the theatre named after him. Laurence Olivier's absence had been marked since he left the National over two years before. He had declined to appear at the farewell performance at the Old Vic, a tribute to Lilian Baylis in which he had been expected to take part. He did not come to the opening of the Lyttleton and declined to speak the prologue to *Tamburlaine* at the first performance in the Olivier. But he could scarcely disappoint the sovereign. With the instinct of a professional he had got to know the stage with a little quiet advance practice, arranged through the housekeeper, Harry Henderson. 'Every morning at eight he came to the theatre and I let him in to rehearse his speech, with only the cleaners there. He used to ask them if they could hear him all right.' On the night he showed no sign of the serious illness that had plagued him since he left nor of the mixed feelings he must have experienced on mounting the Olivier stage with which he now had nothing to do. 'For this moment we must be grateful to the timing and the durable cladding of Mr Peter Hall's foot when he put it in the door,' he said, naming some of the campaigners who had brought a national theatre to pass, including his old foe, Lord Chandos, Baroness Jennie Lee, Lord Goodman, Lord Cottesloe and others. His tribute to the architect was fulsome even by his standards: 'Our very eyes and all happy senses will for ever be rewarded by the craft and genius of the actual creator of this situation in which we find ourselves – Sir Denys Lasdun . . . To those who will follow, I wish joy eternal of all of it.' In actorly style, he thanked the audience 'for your kind attention and for the glory and lustre of your presence. Welcome.' They were the last words he ever spoke from the stage of a theatre.

10

1977–8: A Beleaguered Fortress

Six contemporary playwrights had been commissioned to provide new works for the opening season of the South Bank. The plan was disorganized by its repeated delays and the plays were of uneven quality. The best and first to be delivered, Harold Pinter's *No Man's Land*, was brought back for a token dozen performances in the Lyttleton before departing for the more lucrative pastures of Broadway. John Osborne's commission had resulted in a curiously artificial play from him about an artist commune living in a converted railway station. *Watch It Come Down* had opened at the Old Vic to baffled reviews – 'Osborne off the Rails' was the inevitable headline – and moved to the Lyttleton where it had twenty-nine performances before Hall took it off, much to the displeasure of Osborne, who argued that it was part of the function of a national theatre to keep at least one non-box-office play in production (in fact his play had averaged respectable 77 per cent audiences).

The third commission, and the first to be premièred in the Lyttleton, was *Weapons of Happiness*. Its author, Howard Brenton, had been nurtured partly at the Royal Court, where he was resident dramatist, and partly on the Fringe, particularly in association with David Hare, who directed the play. It contrasts two kinds of revolutionaries: an old Czech communist, broken in the purges of the 1950s, and a young English girl Marxist with romantic ideas of revolution, who leads a sit-in at her factory. It added up to a pessimistic critique of the state of part of the nation, at least, and showed that the National's doors were open to a left-wing political playwright. Communism was also the topic of Robert Bolt's *State of Revolution*, which examined the role played by Lenin, Trotsky, Stalin and others in the 1917 Bolshevik revolution and showed that the saintly Lenin of legend was no less ruthless a tyrant than his rivals. The part gave Michael Bryant, beginning a long career at the National, the opportunity for a physically convincing character study.

The next commission, which also caused the most controversy, was from Alan Ayckbourn. After *Relatively Speaking*, his first London production in 1967, he seemed to take on the mantle of Terence Rattigan as a prolific master of West End comedy. His ingenuity in setting scenes in two separate households on stage simultaneously was now outdone: he made it three. *Bedroom Farce* is set in three bedrooms in the separate houses of three couples connected through a party. It is given by one couple, attended by the second couple and wrecked by the destructive behaviour of the third. The action switches from bedroom to bedroom without ever involving what, in Aldwych farce days, would have been called 'hanky-panky'. Indeed, it is the absence of hanky-panky from their marriages that springs the action. Maria Aitken and Stephen Moore milked high anxiety of its tragi-comic possibilities as the feuding couple who can neither get on nor break up. The play was jointly directed by the author and Peter Hall, which made for confusion when first one, then the other, would change what had been set at the other's rehearsal. 'When we went on tour I suggested that they should both leave us alone while we tried to find out how best to do it with an audience,' said Maria Aitken. New plays had provided few laughs at the National and audiences seized on this expert comedy gratefully. The production set a Lyttleton Theatre record with 185 performances to 139,000 people. After eighteen months in the repertory it transferred both to Broadway and the West End where, some carping critics maintained, it belonged in the first place. Of course, it was true that Ayckbourn needed no help from a subsidized theatre to get a showing. But the converse argument did not hold: that people attending the National should never be entertained by the sort of plays they could see elsewhere. To ask, What is the National Theatre doing putting on Ayckbourn? – as some critics did – was to take an extremely narrow view of what a national theatre is for.

Audience figures over the first year showed that the South Bank was no different from the West End when it came to finding hits. The popular, long-running successes were *Plunder* (86 per cent average audiences), a revival of *Blithe Spirit* directed by Harold Pinter (92 per cent), the revival of Tom Stoppard's *Jumpers* (99 per cent) and *Bedroom Farce* (84 per cent). Not politics, poetry or psychological profundity but proficiency of comedy technique were what kept the theatres consistently filled. With 2,000 seats to sell nightly, the staple diet of the two main houses was bound to be revivals – new plays inevitably had a higher failure rate. The notable revivals included a richly-cast *Volpone* in which Paul Scofield made his South Bank debut, with Ben Kingsley as his Mosca and Gielgud as Sir Politic Wouldbe. The theatre's first exhumation of a rarity, *The Madras House*, directed by William Gaskill, was a carefully detailed reconstruction of a theatrical edifice of 1910. Appropriately enough, it did credit to Harley Granville-Barker, who maintained that a national theatre should offer a 'library of standard literature' of all periods. His study of a wealthy Edwardian merchant family, with Paul Scofield at its head, was realized in solid mahogany interiors by Hayden Griffin which were wheeled complete on to the Olivier stage (the flying system still being inoperable). Here was a proscenium play if there ever was one, which managed to reduce the focus of the open stage to human proportions by ignoring the void around it. Barker's fate had been to lie forgotten in Shaw's shadow, but Shaw, too, now suffers selective neglect. His second play, *The Philanderer*, of 1893, received a mere eight matinée performances in Barker's 1907 season at the Court and had had only four London productions since, until the National revived it. It proved to be no apprentice work but a sparkling debate on relationships between the sexes, with the philandering hero (a lightly disguised 38-year-old Bernard Shaw) rebounding between two emancipated New Women. Besides its Edwardian successes, the National also had its Irish ones. The largely Irish company directed by Bill Bryden in *The Playboy of the Western World* at the Old Vic scored an even bigger success with it in the Olivier and went on to revive Sean O'Casey's play of the 1916 Easter Rising, *The Plough and the Stars*, which is seldom done at all, let alone as well as it now was, outside Ireland.

Nevertheless, one seldom heard anything but adverse comment about the National in its early years in the new building. It was a beleaguered fortress and although the public had taken to the front-of-house, with its foyer events and mingling space, the back-of-house went on causing great discontent to those who worked there. The actors, although over 100 strong, were heavily outnumbered amongst a staff of 750 (rising to a peak of over 900 in 1977–8). All shared the same industrial-style canteen and a 'green room' which resembled a public bar full of outsiders, not an actors' retreat. The dressing-rooms, whose windows could not be opened because of the air conditioning, were another bugbear. For an actor a dressing-room is a sort of home, neat and tidy or scruffy and disorderly according to temperament. The cubicled cells, spread over three confusing floors, never acquired the homeliness they have in old, cramped theatres. Albert Finney and Denis Quilley used to ring each other up in the 'half' before *Hamlet* or *Tamburlaine* rather than risk getting lost by trying to find each other's dressing-rooms on different floors. People complained of getting lost between stage and dressing-room and there were stories, never quite substantiated, of disoriented actors rushing panic-stricken through the maze of identical-looking corridors to emerge on the wrong stage in the wrong play. 'Physically it was an inimical place with none of the atmosphere that a theatre should have,' said Quilley. There was little sense of unity between the actors and administrators, who were segregated in two floors of offices at the top of the building, nowhere near the dressing-rooms or the stages. Very little mixing went on. Even in the canteen it was noticeable that different casts kept to themselves at separate tables. They hardly met fellow actors who were appearing in different plays in the same building. 'You felt you were part of a travelling company that had just touched down,' said Maria Aitken. 'Other companies were hermetically sealed off from your own. It was rather like working in TV.'

Ultimately, what really matters about a theatre to an actor is the stage and its relation to the auditorium. This was supposedly the most carefully planned theatre complex in the country, yet everyone seemed to find the Lyttleton particularly unfriendly. The stalls are an unbroken block of 550 seats without a centre aisle. The circle, seating 324, is set at such a height that it seems difficult to play to both. A row of extra seats, strung along the side walls of the auditorium at balcony level, one in front of another like seats on a bus, are supposed to link the circle with the stage in the way that theatre boxes do. They have no such effect and command a very poor view of the stage. For audience and actors alike, the auditorium lacks focus. For Albert Finney, who took *Hamlet* there direct from the Old Vic, 'it was like exchanging a horse-shoe for a shoebox. The stage felt very wide and the auditorium felt very deep and I didn't feel like me at all.' Dennis Quilley, who made the same transition as Claudius, was equally unhappy. 'As a theatre, it was a disaster. In all three fundamentals, the size, the shape and the acoustics, it went wrong – quite an achievement. It did not work acoustically, aesthetically or socially.'

When both of them moved into the Olivier with *Tamburlaine*, they found the arena-like space stimulating but difficult to work in. The sight-lines leave masked considerable areas at the back of the stage. And the reflection of sound makes for blurred hearing in certain parts of the house, especially the front rows of the circle. It had been claimed that every seat is within 75 feet of the stage. But the psychological expanse is much greater. From halfway back or more in the circle, figures on stage are reduced to pygmies gesticulating in an overwhelming void. Instinctively actors throw their voices to cover the big expanse, which does not make for intimate playing. 'From the point of view of vocal effort, it was the nearest thing I know to playing in the open air,' said Quilley. 'It is an exciting, vibrant sort of space, with a certain magic about it, but it seemed extremely tiring to work in. Albert Finney had a similar reaction: 'If you stand on the stage of a "proper" theatre, there is a circuit of energy flowing out to the audience and back to the performer again. Here the circuit wasn't completed. The energy going out of me did not come back. Instead of being recharged, like a dynamo, I felt like a battery, running down.'

These were the sort of problems met by the first actors – very experienced actors – who used the new auditoria (neither Finney nor Quilley were in any hurry to return). Both agreed that the problems were increased by the concrete wall surfaces. 'You wouldn't make a musical instrument out of concrete,' Finney pointed out, 'and the concrete was raw, with no coating on it at all, unlike an old theatre like the Vic, where you are aware of all the people who had been there before you.' It is interesting to compare the reaction of Finney and Quilley, the pioneers, with those of Michael Gambon, who became a regular presence on the same stages in years to come: 'The huge sweep of the Olivier is frightening at first sight. You have nowhere to hide. It's like a wild animal – you wonder how you're going to control it. It makes you work very hard, using the full range of your voice. But when it's full of people, it can become almost intimate, unlike the Lyttleton. That has none of the contact, physical and emotional, that you get from a traditional proscenium theatre. The hardest thing to play there is comedy.' Peter Wood, the director who was to put eighteenth-century plays written for the proscenium on both stages, considers the Olivier the more intimate of the two. 'The psychological rapport with the audience is much stronger. People think of it as a stage for epics but a two-handed comedy scene will go like one o'clock in the Olivier.'

The stage-hands' strike of the previous summer had resulted in a new agreement on working the stages, but it had left suspicion and ill-will in the atmosphere, only waiting for a spark to set it off. The spark came at the end of May 1977, in an apparently ludicrous form. The dismissal of a plumber, Ralph Cooper, for failing to repair two wash-basins within a reasonable time, triggered a walk-out and such headlines as 'Two Wash Basins Halt National Theatre' or 'Theatre of the Absurd'. It was not as absurd as it sounded. Cooper was a militant shop steward of the maintenance department, where there was a history of conflict, and the management seized on the wash-basins as an opportunity to get rid of a supposed troublemaker. His fellow shop stewards promptly led 100 backstage and workshop NATTKE members out on unofficial strike, demanding his reinstatement, which closed the theatre for five nights. Kon Fredericks was once more the focus of newspaper coverage. 'As he strides about the concrete complex he has, in the words of *Julius Caesar*, the lean and hungry look of Cassius, unlike Mr Cooper (a fat man),' said the *Daily Telegraph*. Its reporter, to whom this Cassius had refused audience, went on to describe him as 'a former understudy in the nude revue *Oh! Calcutta!* and a confirmed Trotskyist' – probably the ultimate combination of evils in the *Telegraph*'s demonology. The actors invited Kon Fredericks to address them at a meeting chaired by Michael Bryant, who, but for the closure, would have been playing Lenin. The other strikers had refused to enter the building to put their case, so the actors and non-striking NATTKE members went outside to urge them to go to arbitration instead of jeopardizing the future of the theatre. The stewards refused to take a vote on returning to work. 'A lot of it was political agitation, in my opinion. There were people working there only in order to stir up trouble,' said Michael Bryant.

The general secretary of NATTKE, John Wilson, a cautious Scot who was disowned by the militants as too moderate, at last asserted control by threatening to dismiss the eight shop stewards involved from their union posts unless they returned to work. The strike crumbled, arbitration was accepted and Cooper was reinstated pending the hearing. The management had lost thirteen performances and had still got the offending plumber (the arbitration hearing reinstated him on 'final warning'). Everyone went back to work except Kon Fredericks, who refused to accept the verdict and left. After two such confrontations, the public image of the National was one of a strife-torn institution whose labour squabbles about wash-basins and scene-shifting cost a great deal of taxpayers' money. Conservatives now in control of the GLC, like the arts committee chairman, Bernard Brook-Partridge, were not slow to turn this to political account. 'Silly, ludicrous and piddling', he called the strike and said that his committee, which made an annual grant of £350,000 to the theatre, was 'not a bottomless purse for industrial anarchy' of this kind. 'The public, who put £2,400,000 a year into the National Theatre, will not be amused by this disastrous spectacle,' commented Dr Rhodes Boyson, MP, Conservative spokesman on the arts.

When the figures for the first year on the South Bank were totted up, they told an alarming story. The late opening of the Olivier had deprived the theatre of £600,000 of its expected revenue. Circumventing the non-functioning stage machinery had added extra cost. The deficit of £250,000 on the year would have been much higher but for the income from transfers – *Equus*, revived in the West End as well as running on Broadway, alone brought in nearly £500,000. It could be said that playwright Peter Shaffer almost single-handedly bailed out the National in its stormy first year on the South Bank. But the most ominous expense was that of servicing the building. Even before it was fully operational, this accounted for £788,000. The number of employees had increased since the move from 450 to 750. The theatre's grant had already more than doubled, there had been a generous supplementary sum of £500,000 from the Arts Council, and it still had a quarter of a million pounds deficit. The stark, unalterable logistics of the building had come home to roost. Its floor area was about 500,000 square feet, an immense spread ten times that of the Old Vic, but it served only two-and-a-half times as many paying customers. And all this space had to be heated, lighted, air-conditioned, cleaned, serviced and policed, whether a show was put on or not. It was planned when energy was cheap and now it was to eat up more of the funding every year – rising from £1 million the following year to £2.5 million ten years later. No other theatre in the land had to spend a third of its grant on its bricks and mortar – or rather, its concrete and air-conditioning. Many people now argued that it should be funded in the same way as the National Gallery or the British Museum, by direct government grant through the Department of the Environment. 'It must be regarded as a national monument,' pronounced a *Guardian* leader, making the case for direct state funding. This was a dispute that would continue over many years without achieving the change.

It was not long, however, before the National's persistent critics were suggesting that its troubles were due to its own extravagance. It was claimed that the NT designers spent more on one production than two-thirds of English theatre companies received in grant for a whole year. This was probably true; the majority of subsidized theatre companies were so small that they received less than £10,000, many of them less than £5,000. The average cost of productions in the Olivier in 1977 was £29,000. In the Lyttleton it was £19,000. The Royal Shakespeare Company, with a third of the National's subsidy, was mounting 35 productions that year, compared to the National's (reduced) plans for 23. The reputation for extravagance was furthered by the news in early 1978 that the theatre was paying £200,000 a year to extra stage-hands and in overtime to replace the advanced stage technology, the computer-controlled flying system, and the drum revolve, which still did not work. 'A technological folly' said the *Economist*, comparing the theatre to 'a tethered Concorde'. Meanwhile Arts Council policy had changed since the building was commissioned. Instead of allotting 40 per cent of its funds to the 'Big Four' – the Royal Opera House, the English National Opera, the National Theatre and the Royal Shakespeare Company – it had reduced their share to 27 per cent of the total subsidy available, in order to allot more money to the regions.

When the grants for 1978–9 were announced, the National was given £130,000 less than the 'pared-to-the-bone' budget it had submitted of £3.7 million. The immediate response by management was to order the company to be reduced from 137 actors to 106, the programme to be reduced from 23 to 20 productions at lower budgets, to halt all touring, and to drop projected visits by regional companies. On top of the cuts, all theatres were set audience targets of 85 per cent. Then another blow fell – a strike far worse than any before.

As part of the public sector, the National was ordered to keep its annual wage offer within the government guideline of 5 per cent. This was eventually accepted by all departments except the stage-hands and props, after two one-day stoppages in November, causing last-minute cancellation of performances and sending audiences home angry and disappointed. Stage-hands continued to threaten further action, such as that the revolve, on which Pinter's play *Betrayal* depended, 'might not function'. Its opening night was kept in doubt until the last minute. By coincidence, Galsworthy's *Strife*, about a strike in a tin-plate works after which the strikers end up with the same offer as they started with, was premièred in the ugly atmosphere of imminent confrontation that pervaded the country as well as the theatre. It opened on the night that *The Times* suspended publication.

The walk-out finally came on 16 March 1979, involving some seventy backstage staff. They set up a permanent picket line on the access road, with a hut, brazier, placards and all the paraphernalia of industrial strife that were all too familiar during that 'winter of discontent'. There was some intimidation of those going through the picket line. The lorry that was meant to take the new production of *For Services Rendered* to play at Nottingham was attacked and prevented from leaving. Staff members' cars were vandalized in the car park. There were attempts to stop deliveries to the building. On one occasion it was relieved like a besieged fortress by a van carrying provisions, after a signal by radio that the scene dock doors were ready to open. They closed behind it just in time to frustrate the pickets. The atmosphere inside was one of defiance. Hall and his new general administrator, Michael Elliott, who had just joined the theatre from industry, were determined to hold out against the strikers. The theatre had been plagued by unofficial stoppages ever since it opened; to give in to this, the most serious challenge, would be to undermine any control of the militants in future.

To the joy of the London evening papers, which front-paged it, the strikers produced a list of allegations of how the National tossed away taxpayers' money backstage in extravagant and wasteful production. A set for *Hamlet* had been made of lead, another for *Tamburlaine* of brass, a third, for *The Madras House*, had been burned after use despite its costliness. Dresses costing hundreds, even thousands, had been bought and then dyed black to tone them down. Special squeaky boots for Sir Ralph Richardson to wear as John Gabriel Borkman had cost the theatre hundreds. Props were bought or made which were never used.

The journalists who reported this were not going to ask whether second thoughts about costumes or props did not show the care taken to get things right. But the theatre defended itself by pooh-poohing the figures alleged. Nothing had cost thousands, only hundreds, and Sir Ralph's hand-made boots were a bargain at £134. Hamlet had been staged against lead foil, not lead sheeting, the costume that had been dyed black was only a sari worth £85, and so on. The union stuck to its guns: 'We still contend that expenditure on productions like *Tamburlaine* was extravagant,' said the branch secretary. So it had to be, to make a spectacle worthy of the opening of the theatre.

After the theatre had been dark for ten days, it was decided to reopen at any cost. The set for *For Services Rendered* was still up on the Lyttleton stage. Peter Wood redirected *The Double Dealer* around it, since no scenery could be moved without black-legging. The theatre's policy was to play by the rules. The Olivier had only one chair on stage. Despite this, *Strife* was performed to audiences that were offered seats at low prices. It was more of a gesture of good faith than a way of reducing the heavy box office losses. The performances were sporadic and not well attended. People did not fancy walking through the jeers of a picket line in order to enjoy a night out.

Over at the NATTKE headquarters in Lambeth the union executive were once more at loggerheads with their general secretary, John Wilson, who opposed the unofficial action. Things got so unfraternal that the strikers marched in and occupied their union offices. They searched in vain for Wilson, who was hiding in the locked computer room. They demanded that the Transport and General Workers Union should black deliveries of fuel oil to the National building. But there was no support for the strike from any other union, including Equity, or from a majority of the union's own members. A meeting of the entire NATTKE membership at the National, which included many of the office staff, took a vote on whether there should be an official strike ballot. It was heavily defeated. Even the strikers who were present did not want to see the National closed down, perhaps permanently. This was the vote Wilson needed as a weapon to use against his own executive. But when the strike had been going on for over a month he disappeared suddenly to Guernsey. Lord Mishcon was again deputed to take charge of the negotations – to the chagrin of hardliners in the management. 'I had to decide how far we would go,' he said. 'The union trouble-makers wanted a bloody revolution. Wilson was being bullied by the strike leaders, who wouldn't allow him to make an agreement. I felt we should look for a compromise.' The compromise formula suggested by Mishcon was that all those outside would be dismissed but reinstated immediately if they signed an undertaking recognizing that unofficial action was a breach of contract. There was fruitless to-ing and fro-ing to ACAS, the conciliatory body, even unofficial contacts between some actors and the strikers, who suggested a private talk with Peter Hall on neutral ground – the back of a taxi – to 'work something out'. Hall refused. He confided to his diary the despairing sentence: 'My heart is no longer in this shit-heap.' As April neared its end, he wound up rehearsals for *The Oresteia* which would have been opening but for the strike.

Then, unexpectedly, on the last day of April, the dispirited theatre workers arrived to find the picket line withdrawn, the huts dismantled, the rubbish swept up and the few remaining strikers handing out leaflets saying that the National Theatre had one of the most right-wing administrations in the industry. The five-week strike was, in effect, over. Why? There may have been backstairs pressure on the strikers to stop providing such conspicuously bad propaganda for the Left just before polling in a general election. Wilson nursed the suspicion that it was Labour Party pressure through the TUC that got the pickets withdrawn. Even if that were so, it hardly mattered. Three days later, on 3 May, the election was easily won by Mrs Thatcher's Conservatives, largely on the promise to break the power of trade unions and end the anarchy. Among those who voted for them was Sir Peter Hall.

Who had won? 'Nobody won,' was the view of Bill Bundy, who as technical administrator helped conduct negotiations with the strikers. 'It left a lot of badly bruised people. Some of them were men I liked and respected, who had had to go along with the ringleaders or get thumped. We were asked if we would take them back and we said no. But we should have negotiated a new operating agreement.' Jules Boardman, deputy general administrator and another negotiator, saw it as a management victory of sorts. 'We stood out against all the pressures to settle. Peter Hall thought the Board would dismiss him, but he never compromised. We had all had enough. Everyone was offered re-engagement but only if they agreed to work by the rule-book.' Very few of the men outside signed on. Michael Elliott, who came from industry and saw the strikers for what they were, took over as general administrator as the strike began. He was shocked by the sour atmosphere of antagonism that he found throughout the building, not only among the strikers outside but among those inside. He and Hall saw the ringleaders off and the atmosphere improved.

A week after the theatre resumed full performances, a dozen demonstrators interrupted *The Double Dealer* by climbing on to the Lyttleton stage and shouting 'scabs' at the actors and audience. The company had been warned that in such an event, they should break off and leave the stage. But Dorothy Tutin had missed the meeting at which these instructions were given. 'I just stood my ground and glared at these men who had dared to invade my territory. I had had my back to the audience when they appeared. It was a shock to turn round and find three strange men there instead of my fellow actors. There was no way I was going to give way. Then Michael Bryant came back, took my hand and led me off and they brought the curtain down.' The cast waited angrily behind the scenes while one of the demonstrators harangued the audience. Nobody knew who these interlopers were – they were not the strikers who had been encamped outside for so long. The audience was also outraged. Simon Gray, who argued with the demonstrators, was told to shut up and sit down, whereupon his wife hit one of them hard. Police arrived and half an hour later the play resumed from the point where it was broken off, with a round of applause. The publicity which the event attracted next day was no help in persuading audiences back to a theatre which had scarcely been functioning for six weeks. It had lost £250,000 in box office revenue. With the militant ringleaders gone, life backstage settled down to comparative peace. Standing firm against the bullying was obviously the right, indeed only, policy to avoid further bullying. But it came near to closing down the theatre completely.

At that point there was an Arts Council inquiry in progress into the costs of running the National in its new home in order to determine its future level of funding. The National Theatre Board claimed that the delays in completing the building and its technical shortcomings had saddled the Board with an accumulated deficit which it put at £336,000. It pointed out that the building's demands were inflexible; the only economies that could be made were in the programme. It supported its case with statistics that demonstrated the theatre's success with the public: despite all the handicaps and interruptions, it had sold 1.6 million tickets, earning £7 million, in its first eighteen months in operation. But it still could not promise to be 'a theatre centre for the nation' unless it received £6 million a year in subsidy in order to finance a full programme of activities.

Again it was suggested that the cost of maintaining the building should be separated from that of running the theatre and taken over by 'an agency other than the Arts Council'. Other bodies submitting evidence, such as the Arts Council itself and the GLC, supported the proposal to finance the running of the building by a special grant. On the model of public buildings like the National Gallery, it should be the Department of the Environment's responsibility. But how would theatre expenses be separated from maintenance and which members of the maintenance staff would be working for which employer – the NT or the DOE? Before the Arts Council inquiry had reached any conclusions the Government proposed its own solution – to give an extra £700,000, annually through the Arts Council, to cover maintenance of the building, provided that the National Theatre Board took over the lease. 'This type of solution is to be preferred to any of the alternatives,' wrote the Arts Council Chairman. Already the Board was having serious doubts about being placed under the aegis of another government department, which had no experience of theatre administration and would not necessarily provide any more money, possibly not as much. In short, better the devil you know . . . The Arts Council wound up its inquiry recommending a once-for-all grant to clear the accumulated deficit, which at last was done.

It was the end of the beginning. It had been a very rough ride and had come near to unseating Peter Hall on several occasions. It was a measure of his resilience that he hung on and kept his grip. Those who attributed this to a thick skin and a driving ambition did not fairly assess the man. His diaries for the period 1978–9 could be a case-book of paranoia. Looking at them dispassionately, one wonders if he would not have been wiser not to direct productions while steering the ship through so many storms. Taking rehearsals, he often declared, was his main solace for the hours spent on administration, but when he was so distracted by backstage problems that he could no longer lose himself in directing plays, the results showed on the stage. *The Country Wife* opened in November 1977 – a time of financial crisis – to 'horrible notices – unfortunately I think they're right'. He admitted to himself that he was ashamed of his work and had lost his confidence, as he went straight on to rehearse *The Cherry Orchard*. Before the first preview he gave notes to individual actors for six hours without stopping – hardly a sign of having completed his work in rehearsal. He believed the audience were waiting for the latest disaster from the National Theatre. The notices were mixed, even Ralph Richardson's Firs attracting criticism. Albert Finney, who had soldiered through these productions, now insisted on playing Macbeth, asking Hall to direct him. Hall reluctantly agreed, feeling that he owed it to Finney. Before that production opened he took the extraordinary course of telling the cast that they must not expect success. 'I am now militantly classic, which is not popular at the moment when everybody expects to see Shakespeare directed from one single interpretative viewpoint. I don't believe in that any more, so there can be accusations of ordinariness.' It was a self-fulfilling prophecy. The notices were 'as terrible as any I have ever had, malicious and mocking . . . The critics just now don't like me, nor the Olivier, nor *Macbeth* . . . The production is unfashionably simple – and I am out of fashion too.' It was a fairly desperate course to blame his production's lack of success on a dislike of the play and on being out of fashion. Albert Finney remembered the production as 'dreadfully operatic' and he attributed this to the size of the Olivier stage. 'Because of the big space, you need a bigger throne. That means the man who sits on it needs a bigger costume. The result is to make you, the actor, operatic.' After three disappointments in a row, Finney went his way, not to return in Hall's time. Much had been hoped of their partnership. 'People thought we would make a good combination of brawn and brain – I was the emotional actor, he was the academic director. But I don't think it ever caught fire. I don't know if it was the coldness of the concrete, the size of the theatre or what.' Finney put an end to it, somewhat resentfully because he had put so much energy into the project.

There seemed no end to the early discouragements. Despite the knighthood given him in 1977, Hall knew that in government circles he was their least favourite administrator of a politically unpopular institution. He began to feel like a sacrificial victim, set up to be blamed for all that had gone wrong, didn't work or cost more than had been expected connected with the building. 'It would make a rotten hotel,' he declared irritably. He resented all the published criticism of the National in the papers and in the book which appeared in April 1978, *The History of the National Theatre*, by John Elsom, who had taken it over from Nicholas Tomalin after his death in the Arab–Israeli war. To cap it all, the commentator on one of the Thames pleasure cruises, passing the front of the building, had taken to pointing it out audibly over the loudspeaker as 'that monstrosity run by a pig called Peter Hall'. In the background, his domestic life was in the throes of the final break-up of his second marriage.

He had had a rotten year. More than once he contemplated getting out. 'I wrote a letter of resignation, tore it up and generally wondered what the hell I was doing' (29 January 1978). 'We agreed [Trevor Nunn, director of the RSC, and Hall] that we didn't any more want to head huge organisations . . . These monsters are having to get bigger and bigger in order to justify their subsidies . . . I ought to leave the National, Trevor ought to leave the RSC and Brook, Trevor and I ought to start a theatre together' (20 June). A simple space and twenty-five actors – that old ideal had raised its head again. In August he appointed three capable assistant directors – Christopher Morahan, a former head of television drama at the BBC, to run the Olivier, Michael Rudman, director of the Hampstead Theatre, to run the Lyttleton, and Bill Bryden, home-bred at the National, to run the Cottesloe. It was a move that he would have made earlier, but his previous overtures to Terry Hands and to William Gaskill had not borne fruit. Even with such help at hand, Hall, turning forty-eight, was anxiously interrogating himself with the insecurity that lay not far below his resilient-seeming surface: 'I've tried to be a superman over the last three years in the face of villainous hostility from sections of the profession who have tried to isolate me . . . I must cease to behave like a demented superman . . . Maybe my *hubris* is to want to try everything – plays, films, operas, the harsh, the epic, the political, the comic. Perhaps that is just stupid.' Perhaps. But that, for better or worse, was the kind of man he was.

11

1978–80: Mozartian Smut and Roman Rape

The emphasis that Peter Hall placed on new plays far outweighed any other category at the National – his policy statements never referred to the Granville-Barker concept of maintaining a library of standard dramatic literature. Under his regime the National was to present more new plays than any other kind. It was a risky policy and in the early years the plays got little encouragement from the critics. The first play by David Hare to be premièred at the Lyttleton was *Plenty*, in which the Second World War influences the actions of every character long after it is over. The heroine, Susan Traherne, has been dropped into occupied France as a courier for SOE (Special Operations Executive). As a result, she says, 'We get rather restless back in England. The people who stayed behind seem childish and a little silly.' It is typical of Hare's shock technique that the play opens with a blood-stained naked man lying full-length downstage, who is ignored by Susan and her confidante, Alice. He turns out to be the diplomat husband whom she is leaving and who has temporarily succumbed to the effects of whisky and Nembutal. In flashback scenes she is shown trying to come to terms with the anticlimax of her life as a diplomat's wife in a post-war Britain that is gradually adjusting from austerity to plenty. She is not adjusting. Disgusted by the compromises of diplomacy, she tries to rediscover the spirit of wartime by keeping a tryst with another former agent in a Blackpool hotel. The depth of the Lyttleton stage permitted a transformation scene which said more than any dialogue could do. As her companion steals away leaving her asleep, the door opens to admit a shaft of brilliant green light. The hotel setting disintegrates and behind it comes up a vibrantly lit French hillside at the time of Liberation, August 1944. Susan is nineteen again, dressed in a French print frock, exhilarated by the promise of the moment: 'We have grown up, we will improve our world,' she says to the French peasant beside her. It was a poignant ending, illuminating all the hopes that had failed, and not only for Susan. The play furnished Canadian actress, Kate Nelligan, with an impressive role, but most critics were unresponsive to the play and audiences were slow to discover it. To its credit, the National stood by its playwright on this occasion and kept the play in the repertoire until word of mouth brought in audiences and it played to full houses. Hare was henceforward a leading member of the NT stable of playwrights.

The next contemporary writer presented was Edward Bond, the Marxist revolutionary of the Royal Court, who had proved his ability to disturb and offend audiences in the sixties with works like *Saved*, *Lear* and *The Fool*. His new play, *The Woman*, which he also directed himself, was a difficult experience for those involved in it. He asked members of the company for their political views and objected to his assistant director, Sebastian Graham-Jones, on the grounds that he had gone to Harrow. Bond was left with sole responsibility for the cast of forty-three, a severe test for a director more experienced and tactful than he was. *The Woman* was the first play to be written specifically for the Olivier stage and was based partly on *The Trojan Women* of Euripides. Hecuba blinds herself rather than witness the sack of Troy, which she had nearly saved by coming to an understanding with the wife of the Greeks' leader, Ismene, showing how much less destructive by nature women are than men. Given a less traumatic production, the play might have been more successful than it was. Bond departed with all his prejudices against the National intact, and after thirty-five performances to half-empty houses the National was not eager to renew the partnership.

Harold Pinter's *Betrayal*, which one might have expected to be greeted as exactly the sort of play the National had been waiting for, was met with the worst notices that the author had received since the notorious reception given to *The Birthday Party* twenty years earlier. Then he had been accused of incomprehensibility. Now it was the unwonted straightforwardness of his narrative that seemed to baffle the critics. What was this, they asked, but a commonplace story of adultery between a wife and her husband's best friend (which the husband has known of for some time)? It was presented with none of the evasions and suppressions for which Pinter was renowned, except that the story was told back to front, beginning at the end. The play was dismissed as slight, ordinary, boring, and concerned with trivial people. What, if anything, had gone wrong? It could hardly be the production. It was directed, as usual, by Peter Hall, with the author at his elbow; designed, as usual, by John Bury, and strongly cast with Penelope Wilton, Daniel Massey and Michael Gambon playing the wife, husband and lover. Pinter told the cast, disconsolate at the notices, 'I think it is a very good play, superbly done, and that is all I have to say on the matter.' Two weekly critics saw the play in a very different light from their colleagues. Benedict Nightingale in the *New Statesman* called it 'one of Pinter's most successful exercises in presenting the least and evoking the most', while Peter Jenkins in the *Spectator* saw it as a play that 'dealt with its subject with the blinding honesty of a true artist'. The American critic, Jack Kroll, found it 'brilliantly simple in form and courageous in its search for a poetry that turns banality into a melancholy beauty'. Those who compared it unfavourably with *No Man's Land* seemed not to notice the similarity in technique, in making the audience work on the quite simple material that is presented. There is a great deal left ambiguous in *No Man's Land* but it does not prevent the audience from following the shifts in the relationship between Hirst and Spooner. The development of *Betrayal* is of the same order. All three couples have suffered betrayal, husband and wife, wife and lover, and the two best friends, husband and lover. The play explores what that has cost with a clinical technique that is quietly appalling. But it proved to be Pinter's last full-length play to be presented at the National, transferring to a five-month run on Broadway – a respectable, but not wildly exciting outcome.

Simon Gray's first innings at the National was another disappointment. *Close of Play* seemed a sad, depressing piece from the author of such sparkling and sharp comedies as *Butley* and *Otherwise Engaged*. It is chiefly remembered for the affecting sight of Michael Redgrave confined to a wheelchair, able neither to move nor speak – except for one line – as the paterfamilias at a family reunion. This disability made him the ideal father-confessor for this collection of life's walking wounded because they knew no demands and no censure would be forthcoming from him. As a picture of family bondage, it was economical and ironic but hardly the stuff to fill the theatre, despite elegant playing under Pinter's direction.

One of Peter Hall's aims was to present neglected European drama. He commissioned a 'translation bank' of six major plays adapted by English playwrights. Early fruits of this policy were Christopher Hampton's version of *Tales of the Vienna Woods* by Odön von Horvath, John Mortimer's version of the Feydeau farce, *The Lady from Maxim's*, and *The Guardsman* by the Hungarian, Ferenc Molnar, translated by Frank Marcus. Tom Stoppard's adaptation of *Das Weite Land* by Arthur Schnitzler was so far-reaching that it amounted almost to a new play by Stoppard, set near Vienna in 1911 and now entitled *Undiscovered Country*. Stoppard explained that as he got to know the play in a literal translation, 'the temptation to add a flick here and there became irresistible so I did not resist it'. So his text remained faithful more in spirit than in letter to Schnitzler. The play is concerned with a society strait-jacketed by a rigid code of honour which nevertheless regards infidelity as an enjoyable, light-hearted pastime, rather like its tennis parties and walking trips in the Dolomites. Like Pinter, Schnitzler was interested in the effects of systematic sexual betrayal. The apparently heartless Don Juan of a hero reproaches his wife because a young pianist they know has shot himself out of unrequited love for her. When she sacrifices her fidelity and becomes 'just like the others', however, her husband challenges her lover to a fatal duel – not out of love or jealousy, he explains. 'I couldn't give a damn about any of that, but I won't be made to look a fool.' The play, directed by Peter Wood, gave John Wood, completing an all-too-brief stint at the National, the chance to be brilliant and heartless as the hollow husband.

Peter Hall had always believed that it would be fatal for the newly launched national theatre to play to less than full houses. When the backstage strike petered out in 1979, the theatre had virtually lost its audience during the weeks when performances were either cancelled or given in inappropriate sets. People had to be won back by popular programming. His first choice of a crowd-puller opened that September – Arthur Miller's *Death of a Salesman* with the unexpected casting of Warren Mitchell as Willy Loman, the salesman whose dreams have crashed. Under the American director, Michael Rudman, he gave a compulsive performance that conveyed the gnawing sensation of fear. Despite the discomfort that Miller offered his audience, it played to more people than any play since *Bedroom Farce*. It also won for Mitchell most of the Best Actor awards going. To convince the public, which identified him with Alf Garnett, that he was a small, cornered victim of the American system, terrified beneath his façade of lies and bluster, was a feat of character acting. Thirty years after he first disturbed the complacency of a materialist, success-worshipping society, Miller was then deeply unfashionable in his native land and his new plays could hardly get New York productions. He acknowledged this when he later wrote: 'The National Theatre has done terrific productions of my plays at a time when they were not welcome on Broadway, for which I owe it my allegiance and gratitude.' Soon afterwards followed a fine production of *The Crucible* by Bill Bryden in the Cottesloe, and much later *A View from the Bridge* and others.

New plays had seldom been money-makers. When we come to one that notoriously was, it is difficult to realize in retrospect how risky a venture *Amadeus*, Peter Shaffer's play about Mozart and Salieri, must have seemed before it opened. It was opposed by a majority of the associate directors, including Rudman, who called it 'the longest sleeve-note ever written'. The text was inordinately long and, as usual with Shaffer, was in a state of constant revision. There was a prolonged dispute about where it was to be staged and by whom. The partnership of Shaffer with John Dexter, which had been so fruitful in realizing *The Royal Hunt of the Sun*, *Black Comedy* and *Equus*, was breaking up in disagreements. Dexter wanted to do the play in the commercial theatre, partly out of antipathy to the South Bank building and its regime, and he was not immediately available. Shaffer offered the rights to the National in March 1979, on condition that it was done within a year, if not by Dexter then by Peter Hall. 'There's never been a play I wanted to do more,' Hall admitted to himself, but he suggested that it would be better if Shaffer and Dexter 'made it up'. That was not to be, and Hall was finally asked to direct. In August, the two men went on a week's pilgrimage to the Mozartian cities of Salzburg and Vienna. Both cherished an informed devotion to Mozart; Shaffer had once spent time as a music critic and Hall had been doing regular Mozart opera productions for Glyndebourne. The notorious shock-effect of the play, its presentation of Mozart as a giggling, childlike vulgarian and show-off was, from the point of view of dramatic structure, a minor issue. The play was originally entitled *Salieri* and its real subject is the older, then more successful composer's quarrel with God for giving Mozart a divine voice while granting him, the worthier human being, only mediocrity. Many of Shaffer's characters interrogate an apparently uncaring God and in this case he associated Salieri with the masked stranger who is supposed to have haunted the dying composer while he was writing his Requiem. It was potent material for theatre, indeed for opera, and it was as opera that Peter Hall responded to it. 'I will give you an operatic production,' he told Shaffer, and that was indeed the way the play was written. It begins with an overture in whispers, the voices of Viennese gossip echoing the rumour of Salieri's deathbed confession that he poisoned Mozart. Arias for Salieri, duets for Mozart and Constanze, choruses for the emperor's court of yes-men duly follow. Snatches of Mozart's music, carefully kept in the background, reinforced the operatic quality. So did John Bury's design which introduced a genuine proscenium arch at the rear of the Olivier stage, like a gilded Rococo frame for the court scenes, which were bathed in golden light and reflected in gilded mirrors.

It is difficult to make a distinction now between the original version of the play given in the Olivier in November 1979 and subsequent altered versions done in New York the next year and in the West End the year after that. Instead of the masked stranger being Salieri's servant, he was Salieri himself (later, in the film version, Salieri was given the task of writing down the Requiem at the dying Mozart's dictation). Shaffer was not writing history but drama – he once described the play as 'a fantasia on Mozartian themes'. But purists saw his portrayal of Mozart as a dirty-minded crude child as blasphemy. There was some historical warrant for Mozart leaping about miaowing like a cat. But whether he talked as smuttily as he wrote in his letters is simply unrecorded. In later versions Shaffer toned down the scatological language because, he admitted, 'I could sense that unsettled the audience and that was not the point I was trying to make.' All the same, the play aroused in some quarters the violent antipathy that had been foreseen by those who tried to discourage Hall from putting it on. The then *Sunday Times* critic, James Fenton, wrote: 'Shaffer's Mozart is depicted in an offensive and banal way because he is seen through the eyes of a very, very bad dramatist indeed, perhaps the worst English dramatist since John Drinkwater.' His summing up of the play was 'a nauseating load of – to use a word much loved by Peter Shaffer – shit'. He was not alone in denying any intellectual merit in the play. Even generally favourable reviewers dropped phrases such as 'a costume thriller', 'facile rhetoric' and 'superficial theatrical magic' into their notices as if insuring themselves against being taken in by a cunning master of stagecraft.

This is not the place to debate the play's intellectual stature; but of Shaffer's brilliant stagecraft there was no room for doubt once the piece was put in front of an audience. Simon Callow, who was the first actor to play Mozart, wrote: 'I had again the experience I've only had on two or three previous occasions, a feeling that the audience were getting something that they had done without for too long . . . Not one performance failed to ignite an electric charge in the audience.' He found his greatest problem was to make it credible 'that inside the giggling, shit-shanking, hyperactive little man was *The Marriage of Figaro*'. If Shaffer's characterization is right, this must also have been hard for Mozart's contemporaries to believe. Callow played it 'romping like a drunken porker across the stage', wrote John Russell Taylor in a memorable image. His successor in the West End production, Richard O'Callaghan, was more inclined to puppyishness, with an hysterical giggle. It was the part of Salieri that offered the greater scope and won the awards – for Paul Scofield at the Olivier and for Ian McKellen on Broadway. Scofield's performance was aristocratic and technically dazzling in its depiction of Salieri's bitter old age. His successor in the West End, Frank Finlay, was by comparison 'a small-town boy, ungainly and provincial, hanging on to his job, fighting for his life', as Irving Wardle put it. It is a measure of Shaffer's skill that besides these two actors, both Ian McKellen and John Wood had scored big successes with individual interpretations of the part within two or three years. Altogether *Amadeus* won thirteen awards, including five Tonys. After playing to 129 sold-out houses at the National, it ran for more than a year in the West End. It was produced throughout Western Europe and in Australia and translated into twenty languages. The productions in the commercial theatre earned the National nearly £500,000 and rescued it from its financial predicament resulting from the stage-hands' strike. Once again Shaffer bailed it out.

Alan Ayckbourn's next offering to the National was *Sisterly Feelings*. This time he exercised his ingenuity in writing alternate plays which set out from the same initial scene (the aftermath of a funeral) to travel by different routes to the same final scene (the aftermath of a wedding). The two sisters, Abigail and Dorcas, toss a coin at the end of the first scene to decide which of them should take a lift in a car, leaving the other one alone with the good-looking Simon. Another point of choice arrives when one of the actresses has to make a spur-of-the-moment choice either to stay with Simon or to go back to her original partner, thus choosing one of two alternative second acts. So there were four possible versions of the play. 'I was intrigued by the possibility of writing a piece that contained variable scenes that could be spontaneously chosen during the action,' Ayckbourn explained. 'The plays are about choice. How much do we really control our lives? And do we really make decisions or just think that we do?' With family tree and an explanatory map of the alternatives in the programme, it seemed more like a game than a play. Audiences were invited to come back and try it again the other way round, but 'the second visit made me realise that one had really been enough,' concluded the man from the *New York Times*. What the author had not allowed for was that the actors themselves preferred one set of scenes to another, which led Michael Gambon to introduce among the props a double-headed penny of his own devising. With Penelope Wilton and Anna Carteret as the sisters, the play ran from 1980 to the following year.

Next to join the repertoire were two plays that, though technically not new, were more risky than usual. *The Elephant Man* was based on the physical freak, Joseph Merrick, who became a celebrated ornament of the London Hospital in Whitechapel in Victorian times. The play had been seen briefly at the Hampstead Theatre in 1977 before appearing both off and on Broadway, where it won awards. Written by Bernard Pomerance, an American living in London who had discovered Merrick's skeleton preserved at the hospital, it proved to be the vehicle for what was called a performance of genius by David Schofield. Instead of assuming freakish make-up, as was used in the film, Schofield was shown naked and physically normal at the opening; by grotesque contortions of face and body, he conveyed the condition of Merrick, while visibly remaining a gentle, sensitive human being.

Brecht's *The Life of Galileo*, which opened in the Olivier in August

1980, was a distinctly dark horse. English productions had been few – the last in London was twenty years earlier. Such was the indifference, if not hostility, to Brecht among English actors and audiences it could well have emptied the theatre. John Dexter was asked to direct it with the casting of the name part already settled. One day in the canteen Peter Hall had gone up to Michael Gambon and told him 'I want you to play Galileo.' Gambon had proved his mastery of comedy technique in many an Ayckbourn play, but the long, magisterial soliloquies of a scientific genius made quite new demands. 'I read the play and swallowed hard,' he recalled. Dexter knew Gambon as a rather Bolshie spear-carrier and small-part actor in the Old Vic company. Such was the fear that the disciplinarian Dexter inspired there that, Gambon recalled, 'Out of terror I once excused myself for being late at a rehearsal by telling him my mother had died. He gave me a week off.' Jocelyn Herbert's complex geometrical setting accommodated a papal investiture and a carnival, with a cast of forty-five. All this was meat and drink to Dexter who brilliantly animated the space, using a projection screen that descended to fix terrestrial time and place and to project the heavenly bodies. Lit with flair by Andy Philips, the production was the first to use the Olivier's stage with complete assurance. But for all its visual qualities, it is a one-man play, following Galileo through the years spanning his great discoveries, his recantation and his compromise with the Church's authority in order to go on working. The part requires idealism, cynicism and self-disgust in equal measure and the ageing problems are formidable. By common consent, Gambon cleared these obstacles magnificently. James Fenton, the scourge of *Amadeus*, revisited *Galileo* in order to discover what it was that Gambon did in order to accomplish his transformation in the course of the play. He failed. 'He turns his back on us and keeps it turned for a while. When his features become visible again, they are ravaged by the combined effects of disease, indulgence and intellectual disgrace. It is not a question of make-up. It is something he has done with his brain,' he wrote. 'The trick must be . . . great acting.' Gambon admitted he had lost his nerve before the first night and was thankful he did not know Olivier was in the audience to see one of his apprentices from the Old Vic make good. When he returned to his dressing-room afterwards, his fellow actors gathered at their windows around the light well and applauded him – a tribute which he brought to an end by shouting brusquely, 'Shut your row!'

Galileo was the biggest popular success a Brecht play had had in London, playing for over a year. Howard Brenton, who had made the translation, had just completed a new play of his own which was expected to be political dynamite. *The Romans in Britain*, like most of his work, was a response to topical events, the violence in Northern Ireland, as well as a re-examination of ideas of empire by looking back at early invasions of Britain. The play set out to make real the kind of Celtic Britain that was invaded by Julius Caesar in 54 BC. Its *coup de théâtre* occurred when the Roman troops, who have run wild, laying waste a Celtic settlement, suddenly reappear as a khaki-clad British patrol, who proceed to mow down the one survivor, a female slave, as a terrorist suspect. On their heels comes Caesar, now in the uniform of a senior British officer, making asides about reducing violence to 'an acceptable level'. It was an unexpected and disconcerting parallel to suggest between then and now – if you could accept it. The second part of the play concerned an SAS man waiting to contact an IRA commander, dreaming of the Saxons whose invasion followed the Roman withdrawal. Before dying at the hands of the IRA, the British officer says rhetorically: 'In my hand there's a Roman spear, a Saxon axe, a British army machine gun . . . the weapons of invaders, Empire,' and he is asked, 'What nation ever learnt from the sufferings it inflicted on others?'

But it was not the argument that imperialists destroy the civilizations they conquer which caused the outrage. It was one of the play's many examples of casual brutality. Three Roman soldiers come across three young Celts bathing naked, kill two of them and subject the third to sexual assault. While two of them hold him down, the third attempts to rape him anally. It was this symbolic scene, not the political message of the play, which made it a *cause célèbre*.

Howard Brenton, a mild-mannered and gentle man despite the violent scenes of fantasy that occur in his plays, claimed: 'The analogy between Northern Ireland today and one of Caesar's raids is that in both situations, the soldiers are operating in a country that is hostile to them. It is not so much the representation of a rape that is horrifying, it is the uncaring casualness with which the soldiers behave. This kind of incident is common both to historical times and our own. I thought a lot about My Lai when I was writing it.' The text aroused hostile reactions from several of the associate directors who read it and more moderate approval from others. Brenton rewrote and a further debate took place among the directors. None of its opponents had been converted but this hardly mattered. From the beginning, Peter Hall, who had commissioned Brenton, was determined that the play should be done. Since he was not free to direct it himself, and since none of the associate directors wanted to take it on, it was offered to a newcomer, Michael Bogdanov, whose work at the Young Vic had caught Hall's eye.

Bogdanov was enthusiastic about the play as an indictment of imperialism, but there were some serious doubts among his cast about the rape scene. According to Michael Bryant, who played Caesar, 'A number of us begged the author to cut that scene because we thought the importance of the play's content would be overshadowed by it. We feared that people would only talk about that incident, which is exactly what happened. It became known as "the buggery play". But the author decided that it must stay in. Of course we accepted his decision.' They also discussed how to present the moment of rape – upstage in dim light or downstage fully lit? 'We felt it would have been deceitful and rather tacky to try to ameliorate it,' said Brenton. For all his enthusiasm for the play, Peter Hall only had time to attend one preview before flying to New York to direct *Amadeus* on Broadway. Having watched it, even he had his doubts about thrusting the rape, so to speak, in the audience's face. He said to Brenton and Bogdanov: 'I have to put this to you. Cut down the swearing and put the rape behind a tree and you will have a hit. Otherwise we will have trouble.' Brenton emphasized that Hall applied no pressure to them. 'He said this, just once, and never referred to it again. He wasn't even asking us to change the way it was done. We decided to play the scene as it stood and take the consequences. I still think we were right to stand by it.'

There might have been more pressure to modify it had the Board known in more detail what the production involved. Hall had told them in general terms that it was 'strong meat' and stated his complete faith in the integrity of the play and of its author. Lord Rayne's policy that the Board should be consulted over any question of obscenity could well have been invoked in this case – it was practically a test case of the Board's responsibility in such matters. If the Board as a whole had attended a preview, there is not much doubt what their response would have been. 'Some of us were not happy with what was shown on the stage. If they had asked us, we might have advised against it,' recollected Lord Rayne. 'I think we should have been warned.' The long-serving Lord Mishcon, put this more strongly: 'We expected consultation about such a play. Had we been consulted, I think there would have been a majority of the Board against it.' Other Board members defended the play and the scene. John Mortimer advised them to 'keep right on to the end of the woad'. Anyway, it was not the practice to invite the full Board, which meets only four times a year, to previews. *The Romans* proved its impotence to control the director, even to the restricted degree that it claimed to do.

But if the Board did not manage to attend a preview, a party of GLC members, headed by Sir Horace Cutler, the Conservative leader of the Council, and his chief whip, Geoffrey Seaton (both of whom served on the National Theatre Board *ex officio*), did. Cutler and Seaton were appalled by what they saw and walked out. They sent Peter Hall, now in

143

New York, a telegram registering their protest at his 'singular lack of judgment', followed by a letter which called the play 'disgusting, immature and devoid of merit'. Their comments were retailed for publication in the evening newspapers on the day the first-night notices appeared. These had ranged from bad to awful: 'Rape of the Senses', 'National Clanger', 'Roman Scandal' . . . Some of the hostility was grounded in what the critics saw as the false parallel between Roman and British occupation; more often it was in revulsion at what one notice called 'Torture, plague, necrophilia and suicide, intermixed with gangrene, blood-letting, hanging and patricide – all of it full frontal'. To be exact, the rape scene was not singled out as more offensive than the rest of the violence, although the *Daily Express* called it 'the highlight (lowlight?) of the distasteful proceedings'. But it was the main burden of complaint by Sir Horace Cutler in front-page stories illustrated with pictures of the naked Celts. Headlines ran: THIS IS A DISGRACE – If I Wanted This Sort of Thing I'd Go to the Worst Parts of Soho. GLC CHIEF THREATENS GRANT CUT OVER THE NATIONAL'S SHOCKER. 'I have no doubt that the GLC will be reconsidering its position *vis-à-vis* the National Theatre,' Sir Horace told the *Evening News*. 'I am not prepared to see rates and taxes spent to support plays which in my view have no artistic merit.' Mr Seaton was quoted as saying: 'The feeling in the GLC is that the grant should be suspended forthwith. It may be that the cheapest thing for the National to do would be to remove this so-called play from the repertoire immediately.' That was telling them. The GLC grant that year was £630,000, of which the final instalment, £157,500, was due to be paid in two months' time and now, it was suggested, might not be.

But another player was about to enter on the scene. In the *Daily Mail* review of the play Jack Tinker suspected that 'Mr Brenton conceived the entire enterprise in the hope of giving Mary Whitehouse a very nasty seizure.' On the morning those words appeared, his telephone rang. 'I heard a strange voice ask: "Is there full anal buggery in this play?" I asked who was speaking. "Mary Whitehouse," said the voice. It was obvious that there was going to be trouble.' Mrs Whitehouse did not wait to see the play (she never was to see it). She laid a complaint with Scotland Yard which was referred to the Obscene Publications squad. So began the attendance of investigating police officers at the performances, which so delighted the cartoonists that for days one could scarcely open a newspaper without finding a drawing of a naked policeman on stage as an extra in pursuit of his inquiries.

The Theatres Act of 1968, which replaced the Lord Chamberlain's licensing of plays, made it an offence to present an obscene play, but prosecution could only be brought with the consent of the Attorney-

144

General. Thanks to the repertoire system, *The Romans* was not due for performance again for a week, during which the scandal escalated in the Press. The next performance was a sell-out. An unusually high proportion of the audience consisted of police and reporters hoping for trouble (the *Daily Mail* sent no fewer than eight of its writers to provide their reactions as average citizens). Debate proliferated in letter columns and editorials, regardless of the fact that very few people, 4,000 at the most, had yet seen the play. Most popular newspapers were quick to condemn the National for staging it. In the *Sunday Times* the often-nauseated James Fenton, a poet whose prose lacked noticeable charm, called it 'a nauseating load of rubbish from beginning to end, written in ludicrous pseudo-poetic yob-talk'. If he were Sir Peter Hall, he reflected, 'I would take myself out to dinner and tactfully but firmly sack myself.' Hall was steadfastly defending the play to reporters on the sidewalk of Broadway as a work of great merit, 'or I wouldn't have put it on in the first place'. The Board's only playwright, John Mortimer, pointed out how much worse were some of the things that happen in *King Lear*, *Titus Andronicus* and other highly regarded works. Sir Harold Hobson, former critic of the *Sunday Times*, called the threats to stop the grant 'monstrous'. Benedict Nightingale recalled that the stoning of a baby in a pram in Edward Bond's *Saved* had by now been accepted as an integral part of the play – 'Yesterday's shock-horror headline had become today's challenging masterpiece'. He doubted, however, that *The Romans* would prove the same point. 'Its message is hardly more than that imperialism is a crying shame, not to say a pain in the arse.' The *Guardian* offered the cold comfort that the National was taking the sort of risk 'that must be run if it is to perform its job half adequately'. Bernard Levin almost alone declared that, to his surprise, it was 'a very fine play indeed'. It was a nerve-testing time for all concerned – including the Board, whose members kept their private opinions to themselves and united to face the theatre's critics. According to Sir Derek Mitchell, a senior civil servant who had been a member since 1977, 'The true objection to staging it, some of us felt, was that it placed the theatre's finances in jeopardy. We and the Arts Council were getting angry noises from MPs as well as from Mrs Whitehouse. But although Peter Hall had not exactly confided in us what we were in for, all these pressures were withstood.' The Board was in a difficult position. It could hardly say that some of its members did not approve of the play but had not been consulted. Their only tenable position was that it was an artistic decision, with which they would not interfere, by an artistic director who had their overall confidence.

A week or so later it was announced that the Director of Public Prosecutions had decided that a prosecution of the theatre 'would not be justified' (the play as a whole would have had to be found likely to deprave and corrupt those who were likely to attend it). On the same day the GLC's arts director told the Council that he did not recommend the withdrawal of any of its current or future grant, 'unless one mistake becomes a habit'. No performances of *The Romans* were cancelled but one was interrupted by unidentified demonstrators. A pack of hecklers rose from their seats and threw bags of flour and fireworks at the stage, while others shouted 'Get poufs off the stage!' – hardly the cry of an habitual theatregoer. They escaped before they could be interrogated. One morning the front windows of the theatre near the box office were daubed with graffiti. But the play ran its course of twenty-four performances and was seen by about 20,000 people. For all its notoriety, it was hardly a *succès de scandale*.

'I would have expected a new play of minority appeal to do 60 per cent. Because of the fuss, we did 75,' said the director, Michael Bogdanov. The fuss now seemed to be over. The cast were celebrating at a Christmas party when he was called to the stage door. Mrs Whitehouse's solicitor was waiting for him with a summons. Having been refused leave to prosecute under the Theatres Act, she had decided to prosecute the play's director privately under the Sexual Offences Act for 'procuring an act of gross indecency' in staging the rape scene. It was over a year before the case came to trial at the Old Bailey in mid-March 1982. In the interval, writers, actors, critics and others were assembled as witnesses for the defence. The case had all the makings of another *Lady Chatterley* trial, involving as it did art, sex, morality and public expenditure. But any of those who may have looked forward to a debate on the place of anal intercourse in serious literature or whether you should allow your wife or servant to attend the National Theatre were soon disappointed. The case collapsed inside three days. Bogdanov had based his defence on the distinction between stage illusion and reality, which seemed obvious enough. But it was a distinction that did not seem to have troubled Mrs Whitehouse or the solicitor, Mr Ross-Cornes, who had attended the play on her behalf. He had taken a seat far back in the Olivier circle, where he seems to have accepted theatrical illusion for reality. Cross-examined for the defence by Lord Hutchinson – 'I put it to you that what you saw was not a penis, it was a thumb' – he was nonplussed. The employment of such subterfuge seemed not to have occurred to him before. The prosecuting counsel, Mr Ian Kennedy, turned to his junior with the question, 'Is that true?' and asked for an adjournment. Soon afterwards he announced that the prosecution would be abandoned. Not so fast – it proved quite hard to stop it. It required no less than the intervention of the Attorney-General to invoke the rare and ancient procedure known as *nolle prosequi* (unwilling to proceed). Before doing this the Attorney insisted on a private demonstration by counsel, one of them on all fours, of exactly what actions had been represented on stage in our National Theatre. This scene must have been a curious one, even by the standards of the Old Bailey.

Both sides claimed victory. Mrs Whitehouse called it 'a great day for the country and the theatre' on the grounds that the trial judge had ruled that the Sexual Offences Act applied to events on stage, so that a simulated sexual act could amount to an act of gross indecency. Indeed Mr Justice Staughton had ruminated that Parliament *could* have exempted the theatre from the Sexual Offences Act if it had wished, but had not done so. 'Whether the omission was accidental or deliberate I do not know and cannot inquire.' Other legal minds opined, however, that nothing of the sort had been established because the *nolle prosequi* effectively removed the case from the record and from the status of a legal precedent. This fine point was small comfort to anxious theatre owners, who had previously assumed that they were immune to prosecution for simulating criminal acts, such as murder, on the stage and had launched a Theatre Defence Fund to assist Bogdanov's defence. Were they now to conclude that, at the end of *Hamlet*, they and all the leading participants could be prosecuted for simulated homicide?

The National Theatre could hardly claim to have been vindicated, only to have been let off. Howard Brenton, who felt that, as it was his play, he was the one who should have been prosecuted, was very relieved to see Bogdanov walk out of the dock a free man (he could have faced a penalty of up to two years' imprisonment). But the real penalty was the abuse both had been subjected to. Bogdanov recalled how his family had suffered from 'letters, phone calls, threats to burn down my house and to maim my children. It upset us tremendously. My children were taunted to the effect that their father was a queer who put on homosexual plays. We had to go ex-directory, we had police surveillance, we moved. You begin to think that the person they are talking about is not yourself but some horrific monster. It was a tremendous relief when it was over.' Bodganov's legal costs were met by the state. Mrs Whitehouse's, estimated at £20,000, were not.

At the end of it all, the question that needed answering was, was it worth it? Would it have been better for the National if the Board, as in the case of *Soldiers*, had overruled its director? There will always be two opinions on such matters. The National had demonstrated the principle that it would stand up to public pressure and stand by its commitment to its artists and its productions. Admirable as a general principle, its rightness in any particular case depends on the worth of the play. *The*

Romans was not performed again in the succeeding ten years, although it remains in print and is quite widely studied. It does not at present look likely to join the list of historic theatrical causes such as Shelley's *The Cenci*, Ibsen's *Ghosts*, Shaw's *Mrs Warren's Profession*, or Miller's *A View From the Bridge*. Had it been put on in the Cottesloe, the fuss might have been much milder. The fact that it was put on in the showcase of the Olivier suggests that it was a deliberate gesture to disassociate the theatre from the Establishment consensus. What the National may have gained thereby in reputation as nobody's poodle, it paid for dearly. For long afterwards *The Romans* clung to the National's name like The Bricks did to the Tate Gallery's.

There was a quaint consequence, as far as the Establishment was concerned. A year after the Old Bailey trial, as the National approached its twentieth anniversary, Lord Rayne floated the suggestion that it might be honoured with the title 'Royal'. He got a frigid response. Invited to the Home Office, he was met by a senior civil servant who mentioned the fact that it was he who had had to consider whether or not to prosecute *The Romans*. Clearly it was too soon after this unfortunate business to think about giving the sign of royal approval. A decent interval would have to elapse. By such discreet signals Britain deals with matters which, under other systems, end in a play's outright suppression or with its author in jail.

12

The Cosy, Communal Cottesloe

The Cottesloe Theatre was the last and the least heralded of the auditoria to open at the National, but it turned out to be the most successful of the three; not as a studio for presenting experimental evenings or work in progress, but as a small unconventional theatre which staged some of the best new British and American plays of the seventies and eighties.

Iain Mackintosh's design, a courtyard-style auditorium with shallow galleries, deliberately left the floor space adaptable to many different seating plans. 'The science of theatre building must come from studying what it is that brings about the most vivid relationship between people,' wrote Mackintosh 'Is this best served by asymmetry, even by disorder? If so, what can be the rule of this disorder? The Cottesloe design proposals are aimed at giving theatre people enough, but no more than is essential, to experiment in those mysteries.' The experiments carried out there have varied from a flat floor to a steep rake, from a lateral end-stage to a traverse stage set longways down the middle, from theatre-in-the-round to having no stage at all. In the latter case, floor space was shared with the promenading audience. Decoration (and comfort) are minimal. The Cottesloe has always been a powerful theatrical Black Hole.

The paradox is that this modestly-equipped space should have so quickly become nearly everybody's favourite part of the building; the favourite space to work in, and to experience theatre in. Considering the immense pains expended on the rest of the National, it is slightly absurd that this afterthought, this overlooked spare pocket, whose existence was frequently threatened with the accountants' axe, should have proved to be for several years the National's most exciting achievement.

That it did so was partly due to the energy and vision of its first regular director, Bill Bryden, an intense, black-haired, romantically

Celtic-looking Scot, who talks in an impatient rush of words and inspires confidence in the actors with whom he works. He had joined the National late in its Old Vic days at Peter Hall's invitation. He soon became an associate director at the Old Vic, responsible for some unhappy ventures, such as *Watch It Come Down* and *Il Campiello*, before he made a name for himself directing the 'Irish company' in *The Playboy of the Western World* and *The Plough and the Stars*. When the Cottesloe was at last ready to open, in the spring of 1977, he got the directorship by default. (Hall's first choice, Stuart Burge, was not available.) Bryden's good fortune was that in early 1977 Hall was too preoccupied with the other theatres to give it much attention. 'No one really knew what to do with it,' Bryden recalled. 'Peter Hall told me to go in and play a captain's innings for a year. He let me have *carte blanche*.' Bryden took advantage of his free hand to recruit a semi-permanent company of actors whom he had worked with in his periods at the Royal Lyceum, Edinburgh, and at the Royal Court. He presented plays in straight runs for three weeks to a month each, instead of in repertoire. This meant that his actors could not be cross-cast in the Lyttleton or Olivier. They became 'Cottesloe actors' and the company became virtually a permanent group working together in a very free atmosphere. Sebastian Graham-Jones, who was Bryden's assistant director on many of the big productions such as *The Mysteries* and *Lark Rise to Candleford*, recalled: 'Everything we did was collaborative. Everybody felt they were of equal importance and could speak their minds. If an actor had a good idea for doing a scene, it would be done that way. If they thought something wasn't working they would say so.' According to Gawn Grainger, 'It was the nearest thing that we ever had in the new building to the old Laurence Olivier company spirit.'

The other dimension in which the Cottesloe was different was in its audience. It soon acquired a hard core of enthusiasts who went to virtually every production, a brand loyalty that must have been the envy of the *ad hoc* companies playing in the other two theatres. In the early years of the Cottesloe you could not reserve any of the seats. Everyone was, so to speak, a 'groundling', even on the balconies, obeying the principle of first come, first served. Indeed, with its strongly Fringe-like ethos, its separate entrance by a side door, its informality, its modest passage-like foyer and bars and its spartan atmosphere of dedication, the Cottesloe might as well have been in another building entirely. Connection with the grandiose spaces next door seemed minimal.

The first play to be produced there was by the National Theatre's first resident playwright, Stephen Poliakoff. Ironically, he was offered the role and title in 1976, when there was nowhere for a writer to work, let alone reside. The stipend – actually a £1,500 bursary from Thames Television – was awarded on the strength of his early work, *Clever Soldiers*. Poliakoff (whose Russian family, headed by his grandfather, an inventor, left the Soviet Union in 1924) was a precocious talent, then only twenty-two. His next plays were about contemporary teenagers and made him a name at twenty-four. When building delays postponed moving in, he was asked to write for a season at the Young Vic. The result was the first version of *Strawberry Fields*, which was later expanded to open the Cottesloe officially on 31 March 1977. The theatre was first occupied, at weekends only, earlier in March with a visiting production by Ken Campbell's 'Science Fiction Theatre of Liverpool', whose epic *Illuminatus* rambled on for some eight hours of anarchic comic fantasy.

Strawberry Fields is a serious play that begins deceptively with a prim, demure and inhibited English Rose, named Charlotte, who travels the motorways with a van-full of leaflets on behalf of the 'English People's Party', which protests against the spoiling of England by pollution, traffic, black immigration and overcrowding. Later she is revealed as an ultra right-wing fanatic, who thinks nothing of pulling a gun from her handbag on a young policeman and shooting him. At a time when their elders still thought of the young as imbued with sixties attitudes and hippie-ish dreams of love-not-war, this vision of potential right-wing terrorism came as a shock. The motorway carving an ugly, inhuman path through the country contributed to the darkness of the vision. Poliakoff's dialogue was as heavily laden with disgust and impotent rage at the state of England as John Osborne's, but expressed in the neutral, restrained language of the well-brought-up middle class who 'felt things strongly' to the point of paranoia. It packed a disturbing power and sometimes played to standing room only. 'It was written to catch a mood of the time,' said Poliakoff, a thickly bearded intellectual who could have passed for a student still. When the post of resident playwright lapsed at the end of the year, he was asked to stay on a part-time basis but found the atmosphere unencouraging. 'I felt creatively lonely there. Although there were a lot of underemployed actors, it was difficult to write for them because of the difficulty of fitting anything into the repertoire. I also disliked the Cottesloe and its total blackness intensely.' As a result, his next play, the very much more substantial *Breaking the Silence*, was done by the RSC, and it was 1987 before another Poliakoff play, *Coming In to Land*, was seen at the National.

Bill Bryden was busy preparing the production that succeeded *Strawberry Fields – The Passion*, one of the cycle of York Mystery Plays or 'mysteries' that had originally been given by the medieval craft guilds on carts drawn through the streets of York, halting at certain places to enact their play. It was a major example of English community theatre at least a century before the Elizabethans. The texts were written in rhythmic, rhymed verse designed to be declaimed against the distractions of city life. Bryden had asked Tony Harrison, the Yorkshireman who had translated Molière for the company with such success, if he would edit and clarify the Middle English text. He agreed, on condition that Christ and his followers would speak in North Country accents, as the original players had done. *The Crucifixion*, which forms the central part of *The Passion*, is admired for the unsentimental practicality with which the four 'knights', or Roman soldiers, set about the task of nailing the victim to the cross and erecting it. On Easter Saturday, before the Cottesloe was available, the cast gave an open-air performance on the terrace and steps of the National well within earshot of Waterloo Bridge. The sound of a band and the sight of a man crucified beside the Thames in the middle of a busy city had the holidaymaking crowds lining the riverside, the terraces and the edge of the bridge.

As in medieval York, people stood and watched the group of actors moving past them. How could this feeling of movement be preserved when the play was done indoors? The solution was to move the succeeding scenes of the cycle from one part of the theatre to another, making the audience follow. Bryden and his designer William Dudley decided to remove all the seating from lower level of the auditorium and use it as a space to intermingle performers and audience. Thus Cottesloe 'promenade productions' were born. Those who wanted to follow the action round the auditorium stood at floor level. Others sat, or stood, in the two galleries, rather as people in medieval York watched from their upper windows and balconies. A special atmosphere was created inside the theatre by filling the space above the floor with an extraordinary galaxy of homely-looking lights. Workmen's oil lamps, up-ended colanders, perforated dustbins and cans, paraffin stoves, even cheese-graters were strung from above at varying levels filled with lights that flickered like candlelight. A light haze of smoke diffused the twinkling light, which might have been that of some medieval guildhall. On arrival the audience found the actors already present, wearing the present-day gear of the trades that their forerunners might follow today – a carpenter, house-painter, butcher, baker, bus conductor, fireman, gas-fitter, policeman . . . They strolled among the customers, greeting them, establishing their status as tradesmen. The Albion Band, a combination of electric guitars and drums with recorders and sackbuts, struck up country music and folk dances to begin the evening. Overhead, colourful trade-union banners festooned the ceiling. Emblems of their trades and dartboards decorated the gallery-fronts.

When the play began, the actors playing Jesus, John the Baptist and so on put simple robes over their workaday overalls. A blue silk cloth representing the waters of the Jordan was shaken above Jesus' head to show his immersion. But there was nothing token about the Cross that was carried in (it was made of railway sleepers). The soldiers sweated and struggled to haul it and fix it upright. This mixture of realism and artifice was carried to greater lengths when *The Passion* was joined by the other plays from the cycles of York, Chester, Wakefield and Coventry in subsequent years. By 1985 the cycle at the National ran right from the *Creation* to *Doomsday* and *The Last Judgment*. It contained many ingenuities. God the Father was revealed high on the platform of a fork-lift truck. Adam and Eve emerged stark naked from primeval earth; the cast formed the coiling serpent in order to tempt Eve to eat the apple; God descended to earth in a cloth cap and braces, with a pencil behind his ear, to give Noah the measurements for the Ark, which was constructed from a mixture of wooden benches and umbrellas. *Doomsday*, which followed the Crucifixion, showed the Resurrection of Jesus as a piece of escapology from a chained crate, and at the Ascension a fork-lift raised Jesus up trailing a billowing white cloth. At the Last Trump, trapdoors opened releasing the dead from their graves wearing neat dark suits and puzzled expressions. At the Last Judgment, the damned were revealed trapped in a large revolving spherical cage, tumbling over and over like clothes in a dryer.

None of this conveys the most remarkable thing about the experience which was the extraordinary sense of participation and shared joy which it produced. One of those 'vivid relationships between people' was established which made it easier, not harder, to suspend disbelief in scenes enacted by actors who were only inches away from the spectators, sometimes completely surrounded by them. It was as if, by assuming the roles and the language of a simpler age, the company had released a simple faith in what it was doing into the audience: when Mary cradled a folded linen cloth, they believed they saw her infant; they winced visibly at the driving of the nails into the Cross. The actors had to clear a space among the milling crowd in which to perform or force their way through them, requiring them to produce a remarkable level of mutual cooperation and confidence. People flocked to see *The Mysteries*. On certain days you could experience all three parts in succession. Critics wrote of it in the most extravagant terms – many called it 'the finest thing the National has done'. 'You could see the audience responding until they ached to be given a part themselves, gradually realising with wonder and visible joy that they *had* been given

153

a part and were playing it,' wrote Bernard Levin. At the end the cast led the audience in a communal dance as recognition that everyone had shared in a common endeavour.

A similar, though not religious, experience was generated by the other main promenade production of those years, *Lark Rise to Candleford*. This was a realization by Keith Dewhurst of Flora Thompson's account of late Victorian rural life during her girlhood in two obscure Oxfordshire villages. The plays compressed each of the books into the events of one day – *Lark Rise* was the first day of harvesting, *Candleford* the midwinter day when Laura, the author as a child, begins work at the village post office. Over the entire theatre from end to end stretched a sky cloth, illuminated by floodlighting so that the light grew from early morning to noon, then faded to the blue of evening and a starry night under a harvest moon. At one end, the skycloth descended to a horizon of field and hedgerows, at the other to the cottage where Laura lived or to the post office where she went to work. The theatre floor served in turn as the cornfield to be harvested, as the village green or as a country lane. Again the audience moved around the space with the actors, watching them reap with old-fashioned sickles, indeed, becoming the corn they reaped. When the reapers sat down in the field for their midday bread and cheese, the spectators thankfully sank down around them. Once again a remarkable sense of reality was created, despite the anachronistic presence of spectators in everyday business suits of 100 years later. 'I strolled into the small village of Lark Rise at 3 p.m., wandered about for a couple of hours and helped to bring in the harvest,' wrote Felix Barker, bringing to life the experience for his *Evening News* readers. 'Then at 7.30 I rode eight miles by donkey cart to Candleford where I picked up a lot of gossip in the Post Office. It was starting to snow when I left around 10.' People went back on several visits to enjoy again the feeling of recapturing a lost time. At the end, many were reluctant to go home. Like the Mystery plays, both Flora Thompson plays were revived many times and never failed to enchant fresh audiences.

Promenade productions were by no means the main output of the Cottesloe. From the beginning it positively hurled new plays at the public – seventeen in its opening year, ten in the second. The choice was eclectic. By the end of five years it had presented new plays by Arnold Wesker, David Storey, Edward Bond, Julian Mitchell, Harold Pinter, Keith Dewhurst, Charles Wood, John Arden and many lesser-known English playwrights. In retrospect it is the performances rather than the plays which stay in the memory – Sir John Gielgud as a ruthless and exquisitely rude retired master of an Oxford college, gleaming with self-approval, in Julian Mitchell's *Half-Life*; Michael Gough as an old-style trade-union leader coming to terms with death in Arnold Wesker's *Love Letters on Blue Paper*; Albert Finney, for once enjoying himself at the National, as an American film director with a John Huston-like charm in Charles Wood's film-making farce, *Has Washington Legs?*; Judi Dench's *tour de force* as a woman being 'awoken' from a 29-year condition of sleeping sickness which Harold Pinter called *A Kind of Alaska*; and Sir Ralph Richardson reliving the fragmentary fantasies of a disgraced politician in *Early Days*, a play written for him by David Storey in which, on certain nights, Sir Ralph seemed to become airborne.

All of these plays were directed by guest directors. Bryden, when not creating promenade productions, introduced a strong American bias into the repertoire. He began with an evocation of the horror and futility of the Vietnam War adapted by Bryden 'and the company' from a book by war correspondent Michael Herr, called *Dispatches*. The Cottesloe again proved its versatility, with its seating arranged round three sides of a sandbagged dug-out and a 'helicopter pad' attached high up on the fourth wall. He produced two early, hardly known Eugene O'Neill plays – *Hughie* and *The Long Voyage Home* – followed by *The Iceman Cometh*, although nothing could make the five-and-a-half hours spent in the company of defeated dreamers in their alcoholic stupor seem anything but an act of piety. Bryden followed up the O'Neill plays with a production of Arthur Miller's *The Crucible*. Using many of his regular team of actors – Proctor was played by Mark McManus, who had been the Jesus of the original performances of *The Passion* – Bryden obtained an intense and powerful ensemble which transferred to the West End.

Bryden was quick to put on the playwright described as the most exciting new voice on the American stage, David Mamet from Chicago. *American Buffalo* had first been staged a year earlier by a Chicago theatre company of which Mamet was artistic director. It takes place in a junk shop where a half-hearted plan is being hatched to rob a coin-collector of some allegedly valuable five cent pieces, or nickels, which carry the American buffalo on one side. Its real interest is the use of Chicago vernacular by the three characters, their speech heavily loaded with four-letter expletives circling round and round its subject in evasive circumlocutions. The proposed robbery is 'the thing'; the victim is 'the man'; crime is 'business'. 'You see what I'm saying?' is their constant refrain but what they are 'saying' is not what they say but what they feel, which can only be hinted at by means of long, oblique diversions. The sound is aggressive but the message is one of fear. People were reminded of Harold Pinter's earlier plays, not inappropriately; the next David Mamet play to arrive at the Cottesloe was dedicated to Pinter. The National was invited to give *Glengarry Glen Ross* its première before it was presented in America. Mamet made his enthusiasm for the National plain and the production justified it. It sold out at the Cottesloe and transferred for a further long run at the Mermaid Theatre. This time there are four main characters winding themselves up to sell some real estate called 'the Glengarry Highlands' (in fact, swampland in Florida) knowing that if at the end of the month they come top of the salesmen's 'Board' they get a Cadillac and if they come bottom of it, they will be fired. Mamet knew his game. 'For a year I worked selling real estate in Chicago. I sold worthless land in Arizona to elderly people who couldn't afford it and I've always treasured that experience. It's really a play about what it does to one to work in that milieu.' What it does is to breed sharks, ready at any moment to attack the unsuspecting client or one another. The violence of the language is an index of the desperation to close a deal at all costs. It is the same underlying fear that haunted Willy Loman. Bryden's production of *Glengarry Glen Ross* was given a vicious cutting edge, especially in the ultra-devious performance of Jack Shepherd as the most ruthless shark in the tank.

Savage confrontation, without the circumlocution, is the genre of another outstanding American playwright, Sam Shepard. In *True West*, done at the Cottesloe in 1981, it was between two brothers, one a thuggish drifter in the American outback who lives by gambling on his fighting dog, the other a Los Angeles screenwriter. This provided the occasion for two explosive performances from Bob Hoskins and Anthony Sher (directed by John Schlesinger). The next Shepard play, *Fool for Love*, did the same for Julie Walters and Ian Charleson (under Peter Gill's direction) as lovers ferociously reunited in a bleak desert motel-room, unable to live with or without each other – they turn out to be half-brother and half-sister. This cowboy-stuntman and his girl make their cage reverberate with slammed doors, battered walls, smashed glass, pain, rage and despair. Doubts whether English actors could ever inhabit such American roles naturally were laid to rest. *Fool for Love* was rated the second best contemporary play in London, *Glengarry Glen Ross* being the first.

In its early years the Cottesloe played host to visiting companies, from the British Fringe and from abroad. None was more memorable than the Market Theatre from Johannesburg which brought over a series of plays by South Africa's leading dramatist, Athol Fugard. His even-handed compassion is not in any obvious way political and his plays are certainly not protest plays. When Fugard was growing up in Port Elizabeth, where his mother ran a café, a black waiter called Sam became a mixture of best friend and father-substitute to him. One day, after a quarrel, Fugard spat in his face, momentarily assuming the racial attitudes of the majority, to his continuing shame ever afterwards. It was many years before he put this situation on the stage in *Master Harold and the Boys* (Harold is Fugard's first name). The teenage Harold turns on his mentor, Sam, and demands that he calls him 'Master Harold' in future. In the ensuing exchanges he makes a crass joke about 'a nigger's arse'. Sam responds by baring his at the boy, and the spitting ensues – shocking in drama, as in life. The scene fascinated audiences who flocked to over 100 performances given first in the Cottesloe, then in the Lyttleton in 1983. The National could take credit for providing a platform for the most audacious theatre company in South Africa.

Until the early 1980s the Cottesloe was the most consistently successful of the National's three auditoria. It had the most hits but it also put on more shows (and more flops) than the other two stages. By 1986, six National productions which transferred to commercial London theatres had come from the Cottesloe: the other two theatres supplied five transfers between them. But it proved far from easy to transfer a Cottesloe success to either of the other auditoria. Calderon's *The Mayor of Zalamea*, for instance, played thirty-nine packed houses in the Cottesloe and transferred to the Olivier, where it looked lonely on the big empty stage and managed to fill only two-thirds of the house. Cottesloe successes gained much of their atmosphere and impact from the intimacy of its auditorium, which they lost on being expanded to fill much wider spaces. When Peter Hall first showed the Cottesloe to his actors he described it as 'the kitchen' of the National, where experiments could be made and, if successful, served up in the main house. It turned out to be not the kitchen, but the small club restaurant, usually hard to get into.

This led to a paradoxical situation. With a seating capacity of around 300, it could not possibly pay its way. Its successes regularly played to 96 or 98 per cent houses, a figure which cannot be improved upon, yet this produced annual box office takings (at the moderate seat prices) of only £250,000. The cost of running the theatre was £750,000. Resulting deficit: £500,000. This small, intimate theatre with its large regular company was, for its size, the most heavily subsidized theatre in the country. Peter Hall noted in his diary: 'Bill Bryden has run the Cottesloe brilliantly . . . but he has done it with a large permanent company which I should not really have allowed – not because I didn't want it but because we didn't have the money.' This was in 1979, six years before the crisis that caused the theatre's closure. Was there an alternative? A smaller company could not have tackled *The Mysteries*. To have raised seat prices to the level of the other two theatres would have gone against the whole spirit of the place. 'We were an expensive operation,' Bryden admitted, 'a big company and not many seats. Some of our scenic designs were expensive, although we borrowed a lot and always tried to economize. But it couldn't have worked without the National's big subsidy and Peter Hall's Medici-like patronage. The Cottesloe is the best space at the National. But it was very hard, perhaps impossible, to balance the books. We were always turning people away at the doors. To make our work financially viable we needed a bigger space.'

When the financial crisis boiled over, early in 1985, it was inevitable that the Cottesloe should be sacrificed. No other branch of the National's activities could offer immediate savings of £500,000. When the blow fell, the full trilogy of *The Mysteries*, including *Doomsday*, had just begun. When the theatre went dark on 20 April, it had been arranged that *The Mysteries*, funded by Theatre Projects, should move for a few months to the Lyceum, Irving's old theatre which had been used as a dance hall since 1939. Meanwhile the GLC offered an extra £375,000 to save the Cottesloe. But when it reopened, it was without Bryden or his company. Perhaps the group had reached its natural ending. Plans for it to mount *The Tempest* came to nothing and there seemed to be no other project ready. So a team unique in the National's history on the South Bank was scattered in many directions, to the sorrow of many of its members and of its loyal audiences.

13

'Who the Hell's in Charge
of this Building?'

There is no disagreement about a national theatre's duty to do the classics. There is general agreement that it should do new plays, though not about which sort. But spectacles created expressly for the theatre and dependent on its large resources of manpower and preparation time – shows that could hardly be put on with the same care anywhere else – constitute a special category about which there is no consensus. They carry extra risks of failure and extra penalties in the event of failure. Three such high-risk operations were undertaken in successive years at the National, three 'musical offerings' – *The Oresteia, Guys and Dolls* and *Jean Seberg*. It took the obsessive enthusiasm and determination of one man at the highest level – Peter Hall in the case of *The Oresteia* and *Jean Seberg*, Richard Eyre in the case of *Guys and Dolls* – to get them put on at all.

Peter Hall joined the National Theatre with the firm intention of doing *The Oresteia* there. 'I had wanted to do it ever since I had one line in a production of *Agamemnon* at Cambridge in the original Greek.' He had approached Tony Harrison about a translation in 1973. When the Olivier stage, with overtones of a Greek amphitheatre, was unveiled, his ambition to stage Aeschylus' trilogy on it became obsessive. Rehearsals began in March 1979, and were abandoned a month later because of the strike. Then, by an anguishing coincidence, the RSC mounted *The Greeks* (the Orestes cycle). So it was not until 1981 that the long-brooded-on project became real. Before then Hall had reached several convictions about the way to present the story first performed in 458 BC.

The first and crucial decision was that it should be done in masks, as in ancient Greece. 'I don't think the plays work except in masks. This is not because of the size of the Greek amphitheatres, it's because of the size of the emotions. They are so violent, hysterical, horrific, they could not be expressed without masks.' As in ancient Greece, the cast was to be all-male: Clytemnestra, Cassandra, Electra, the Furies' chorus all being spoken by men behind female masks. The music was also crucial and Harrison Birtwhistle, the National's regular composer at that time (responsible for *Hamlet*, *Tamburlaine* and many other Hall productions), was commissioned to write it. The designer, Jocelyn Herbert, produced many different kinds of mask for the actors to try out experimentally before the designs were settled.

Tony Harrison, who also wrote libretti for the Metropolitan Opera, was the National's unofficial house poet. This was his fourth assignment as a translator-adaptor. *The Misanthrope*, given twice at the Old Vic in 1973 and 1975, had been followed by Racine's *Phèdre* (transposed to British India and retitled *Phaedra Britannica*), and *The Passion*, the first instalment of *The Mysteries* from the Middle English of the York Mystery Plays. He was a Greek scholar and president of the Classical Association. Rather than render Aeschylus into modern English, he went back to Anglo-Saxon, the language of *Beowulf*, for his inspiration. 'Just as the masks are in visual terms a means of conveying the dramatic rhythm of the original, so the ghostly Anglo-Saxon rhythms I chose, with their heavy emphasis on consonants, were intended to convey the particular weight of the original Greek,' he wrote in a programme note.

The inappropriateness of informal conversational English issuing from an over-life-size tragic mask was obvious. The question was, what *would* be appropriate? The 'heavy' alliterated Anglo-Saxon lines chosen by Harrison led one knowledgeable critic, Benedict Nightingale, writing in the *New York Times*, to say: 'Actually the most oppressive mask, the one that acts as a barrier between us and Aeschylus, turns out to be Tony Harrison's translation.' The continual thud of Anglo-Saxon monosyllables joined together creates an unfamiliar vocabulary strange to the ear: he-god and she-god, he-child and she-child, godstone for altar, godsop for sacrifice, lifelot for destiny. Marriage is 'bedbond sanctified by the she-gods of lifelot'. Scarcely two lines go by without mention of blood: bloodclan, bloodright, blood dues, bloodglut, bloodspill, bloodspot, bloodclot . . . even bloodquag, are constantly on the lips of the chorus. Amongst these 'Anglo-Saxon' coinages the characters sometimes break into contemporary expressions such as 'Don't get you – don't know what you mean' or 'the gods in their wisdom will sort it all out'. The audience in their wisdom also had to sort it all out and it was one thing to do this from the printed page and another when it was intoned through heavy masks for over five hours in a large auditorium.

Critics were more than usually divided about the degree to which the combination of verse-style, mask and music succeeded in bringing

Aeschylus to life. Some liked the masks but not the verse; some liked the verse but not the masks, which they complained muffled the speeches. Most liked the percussive music, punctuating the action with beats, plunks, bangs and shrieks and wails. Several seemed unable to decide whether they had enjoyed the experience or not. Comparisons were made by well-travelled critics with recent *Oresteia* productions in Vienna and Berlin done *without* masks. 'The audience, confronted by recognisable human beings, had rather less difficulty than here in keeping their eyes open,' according to Michael Billington, who went on to praise the last part of the trilogy, *The Eumenides*, the trial which Orestes undergoes as his mother's murderer, which at last achieved 'a natural excitement'. Perhaps it took that long to acclimatize one's eyes and ears to the technique employed. Certainly gaps appeared in the audience after the intervals, but over a period of time audiences built up and sixty-five performances were given, instead of the twenty originally scheduled, to houses which became packed towards the end of the run. The sixteen actors who had submitted to such long and tightly disciplined training – the chorus-speaking was rehearsed to a metronome – voluntarily gave up individual programme credits. 'This seems in keeping with the spirit of a masked production, and of a text in which the main role is the Chorus, at some point played by them all,' explained a programme note.

In the summer of 1982, the National Theatre was invited to Epidaurus, the first foreign company to be so honoured, as a climax to a year of gruelling work on the plays. The great bowl-shaped auditorium among the Greek hills had seen many performances of Greek drama since it was built about 340 BC, but none in English before this. The Olivier production easily fitted the circular 'orchestra' or acting area at the foot of the tiered seating and the stage building, or *skene*, behind. The company were awed by the scale of the setting but acoustically it proved to be perfect, as the Olivier signally failed to be. Altogether the production must have been seen by over 70,000 people, a remarkable figure for Greek tragedy.

The question that hung over *Guys and Dolls* the following year – the cherished project that Laurence Olivier was not allowed to attempt years before – was, could an English company lick it? Were the complexities of Broadway musicals better left to the professionals of the genre? And could straight English actors speak a convincing New York Runyonese, as well as dancing tap routines? None of this deterred Richard Eyre, directing his first show for the National as an associate director. Asked to pick 'a major popular classic', he chose *Guys and Dolls* without hesitation. Eyre had been in charge of the Royal Lyceum

Theatre, Edinburgh, and the Nottingham Playhouse in the seventies. A quietly-spoken and unmasterful kind of director in public, he is known for getting his way by unemphatic persistence. His chief impact at the National had been his electrifying production of *Comedians* by Trevor Griffiths which he brought from Nottingham to the Old Vic in 1974.

Why gamble on an American musical, however renowned, with a director, designer and cast (with few exceptions) untried in this field? There were pressures on both the National and the RSC to put on a Big Show rather than to play safe. Eyre put it this way at the time: 'The stakes get very high. The grants are enormous, the seat prices go up and the more they do, the more the theatres realise they have got to provide an "event". It's not enough just to go through the card of conventional classics. Some sort of Substantial Experience has got to be laid on, in capital letters. Obviously *Nicholas Nickleby* was a triumphant example of that.'

There he had it. The RSC's huge-cast, two-part, eight-hour adaptation of Dickens had come to its rescue at a low point in its fortunes at the end of the seventies and earned enough to beat another financial crisis. The National had just been through such a crisis. Loesser's *Guys and Dolls* could be regarded as the revival of a modern (1950) classic, a safer bet than an adapted stage work like *Nicholas Nickleby*. But both shows were large-scale, glamorous and money-earning spectacles. *Guys and Dolls* proved to be, in *Variety* parlance, a socko-boffo of a hit. It was to remain in the repertoire for two and a half years, playing 370 performances (twice as many as any other show) to houses averaging 95 per cent of capacity. Nearly 400,000 people had seen it before it transferred to the Prince of Wales Theatre in 1985 for a West End run of another 370 performances. Altogether it must have earned the National around a million pounds and saved it from the worst financial constraints of the onset of Thatcherism. The show went on to win twelve awards, so the financial success was well matched by critical kudos.

Eyre and his designer John Gunter started work on it in late 1981, and the main lines of the setting were conceived as the montage of neon sky-signs for Maxwell House, Planters Peanuts and Wrigleys that transformed the Olivier's black spaces into an evocation of Runyon's Broadway. Casting was not done as might have been expected, by hiring the leading talents of the musical theatre. It was to be an acting company of which slightly more than half (13 out of 25) had previously appeared at the National. Of the four principals, Bob Hoskins (Nathan Detroit) was a Cottesloe regular, notably in *True West*, Ian Charleson (Sky Masterson) had appeared in two productions, Julie Covington (Sarah) had played in *Jumpers* and *Plenty*; only Julia McKenzie (as Miss

Adelaide at the Hot Box nightclub) came from outside, with a reputation in the musical theatre and for Ayckbourn plays. Seven weeks were allotted to rehearsal during which many of the cast had to learn from scratch to dance and sing in harmony. Eyre insisted that the entire company joined in the tap dance down Broadway at the finale. They were taught to a high standard by the choreographer David Toguri, while a professional croupier taught them crap-shooting. Rehearsals, said Eyre, were 'pure pleasure'. He wanted truthfulness from his cast, not parody. As he pointed out, 'Runyon's world is as hermetic, consistent and original as P. G. Wodehouse's and must be played for real if its spell is to work. But it was not until the first preview reached the climactic number in the Mission Hall, 'Sit Down, You're Rocking the Boat', that they knew it was a winning gamble. This scene became a regular show-stopper, with built-in, choreographed reprise, but on the first occasion the audience simply refused to let the show go on. Hoskins conferred hastily with the musical director to get cast and band back together to the same place. On the official first night the atmosphere in the Olivier was charged with so much electricity that the rare but unmistakable sensation occurred of the floor 'lifting' beneath the audience's feet. It was a good night to be alive and in that particular theatre. Even when you stepped outside, slightly dazed, into the night, the pavement had an unaccountable spring to it.

So *Guys and Dolls* passed into the National's history as a unique high-spot, silencing those who had asked whether such a commercial piece was the kind of thing the subsidized theatre should be spending public money on. The consensus seemed to be that it's all right if it's a classic. Undeniably Loesser's work was as good as anything in its genre, so the National was in the happy position of presenting a 'classic' that made an awful lot of money, and proceeded to exploit it for all it was worth.

The next musical proved the biggest disaster in the theatre's history. In the year of *Guys and Dolls*, 1982, Peter Hall was invited by composer Marvin Hamlisch to direct his new Broadway musical. It concerned the life of Jean Seberg, who had been plucked from a small town in Iowa to star as St Joan in a film epic directed by Otto Preminger. Although the film was a legendary flop, she led the life of a film star for some years in Paris, appearing in Jean-Luc Godard's *Au Bout de Souffle*. In September 1979, she committed suicide and her body was found in her parked car after she had been missing for ten days. These depressing facts had moved Hamlisch and his lyric-writer Christopher Adler to aim to write a musical tragedy, exhibiting the now-nearly-forgotten Seberg as the victim of the American hunger for instant stardom, as well as of the FBI, who had discredited her because of her association with the Black Panthers. Hamlisch had up to this point borne a charmed life as a song-writer. His first Broadway show, *A Chorus Line*, was the longest-running musical in its history. He had won three Oscars for his film scores and had made his life-story into a second hit musical, *They're Playing our Song*. He was thirty-nine, a millionaire and seemed unable to put a note wrong.

These facts could be cited as an excuse for the chain of misjudgments that now followed. Hamlisch had decided that 'whoever did *Amadeus* was the person I wanted'. Since Peter Hall was not free to come to Broadway, Hamlisch would take his 'revolutionary musical drama' to the only place he could do it, the National Theatre. Hall saw this as a unique opportunity for the company to work with Broadway professionals at creating a musical from the ground up. 'I don't accept that a musical must belong in the commercial theatre. Why shouldn't we do *The Threepenny Opera* as well as *The Beggar's Opera*, or *Guys and Dolls* as well as *The Oresteia*?' But these were masterpieces. It was a different matter to risk all on the unknown *Jean Seberg*. Prudently, the show was first explored at a workshop in the rehearsal room during the winter of 1982–3. Some participants thought it might have worked as a small-scale show in the Cottesloe: others thought that would be the end of it. There was no lack of discouragement from Hall's associate directors. 'Everybody warned him it was suicide. But he can be so stubborn,' said David Hare. Hall gave the go-ahead for production in the Olivier the following November on the *Guys and Dolls* scale, at lavish cost . . . another Big Show.

For those who had the good fortune to miss it, the story is presented as a flashback occurring in Jean Seberg's head on the night she is about to take the fatal pills. Her own life, persecuted by Preminger and J. Edgar Hoover, is compared, indeed confused with the life of Joan of Arc, persecuted by the Inquisitor. Both St Joan and St Jean end in the same symbolic flames. Drawing this parallel only served to demonstrate the inadequacy of a failed actress to serve as the heroine of a musical. Seldom has so much talent been wasted on celebrating such a lack of it. Rehearsals were attended by the three Americans – for Hamlisch and Adler had been joined by Julian Barry as dramatist, more as play-doctor than creator. They watched, they chewed gum and sometimes one of them leapt to the floor to rewrite a scene or lyric even while it was in the act of rehearsal. Hamlisch would leap for the piano whenever he was struck by the idea for a new number. Christopher Adler (son of the *Pajama Game*'s creator Richard Adler) who first thought up the idea on reading of Seberg's death, seemed not always in full touch with reality. 'You know who's been guiding us through this all the way? – Jean,' he confided mysteriously to me at one rehearsal. The Americans were used to the hectic atmosphere of constant change that precedes a Broadway opening night. 'They used to come to my office every day, wanting to chuck somebody or other out of the cast,' said Gillian Diamond, the National's casting director. 'By then a lot of us were walking around asking, Why are we doing this dreadful show?'

The Press was not slow to allege that what amounted to a free try-out of the show for its eventual Broadway producers was being financed with public money. The deal with Hamlisch, who owned the rights in the show, was that any production in America would earn the National a down-payment of $200,000 and a 15 per cent share of the box office. This only added to the suspicions that it must be doing the show purely for the money. It was implicit in such an argument that Hall (who also would earn money as its director) could have let this influence his judgement of the show's merits. 'Peter Hall and I had our greatest differences of view over *Jean Seberg*,' said Lord Rayne. 'He said he wanted to do it on its artistic merits, although he had very little support for that view from others. He convinced himself it had the merit he claimed for it. Perhaps he was influenced by the potential it had for Broadway success.'

Once a theatre is committed to a show of such magnitude, everyone needs to believe in it. And once the word gets round outside the theatre that a show is likely to 'bomb', as the Americans put it, this has a cumulative effect. Stories, without foundation, appeared in gossip columns suggesting that there was turmoil backstage, artistic disagreement between Hall and Hamlisch and a disaster in prospect. The show had not been hit by those problems, but by injury. Ankles broken or strained forced the replacement of one actor, and delayed the opening and press night. By the time the critics were invited on 1 December, there had been twenty-two previews, all played to large audiences. So damaging had rumour been that several critics made the point that *Seberg* was not quite as bad as they had been led to expect. 'The ghouls were out of luck last night,' ran *The Times* notice's opening sentence; 'contrary to all the gleeful rumours, *Jean Seberg* is no disaster but an extremely accomplished collaboration by a talented team with a burning belief in their subject. Unfortunately that belief is misplaced,' concluded Irving Wardle. There were several more-in-sorrow-than-in-anger pieces but they were still 'killer' notices. 'The story of a half-forgotten actress of questionable talent who kills herself in the first scene and spends the rest of the show justifying her unfulfilled life,' was the concise plot-summary by Jack Tinker in the *Daily Mail*. Who needed more than that to put them off? American judges were harsher: 'Not a fiasco, just not good enough,' snapped *Variety* tersely. 'Needs to be unjammed before its projected transfer to New York,' wrote Jack Kroll in *Newsweek*. It was left to Bernard Levin to administer the *coup de grâce* (if *grâce* is the word) by calling it 'one of the most frightful stagefuls of junk ever seen in London'.

Paradoxically *Seberg* survived for four months, although houses were two-thirds empty from the time the notices appeared. It ran so long because in the Broadway producers' contract there was a 'minimum-performance' clause, specifying that the National must give the show seventy-five performances if it was to participate in US and film rights which never materialized. So night after night the National lost the use of its main auditorium for better shows in order to maintain one that could only average 30 per cent audiences after being reviewed. Attendances fell by 6 per cent on the year and the theatre made a loss of £268,000 – it would have been £500,000 but for the timely arrival of some American rights payments. How much loss was directly attributable to *Jean Seberg* which cost £400,000 to mount is impossible to disentangle from the published accounts, which nobody is anxious to clarify. The show was withdrawn as soon as the contract permitted – an embarrassment to the last moment when an extra matinée had to be suddenly fitted in to make up the total of performances given to seventy-five. In desperation, the box office staff rang up all the groups to whom discounts are normally offered for block bookings in an attempt to 'paper the house'. So the anticipated money-spinner, a British-made Broadway musical, closed ignominiously playing to parties of bussed-in, non-paying old age pensioners. Worst of all, *Guys and Dolls*, playing to 80 percent houses, had been taken off to make room for it. Compared with retaining *Guys and Dolls* the box-office must have lost £300,000, so the total deficit on the show may have been nearly £750,000.

There must be a lesson in all this, and on the face of it it might even be that subsidized theatres should leave musicals alone. But that would have ruled out *Guys and Dolls* (which the National promptly revived again in order to recoup its fortunes). Perhaps they should leave *new* musicals alone. But that would exclude shows like *Les Misérables*, which succeeded on such a scale that it underpinned the RSC's finances for several years.

The only people who benefited from *Jean Seberg*'s premature death – from the fact that it bombed in London instead of bombing in New York itself – were the American backers who might otherwise have lost all their money. They had pledged $4 million on the understanding that they would keep 95 per cent of it if *Jean Seberg* did not make it to Broadway. To that extent their risk was underwritten for them with National Theatre subsidy. Mounting the show in London cost far less, so it was a thrifty move to do it there first. But was thrift the motive? Hamlisch's intended Broadway producers, the Shubert organization, no doubt breathed sighs of relief at their escape, but Hamlisch lost either way – as indeed he deserved to.

Peter Hall's motives for taking the risk are more difficult to assess. He thought it good for his company and for audiences to widen the spectrum of theatre on offer, and *Guys and Dolls* proved what audiences could be attracted by a musical. But it was still a grave misjudgement to have believed in the stageworthiness of this one. Why couldn't he see it? There could have been a personal factor clouding Hall's vision. *Amadeus* had made his name on Broadway, but he had not yet directed a successful musical, while his former protégé, Trevor Nunn, had scored a resounding hit with the musical *Cats*. As Nunn's mentor, Hall may have felt, consciously or unconsciously, that it was time he did so too and wishful thinking could have persuaded him too easily that he had found the means. Explicable or not, the episode left a shadow of suspicion over the good faith with which the National's programme was being chosen. Hall maintained ever afterwards that, if presented with another *Jean Seberg*, he would do it again, only do it better. But the complaint was not that he did it badly, but that he did it at all.

Fortunately, it was a mistake that could be buried, if not forgotten, in an overall run of National successes. Hall himself had contributed one of these the previous year in a rare, for him, venture into the nineteenth-century comedy of manners, *The Importance of being Earnest*. The fact that the play was foolproof only raised expectations of the National's first production all the higher. It also brought Judi Dench belatedly into the company. As Lady Bracknell she, of course, was challenging comparison with the memory of her great predecessor, Edith Evans. Imitating Dame Edith, whose performance is preserved on film, was almost a national pastime. How will she say 'handbag'? the Press demanded. There were people who swore she cut the line 'A handbag?' altogether. By the time the moment arrived she had established an entirely different character from Edith Evans's imperiously squashing old snob. Here was a still attractive woman of barely forty, with a propensity to flirt, especially with Algy, whom she clearly fancied. This was a 'game bird' of a Lady Bracknell who freely admitted that in younger days 'I had no fortune of any kind but I never let *that* stand in my way'. On hearing of Mr Worthing's abandonment in the cloakroom for the Brighton line, she removed her spectacles very slowly and repeated 'A handbag?' very quickly, with slight surprise but no disbelief and no pushing to get a laugh. Like the rest of her performance, it was played for real.

Another foolproof comedy that had joined the repertoire soon after *The Importance* was *The Rivals*, directed with his usual finesse by Peter Wood, which made the play seem at ease outside a proscenium, on the Olivier stage. Sir Michael Hordern found in Sir Anthony Absolute exceptionally human and wistful nostalgia for a randy youth, and Geraldine McEwan raised Mrs Malaprop to a glittering level of lunacy, helped out by a few extra malapropisms such as her final line: 'Men are all Bavarians!' But the next venture with an Ayckbourn comedy, *Way Upstream* in 1982, had an ill-starred voyage. This drama of oppression and tyranny among the weekend cabin-cruising classes had been already presented at Scarborough in a boat manœuvred in a shallow tank of real water. When it came to the Lyttleton, the weight of 6000 gallons split a much larger tank from end to end and deluged the stage and sub-stage, doing £125,000-worth of damage and putting the theatre out of action for several days. Repairing the tank and drying out the stage was not the end of the production's problems. The 24-foot cabin cruiser on which the action was set, containing two hidden winch-operators to steer it as well as the two couples on board, proved either too heavy to move or too complicated to control. Ayckbourn, who was directing his own play, could find no one in overall authority to go to for assistance. Hall was directing *The Ring* in Bayreuth. 'There didn't seem to be any other directors in the building . . . The cry I uttered at one technical conference was, "Who the hell's in charge of this building?" '

By this time previews had been cancelled and the press night postponed twice. Newspapers were relishing the fact that the National was up the creek: 'NT's boat play sunk again,' ran one bill. Hall hastened back from Wagnerian strife at Bayreuth to a South Bank complex that was leaking not only water but prodigious amounts of money from loss of performances. In his published conversations with Ian Watson, Ayckbourn laid the blame on fatal economies made at the set-building stage – though the set was not cheap at £25,000. He admitted that if they had told him they couldn't afford it, 'we could have done it without the water'. Eventually he even more sensibly did it without the theatre – on film, for television. But at the end of the costly run of a little-admired play which did poorly, by his standards, he declared angrily that he would never work at the National again – a temporary vow from which he later released himself.

Christopher Hampton came up with an original and diverting play for the Olivier. *Tales from Hollywood* has a list of *dramatis personae* crammed with the great and famous refugee writers who fled from the Nazis to spend the Hitler years in California, where they suffered in a subtler way from varying degrees of love-hate for American culture. In the play they consist of Thomas Mann and his novelist brother Heinrich, creator of 'The Blue Angel', Bertolt Brecht and Odön von Horvath, whose *Tales from the Vienna Woods* Hampton had translated for the National in 1977. In fact Horvath died in Paris in 1938 – a tree-branch fell on his head – but Hampton resurrected him as an ironic, detached guide to his fellow-exiles.

As if to compensate for the *Jean Seberg* disaster, Peter Hall had a productive 1984. To mark George Orwell's year the National presented a stage version made by Hall of *Animal Farm*. It was presented through the imagination of an eight-year-old boy reading the book, in the form of the brightly coloured pieces of a toy farm set on a black stage. The actors wore black except for their identifying animal half-masks, tails and feet. The pigs who take over the farm wore particularly unattractive white snouts and floppy ears as grotesque additions to their all-too-human faces. Heavily orchestrated with songs by Adrian Mitchell, it reduced Orwell's savage political fable to a rather sinister children's fairy story – the bitterly anti-Soviet allegory could hardly survive translation from page to stage. As Napoleon, a pig of few words, Barrie Rutter made a chilling porcine tyrant, whether Stalin or not. Devotees of the original book probably found it hard to accept any conceivable staging of the text, but its popularity was such that it played in all three theatres during 1984–5 to 113,000 people, before touring nine cities in Britain and visiting six more abroad.

Wild Honey introduced a 'new' play by Chekhov to the repertoire, thanks to the ingenious ministrations of Michael Frayn to Chekhov's unperformed six-hour play, which he wrote as a university student of twenty-one and which was discovered after his death. Frayn decided 'to treat it as if it were the rough draft of one of my own plays and to do the best I could with it'. This involved removing characters and sub-plots wholesale and transposing material to give the play dramatic shape. 'It is a presumptuous exercise to rewrite someone else's play,' Frayn admitted in his programme note, but it resulted in a wildly funny, satisfying and sometimes quite Chekhovian drama of a widowed landowner, Anna Petrovna (a feminist forerunner of Madame Ranevskaya), and a reckless, drunken, irresistible Don Juan of a village schoolmaster, Platonov, attended by a stageful of minor characters idly lamenting their idleness. Directed by Christopher Morahan and set by John Gunter, it included the spectacular effect of death beneath the wheels of a train which began its journey in the deep recesses of the Lyttleton stage and ran straight at the audience, continuing by sound effects alone into the auditorium. It gave Ian McKellen great opportunities as Platonov to combine a seducer, cynic, hedonist, a shameless player on women's sympathies and high-minded sufferer from delirium tremens, all of which he encompassed with dazzling turns of speed and changes of tack. The play won no fewer than nine awards for McKellen, Morahan and Gunter.

Like Judi Dench, McKellen was overdue at the National Theatre. After his brief and showy Claudio in the Zeffirelli *Much Ado* in 1965, he had departed to prove himself in other companies perhaps the most formidable and passionate classical actor of his generation. His rendering of Salieri in *Amadeus* won him the plaudits of Broadway but was never seen at home. He had had no love for the National in its early days on the South Bank, calling it 'a siege fortress, rejecting and unassailable'. Nevertheless, in 1984, he had been coaxed inside by Peter Hall to play Jaffier in Otway's *Venice Preserv'd* followed by *Wild Honey*. But the real draw was Hall's *Coriolanus*. Like Laurence Olivier at Stratford, McKellen gave a superbly aggressive and physical display in what some called the best Shakespearean production of that era. It was set in a crumbling Roman amphitheatre round a sandpit arena. About 100 members of the audience were seated behind the action, as if participating in it as members of the plebeian rabble. A crowd with raincoats, handbags and rolled-up evening newspapers taking part in a Roman election was made more acceptable by dressing the actors themselves in multi-period costume. Coriolanus was first seen in a dazzling white suit, before stripping for battle to near-nakedness streaked with gore. The senators wore business suits beneath their robes and Rome was hung with Fascist banners to celebrate the triumph at Corioli. Coriolanus, sword in hand, was finally brought down by casual bursts of automatic fire. McKellen saw Coriolanus as a great athlete, arrogant and ill-at-ease except when finding release in physical action. He spoke of John McEnroe, the temperamental tennis ace, as his possible model. But for all the battles of sword and demagoguery, it was in the supplication scene with Volumnia, his mother, where McKellen confronted the emotional dominance of Irene Worth at her most formidable, that the production touched the heights. It was the immensely long, spellbound pause with which this fighting-machine took his mother's hand and held it, ending at last with a horrified recognition of his defeat ('O mother, what have you done?') which people carried away as the memorable image of a production which ran for 100 performances at the Olivier. At the following year's Athens Festival it was taken to the Herod Atticus theatre, built into the Acropolis, where the Athenians stood and cheered it for ten minutes.

Little noticed among the general run of success in the early eighties was one particularly piquant mishap. In 1981, a production of *Who's Afraid of Virginia Woolf?* was put into rehearsal under the American director,

Nancy Meckler, who thus became the first woman invited to direct at the National. Joan Plowright was cast as Martha, but after opening in Bath and previewing at the Lyttleton her sudden withdrawal was announced on the Press night. A throat infection was blamed but it was later learned that she had withdrawn from the play altogether and was recuperating in France. People wondered whether there was any other reason for her sudden loss of voice and retirement from such a meaty role. There had been such a reason. It was delivered that morning at breakfast-time at the Oliviers' home in the form of a long lawyer's envelope addressed to her. When she opened it, she found to her astonishment a petition for divorce. The petitioner was sitting across the table reading the newspaper, apparently oblivious of this incident or of her reaction.

'But Larry,' she said at last, 'this is a petition for divorce. May I ask why?'

'No wife of mine,' Olivier is reliably reported to have replied, 'will appear at Peter Hall's National Theatre.'

As usual, his timing was impeccably calculated. Peter Hall's National Theatre was thrown into disarray (the play finally opened a month later). Joan Plowright's return to the National Theatre was deferred for four more years. The hatchet remained unburied. One wonders how much satisfaction it gave him.

14

1985: A Year of Crisis and Closure

The gap which had been steadily widening between the financial needs of the arts and the amount the Government was disposed to provide for them became a gulf by 1985. Many arts establishments looked likely to sink into it – and not just the small fry but the biggest flagships, including the National Theatre and the English National Opera. When the Arts Council grants for the following financial year were announced at the beginning of February, the National hastily summoned a press conference, and Peter Hall climbed on to a white plastic-topped coffee-table to make what became known as the 'coffee-table speech'. He announced swingeing cuts in NT activities, including closing the Cottesloe Theatre. He excoriated the Government's parsimony and the Arts Council's acquiescence in it. He virtually declared war between the National Theatre and the Government. It was to continue for the rest of his time there.

On the whole, the National had been well treated in grant terms up until 1980. In return, it had virtuously balanced its books in good weather and in bad. The strike of 1979 cost it £500,000 in revenue, but this was recouped inside a year. In 1980, after the Arts Council inquiry described earlier, £700,000 was added to the grant specifically to enable the theatre to catch up with the neglected maintenance to the building, and was to bedevil calculations for years to come. If it was counted as part of the theatre's annual income, then it could be claimed that grant increases had kept pace with inflation, and this the Government did. But it was really money paid in arrears towards deterioration of the building. It was certainly not money for putting on plays. Excluding this £700,000 from the calculation, the National Theatre's Arts Council grant increased as follows:

1979/80	£4,550,000 base figure:
1980/81	£4,850,000 increase 6.5%
1981/82	£5,500,000 increase 13.4%
1982/83	£5,910,000 increase 7.4%
1983/84	£6,392,000 increase 8.1%
1984/85	£6,576,000 increase 2.9%

When the GLC grant was added, the total grant was £7,336,000 in 1984–5, compared to £5,100,000 in 1979–80. The overall increase in the first five years of the Thatcher regime was 44%. In that period the Retail Price Index had risen by 63%, so it had failed to match inflation by a third.

Given its high building costs, the National had to operate on a big scale in order to give value for money. In its case, parsimony did not pay. This argument won a certain amount of sympathy, at any rate, under the early Conservative Arts Ministers, Norman St John Stevas and Paul Channon. But by 1985, everything had changed. There was a new Minister of the Arts, Lord Gowrie, who also spoke for the Treasury in the House of Lords. There was already a new chairman of the Arts Council, Sir William Rees-Mogg, who as a former financial journalist claimed to have economic expertise. Both were convinced monetarists, in sympathy with the Thatcherite philosophy of drastically reducing public expenditure and promoting market forces. Sir Roy Shaw had also retired from the Arts Council and been replaced as secretary-general by Luke Rittner, who had created what some saw as the Arts Council's 'commercial alternative' – the Association for Business Sponsorship of the Arts. The effect was immediate. The National's grant for 1984 increased by only 2.9%, compared with an inflation rate of over 5%. This increase was derisory compared with the other members of the 'Big Four' – the national institutions which accounted for a third of the Arts Council's funds:

Client	1984–5 grant	Increase (on year)	Increase since 1979
Royal Opera House	£12,300,000	+21%	+76%
RSC	£4,900,000	+36%	+131%
English National Opera	£5,900,000	+13%	+56%
National Theatre	£6,500,000	+2.9%	+45%

It can be seen at a glance that the National was the worst treated of the four. The immediate cause was a government-appointed inquiry into the running of the Royal Opera House and Royal Shakespeare Company, under Sir Clive Priestley, head of Margaret Thatcher's efficiency unit. His brief was to find out in what ways these deficit-making companies were being inefficiently or wastefully run. Instead, Priestley found that they were seriously underfunded. As a result of his findings the Government had no choice but to raise the subsidies for the two organizations – by as much as £1.5 million in the case of the RSC. The National promptly asked for a similar inquiry but was refused one.

Another reason for the relative drop in the National's grant was the Arts Council policy entitled 'The Glory of the Garden' announced in 1984, by which a greater share of its grant money was to be reallocated in favour of the regions. This was all very well if the funds were to be increased overall, but they were not, so the greater share offered to the regions could only be at the expense of the major London companies, including the National. It was not in the interests of the regional companies to complain of a policy which promised them a bigger share of the cake, and it would look selfish of the Big Four to complain of being squeezed to help weaker brethren.

All these factors were analysed by Michael Elliott, in his own internal scrutiny of the National's operations from 1979 to 1984. It showed that the grant had now been reduced in real terms by over £1 million yearly. The National had managed to avoid the sort of deficits run up by the other three national companies through internal economy and high audience levels, which owed much to the enormous success of *Guys and Dolls* (which contributed £720,000 to the box office over three years). Transfers and exploitation brought in an annual income of £275,000, while first attempts to get corporate sponsorship and patronage had brought in £650,000 over three years. The effective scope to increase audiences or seat prices had now been virtually used up. Ticket prices had nearly doubled since 1979, and there were signs that they were beginning to deter the hard core of regulars. The vulnerability of the theatre's finances was demonstrated in 1983. The deficit on the year was £260,000, and would have been £500,000 had not a payment for an American television deal not arrived at a propitious moment. By scraping and cutting corners, the National had survived 1984 and got rid of its deficit. But, Elliott concluded, it really needed an extra £1.5 million in 1985, one million of it to restore the grant to the level of inflation. Otherwise it would go into major deficit.

The carefully-made case was despatched to the Arts Council in November 1984. Response was there none. In December the theatre got advance warning of its grant in 1985. Instead of the £1.5 million asked for, the increase would be £129,000 – a raise of only 1.9 per cent. If 2.9 per cent the year before had been paltry, 1.9 per cent was derisory. 'It made it perfectly plain, after all our efforts, that nobody was going to come to our rescue,' said Michael Elliott. 'The game Peter Hall used to play in the sixties of expanding, running up a deficit and demanding to be rescued, was over. We now had to do something striking to make our point.' With a grant increase of £129,000 to pay increases estimated at £700,000, the National was heading for bankruptcy. It did not own its own theatre and so had no asset on which to raise money. Under recent legislation, Rayne and his Board members were personally liable for the theatre's debts if it should go bankrupt. There was nothing for it but to put together a drastic programme of economy measures: the closure of the Cottesloe, which would save £500,000 a year, a total staff reduction of 100 jobs, the end of touring.

So when he climbed on the coffee-table to announce this, Hall was letting off a calculated bombshell. Rayne's private pleas to the Arts Council and the minister had achieved nothing whatever. He had decided to see what public protest would do. A campaign for the National alone would arouse the old envy of the 'fat cat' by the thin, so he wisely took up the cause of all: 'I want to say how appalled, how outraged I am by the low government subsidy for the arts in general,' he began. 'I am angry on behalf of the subsidized theatre throughout the country. If I don't speak out, I don't know who is going to. It's the same story everywhere . . .' He instanced Birmingham, Exeter, Sheffield, Leicester and Bristol, as theatres having to reduce their output. 'This government has a very clear philosophy: if you cut public expenditure, you do good, you make things work better. They have applied this, mistakenly, to the arts: if you cut the arts they must be better. The government does not understand that the more you put in to the subsidized arts, the more you get out, the more you earn . . . The Arts Council, instead of fighting for the arts, is becoming more and more a straight instrument of Government policy. I believe that the Arts Council has betrayed the National Theatre . . . The Minister for the Arts executes Treasury policy and the Arts Council meekly follows suit. If that continues, we shall not *have* a subsidized theatre.' Calling for a national inquiry into the cost effectiveness of the performing arts, Hall concluded: 'I wonder what happened to vision? Whatever happened to any idea of the future? We are good at theatre as a nation, we're thought to be good at it internationally. I repeat, I don't believe the Arts Council is acting responsibly in carrying out the Government's wishes.'

In singling out Lord Gowrie and Sir William Rees-Mogg as, in effect, traitors to the nation's artistic standards, Hall was striking shrewdly at men who prided themselves on their intellectual credentials and artistic discernment. Gowrie, inheritor of a recent earldom and known to his friends as 'Grey' (his given name being Greysteil), had been a fine-art

175

consultant with strong connections with Sotheby's. But he was also the Government's chief economic spokesman in the House of Lords. Sir William Rees-Mogg was another Balliol-trained monetarist, City editor of the *Sunday Times* before becoming Editor of *The Times*, who lived the life of a Somerset squire. Neither man would answer gladly to accusations of Philistinism. Gowrie listed his hobby in *Who's Who* as 'wine'. Rees-Mogg was the author of *How to Buy Rare Books*.

Hall had drawn attention to the National's special burden, the building which had been erected for it by Act of Parliament. 'Between two and two and a half million pounds a year, ladies and gentlemen, goes on running this building before we start putting on a play,' he declared. 'Things are at such a pass that I have been asked to consider the feasibility of leaving this building and playing elsewhere. It doesn't make any sense for us to lay off actors and stop doing productions, stop touring the country, *stop being a National Theatre*, purely for the sake of keeping a building open.' The cost of maintaining the building, £2.4 million in 1985, took over a third of the total grant, more than was spent on producing plays. The amenities that the building offered as a meeting place, where the public could browse in the bookshop, look at exhibitions or listen to music, eat, drink and sun itself (occasionally) on the terraces, as well as enjoy ample elbow-room, did not come free. Maintaining this commodious style of theatregoing was beginning to interfere with the provision of its *raison d'être* – the plays. Did anyone seriously consider whether the company could move out and take over two conventional theatres, while the South Bank was converted to a conference centre? Probably not that seriously. But to make the point, Michael Elliott told the Press that such a move was 'a real possibility'. Costs, he pointed out, would be much lower in an old-fashioned theatre.

The campaign of public outrage brought forth acres of newspaper comment (mainly favourable to the theatre). In the House the Government maintained that the National had received a 'real increase' in its funding since 1978 – a date carefully chosen to include the £700,000 special grant for maintenance mentioned above. Michael Foot then asked, 'What is the use of having a great and adventurous National Theatre and a Cabinet of barbarians?' In a debate on the adjournment on 25 February Clement Freud showed how much the National had done to help itself by raising £1 million in the past two years from exploitation, sponsorship and patronage – considerably more than the more favoured RSC had done. Did the Government want the National Theatre to fade away? William Waldegrave, the junior minister, answered on behalf of the Government 'a resounding no', but argued once more that the arts could not be given privileged status among the

Government's priorities. He did not see the objection to private sponsorship of its main-line activities. 'As the Emperor Vespasian said when he put a tax on the urinals in the city of Rome, money does not smell,' concluded this fellow of All Souls.

The Government's case was in essence that £7 million was an awful lot of money to run a theatre, and if the National needed more, it should go out and raise it. The issues that were debated then are still unresolved, so they are worth setting out in some detail. Sir William Rees-Mogg rejected Hall's charge that he was not fighting the Government for more arts money. Instead of the £105 million allocated to the Arts Council in 1985–6, he wanted £120 million – although he appeared to be peacefully resigned to the likelihood that he was not going to get it. 'The idea that standing on a coffee table is going to change central government policy, months after it has been fixed, is absurd,' he wrote. Peter Hall was making an unreasonable outcry about 'very small sums indeed. Ought we to be starving Liverpool and Sheffield in order to feed a few extra crumbs to London?'

Lord Gowrie protested that one should not protest too much. 'I know very well that the arts share of total public expenditure is small. But it would be a damaging and incomprehensible signal to other parts of the economy to uprate the Arts Council uniquely and by no less than 20 per cent.' He pointed out that he had made increased funds available to museums and galleries (to repair their leaking roofs) and to the Craft Council, the National Film School and to authors, by increasing very slightly their miniscule payments under Public Lending Right. These improvements, it appeared, did not endanger the fight against inflation. They sent no incomprehensible signals to other deserving cases. Presumably museum curators, craftsmen and authors were discreet enough to pocket the money so quietly that nobody else noticed. His message was that 'the landscape has changed', 'the limits of hospitality have been reached', 'we are in a plateau situation', and that 'plural funding is the name of the game'. Gowrie-isms like these came spouting from him like bubbles from a geyser. But they all boiled down to the same refrain: 'Get out there and hustle.'

On 11 March, Rees-Mogg delivered a lecture on 'The Political Economy of Art' – a title borrowed from John Ruskin. In prophetic vein, he saw that not only had the landscape changed but that history, not the Conservative Government, was working the changes. The Arts Council was a tiny part of the structure of the welfare state, established on the principle that the arts, like education, health and social security, ought to be generally available, regardless of ability to pay. But that whole principle was now under question. The arts could not rely on 'certain and increasing subsidies and' (here he struck his headmasterly

177

note) 'the great drawback to subsidy is that it can weaken the sinews of self-help. Too often subsidy has created dependence and dependence has led to the demand for higher subsidy.' He made subsidy sound like an addictive and harmful drug. He no longer mentioned, if he even remembered, its original purpose of making the arts available to all kinds of people by making tickets cheap. 'Whenever I see Sir Peter Hall, I think of Cardinal Wolsey,' said Rees-Mogg, quoting the line Shakespeare gave him: '*Oh how wretched is that poor man that hangs on princes' favours!*' 'Arts Council subsidies are princes' favours,' said Rees-Mogg.

There were flaws in these arguments. Take Lord Gowrie's doctrine that the arts could expect no special consideration. Why not? If the arts were a profitable industry – and Rees-Mogg himself had proved in his lecture that the Government got more back from them than the £100 million it gave the Arts Council – it would be hard-headed and businesslike to invest more in them. Likewise the Gowrie doctrine of 'go-out-and-hustle' could soon become self-defeating. If everyone went out hustling, how could they all conceivably bring home enough bacon? There was some force in the Arts Council's anti-elitist argument that since subsidy came from everybody's taxes, it should be widely spread rather than concentrated on a few pinnacles, such as the National Theatre. But sponsorship, too, would inevitably be elitist, the big sums going to the big, prestigious pinnacles, rather than the outlying foothills.

The most obvious weakness in the National's case was that it had not established itself nationally. In the past six years, from 1979, it had toured for only thirteen to fifteen weeks a year, visiting ten or a dozen cities for a week, being seen by perhaps 100,000 people. Even then it did not always attract full houses – on one occasion in Bristol it played to 30 per cent. Now, with its cut-backs, it was not touring at all. From outside London it looked like an expensive luxury maintained for those who lived in the capital. And its ticket prices were not so much cheaper than the commercial theatres' in the West End that it could claim to be a theatre for all pockets.

But this was a government that had just been overwhelmingly re-elected, so what proportion of the voting public cared how the theatre was treated? Were there 'no votes in the arts', as Lord Gowrie had said? A country which allocated only £100 million public expenditure to the performing arts out of £130 billion was hardly the keenest of their patrons. Where Britain spent £6 per head of population on the arts in general, the French and the Germans spent over £20. The French Ministry of Culture's budget for 1985 was £778 million compared with Lord Gowrie's £272 million. West Germany supported seventy-four state municipal theatres and there were *five* national theatres in France. To French and German voters, the arts represented national tradition, national pride, and, in the case of France, *civilisation française*, to French eyes the only kind.

In England, as Peter Hall saw it, 'any theatre that puts its case quietly can die quietly'. And, to begin with, the policy of raising a stink seemed productive, although he attracted captious personal criticism: 'Despite his railing against government meanness, Sir Peter collects a salary of more than £50,000 a year and is allowed to spend a very large amount of his time making money on projects of his own,' commented the *Spectator*. 'At no point has he suggested his own pay should be cut. So his devotion to the arts, though real, is not selfless.' Other journalists came out of the closet, eager to be counted as philistines – Brian Walden, for example, declaiming that 'Sir Peter speaks for the theatre elite, which has no contact whatsoever with the strivers in our society, who do not go to theatrical performances.'

Apart from the sniping, the campaign did produce some positive results. Within a fortnight of the announcement that the Cottesloe would close, the GLC arts committee announced a special grant of £375,000 to reopen it. It was rescue, but rescue by an ally itself doomed to be abolished within a year. Next, a meeting of forty-two artistic directors of subsidized theatre companies from all over Britain was held at the National Theatre. They included heads of the Birmingham Rep; the Everyman, Liverpool; the Royal Exchange, Manchester; Nottingham, Oxford and Salisbury Playhouses; the Northcott, Exeter; the Haymarket, Leicester; Ayckbourn's Theatre in the Round, Scarborough; the Crucible, Sheffield; the Royal Court; the Young Vic; and a band of the smaller companies in London and its environs including Fringe representatives such as the Bush, Tricycle and Foco Novo. Many of these theatres had been among the opponents of the National which they feared would take the Arts Council bread from their mouths back in 1976. Now they were all together in the same boat, fighting the same cause, and declared 'no confidence in the Arts Council as presently constituted' by a unanimous vote. The Arts Council meanwhile had just lost half of its drama panel. Seven members resigned, accusing it of 'betraying the arts and lending itself to party politics'. The artistic directors met again, sixty of them this time, at the end of March, unanimously contradicting the government claim that there had been a real increase in funding for 1985–6. By June, at a third meeting, they were being more specific: the 'Glory of the Garden' policy should be abandoned. So the Arts Council found its policy disowned by the very people it claimed to be helping.

As a result of these pressures, the Arts Council was soon talking a different language in a glossy prospectus headed 'An invitation to the nation to invest in the Arts – A Great British Success Story'. The Council announced that it was asking the Government for £161 million for the following year, a hefty rise of £55 million or 53 per cent. Even Sir William Rees-Mogg, he who had sounded so disapproving of subsidy, now proclaimed: 'the Government could do no better than to invest in the arts'. It was such a sudden conversion, could it be sincere? The application was launched at a press conference with a steel band and a string quartet in attendance. It was left to Peter Hall to sound a sceptical note amid the prevailing euphoria. What was the Arts Council going to do, he wondered, when, as he expected, the Government refused to change its mind and cough up?

A few hours later that very day, the new minister for the arts made his first discouraging pronouncement. New minister? Yes, Lord Gowrie had abruptly abandoned that office only a fortnight earlier to resume his career (he soon became chairman of Sotheby's). Nobody, he said, could live in central London on his ministerial salary of £33,000 a year. Earl Grey's departure was unmourned but the arrival of Richard Luce, a junior minister from the Foreign Office whom no one in the arts world had then heard of, was not exactly a case for rejoicing. Luce had not the faintest suspicion that he was bound for the Office of Arts and Libraries until Margaret Thatcher sent for him late one Monday afternoon, when she was in mid-reshuffle. His first public pronouncement was a dusty answer to Rees-Mogg's sudden enthusiasm for bigger subsidy. 'I must make it absolutely clear that there is no prospect of my being able to deliver from government funds the sort of growth which many in the arts are seeking.' To complete the discouragement, he added that, in his view, overdependence on the state 'will stifle creativity'. Rees-Mogg admitted on television that, whatever the outcome of his negotiations with the Government, he had no intention of resigning. The fire in his belly was not difficult to damp down. The Arts Council did not get what he had asked for. It did get a rise of £30 million, but most of that (£25 million) was already earmarked to take the place of the £35 million which the GLC and other metropolitan councils, now defunct, had been giving the arts. So in fact they were getting less than before. A curious gloss was put on the announcement. To quote the *Times* report: 'Mr Richard Luce, fighting his first battle with the Treasury as Minister for the Arts, was said to have worked vigorously to secure a reasonable settlement at a time when he was hampered by some of the lobbying of the arts world. Members of the cabinet, including the Prime Minister, had objected to the outspoken criticism of the Government voiced earlier this year by Sir Peter Hall and regarded the Arts Council's demands for grants totalling £161 million as utterly unreasonable.' The irritable wrist-slapping in that statement was obvious. Despite its brave battle-cries about the good sense of investing in the arts, the Arts Council found it could give its clients an average rise of only 4 per cent. The National Theatre's grant rose by 4.1 per cent. Inflation was 4.2 per cent. The effective result, after so much sound and fury, was a standstill all round.

Had the campaign been worth fighting? The best that can be said is that it may have stopped things getting worse. The Government had improved its offer under pressure, perhaps to avoid another burst of invective and accusation from Hall. But for the rest of Hall's period as director, the National received paltry increases or none at all, as follows:

	Grant	Increase	Increase in RPI
1985–6	£7,503,000		
1986–7	£7,811,000	4.1%	4.2%
1987–8	£7,811,000	Nil	3.9%
1988–9	£7,917,000	1.3%	3.2%

If the grant had kept pace with inflation it would have been £8.8 million in 1988 instead of £7.9 million. There had been a decrease in the real value of the grant by £900,000 that year and a cumulative decrease over the three years of £2 million. So although he won a battle or two, Hall lost the war.

As the outstanding champion who had fought for subsidized theatre on a major scale in the early sixties, he could hardly believe that he was now fighting the same battle again – and losing it. 'The saddest thing of all is having to keep justifying that the arts should be subsidized,' he said. 'I thought that battle was over.' For years to come he was to sound more and more like Canute rebuking the waves. 'We live in bullying times. The only way to stop the bullying is to shout back,' he declared in 1986. But he had to admit his failure to persuade Margaret Thatcher by argument: 'She listened but she didn't understand. She thinks that if you are doing the right plays, people will come to them anyway.' Gas, electric power, public transport and communications, university education and public broadcasting were being privatized or pushed into funding themselves more and more from private sources. If the National Health Service was being squeezed ever more severely, what chance of an expanded National Arts Service? The very concept of a National Theatre was contrary to the prevailing ideology. When Hall declared that a philistine government was undermining 'the soul of the nation' by its policies, he was appealing over the heads of current politicians to the public: the only way to win the day was to change the government. But 'the soul of the nation', or much of it, was busy worshipping Mammon. The National, like many another public institution, had to make compromises with Mammon in order to survive. That meant commercial sponsorship and patronage.

As it might have been: Denys Lasdun's model for the Shell site with the
Opera House (left) and National Theatre (right) across a piazza
(photo: by kind permission of RIBA).

March, 1976: About to move at last into the still incomplete South Bank site.
The frustrations of waiting show on the captain on the bridge
(photo: Hulton-Deutsch Collection).

1976: The one and only time that Olivier took the stage of the Olivier: the official opening ceremony on 25 October (photo: Nobby Clark).

1976: Albert Finney as Tamburlaine the Great in the Olivier Theatre's first epic (photo: Nobby Clark).

1979: John Dexter returns to the National to direct *As You Like It*, giving
notes to Sarah Kestelman, Simon Callow and Marjorie Yates
(photo: Zoe Dominic).

1978: Michael Gambon, an Old Vic spear-carrier, gets his first leading role on
the South Bank in Harold Pinter's *Betrayal* with Penelope Wilton
(photo: Donald Cooper).

1981: *The Oresteia* of Aeschylus in the verse of Tony Harrison. Apollo looks
down on the chorus of Furies in their awesome masks
(photo: Donald Cooper).

1983: *The Rivals*: Sheridan's eighteenth-century humour polished impeccably by Michael Hordern as Sir Anthony Asolute and Geraldine McEwan as Mrs Malaprop (photo: Donald Cooper).

1982: *Guys and Dolls*, the National's biggest hit to date, reaches its finale under the neon lights of John Gunter's Broadway (photo: John Haynes).

Spellbinding performances: Ian McKellen as Platonov in *Wild Honey* (1984)
. . . and Anthony Hopkins as Lambert Le Roux in *Pravda* (1985)
(photos: John Haynes and Nobby Clark respectively).

1987: Judi Dench in full cry as the ageing Serpent of Old Nile in Peter Hall's high watermark production of *Antony and Cleopatra* (photo: John Haynes).

1988: Peter Hall congratulates his successor, Richard Eyre (Press Association Photos).

15

The National Theatre is Whose?

On 22 October 1984, the reorganization of the National Theatre Company into five acting groups, each led by different directors, had been announced. Peter Hall admitted by now that the place and the company were too big, as was the current RSC. 'I think actors suffer in both organizations from a certain impersonality.' The company numbered 135 actors, too many to allow a company spirit to develop. 'One frequently walks the corridors, miles of them, without recognizing a single face,' complained Ian McKellen. Now five companies of 20–25 actors each, who would stay together for 9–12 months, were to give at least three productions, one in each theatre, under the same leadership. The groups were to be led by Peter Hall, Bill Bryden, Richard Eyre and David Hare, Peter Wood and, as the only group to be headed by actors, not directors, Ian McKellen and Edward Petherbridge. All the group leaders were past or present members of the National team, but there was to be greater delegation of power than there had been before. Hall had previously divided command by appointing directors for each theatre but retaining overall control. Now the group leaders were, at least in theory, solely responsible for their choice of actors and of plays. Because of the financial crisis of 1985, the size of each group was cut to seventeen instead of twenty-five actors and the closing of the Cottesloe meant the disbanding of Bryden's already-existing group. Only three groups, not five, could function at any one time within the budget.

The only group to declare its aims was the Eyre/Hare combination. They were, said David Hare, interested in presenting 'large-scale, social plays about the present day'. The first of these, written by Howard Brenton and David Hare, was 'a comedy of Fleet Street' called *Pravda*. Brenton, whose idea it was, had suffered from the pestering of Fleet Street during the *Romans in Britain* turmoil. But, he insisted, 'I didn't write it out of a desire for revenge. I wanted to create a

Citizen Kane of our time.' David Hare spoke defiantly before the play opened: 'A visitor to Britain from Mars would conclude that the relation of government to newspaper here was much as it was in the Soviet Union. What is it about Fleet Street that it gives up what you'd think a paper most prizes – its independence? In *Pravda* we're challenging the Government in the best way we can, on the stage.' The challenge took the form of the broadest ridicule. In Lambert Le Roux, the South African newspaper proprietor who buys his way, via a tabloid newspaper, to the *Daily Victory*, 'a British Institution like Buckingham Palace or the Tower of London', they created a monster of opportunism, greed and ruthlessness to rival Volpone or Richard III, who, said Brenton, was much in his mind when they were writing it. Press proprietors who had come from overseas to bind British newspapers to their wills, such as Lord Beaverbrook, Rupert Murdoch or Robert Maxwell, cannot have been absent from the authors' minds either – or indeed from the audience's. The National was taking on a powerful breed whose money ensured that they were seldom attacked in print. The Board took legal opinion on the risk of a libel writ. Besides the appalling Le Roux, there was a stuffy and ineffectual editor of the *Victory* rejoicing in the name of Elliot Fruit-Norton who could have reminded anyone in the know of Sir William Rees-Mogg, former Editor of *The Times*. Le Roux, as created by Anthony Hopkins, was a character as beguiling in his way as Richard Crouchback. He had a forward-lunging walk and a carnivorous mouth, which grinned and gaped like a shark's, emitting strangled and hideous Afrikaner vowels, as he mockingly made mincemeat of such opposition as came his way. The venial toadies of journalism and politics crumpled before him in their eagerness to take his money.

'Good papers are no good. Why go to the trouble of producing good ones when bad ones are much easier? And sell better too?' demands Le Roux. With so many contemptible hypocrites around him, it was difficult to believe that good papers had ever been produced. 'There's such a thing as a decent journalist but they're never given a chance,' mutters someone feebly. It was a very one-sided play, a polemic which stated more brutally than usual the credo of many contemporary newspapers, as perceived by the public that buys them. Fleet Street was outraged. It did not like the picture of itself as 'the foundry of lies', or as *Pravda*, which, especially in pre-Glasnost days, was a mockery of its meaning – truth. There must have been many a squirm of recognition. 'We don't publish corrections because they don't look good on the page . . . And how could the readers know what was true?' Beneath the play's exaggerated villainy the audience recognized a general truth – that nowadays Britain had an unworthy and untrustworthy 'popular' press – and criticism did not stop with the tabloids. The public reaction was to laugh loudly. 'Just before we opened, Howard said to me. "What if we are the only people who think this is funny?",' remembered David Hare, 'but we were articulating something that people wanted said. Journalists told me they sat chilled at hearing themselves reviled like dogs, to the audiences' laughter.'

Pravda proved to be the most popular straight play the National Theatre has so far put on, playing 168 performances to 181,000 people, comfortably exceeding *Amadeus* in size of audiences (though *Amadeus* transferred, whereas *Pravda* did not). For over two years it formed the backbone of the Olivier repertoire and was recast three times. The one constant was Hopkins, who gave the performance of his life. He had been tempted back to England after years filming in California by being sent the first act to read. 'Hopkins was heroic,' said Hare. 'He was the rock on which the theatre was founded in those years. In all those performances he hardly played to a single empty seat.' (The *average* audience figure was 96 per cent). 'He could do no wrong in it.'

Ian McKellen and Edward Petherbridge were already conversant with running a self-governing troupe of actors, having been the moving spirits of the Actors' Company in the seventies, whose principle was equality between all members. At the National there was already equal billing, on programmes and posters. But every member understudied and the company chose one production by vote. The programme carried a statement from McKellen and Petherbridge: 'In the decade since Laurence Olivier retired from the National Theatre, British theatres have been ruled not by actors but by directors. There has been a total decline in the numbers of acting companies working together for longer periods . . . Even in this theatre there is no pattern of prolonged contracts such as are available to actors in the national theatres of Europe. British actors are even in danger of becoming mere casual employees.' McKellen and Petherbridge included in their company four actors who were better known for their work in television light entertainment than on the straight stage – Eleanor Bron, Sheila Hancock, Roy Kinnear and Hugh Lloyd. They had also invited four directors, 'knowing their versatility and experience will make exceptional demands on our acting'. Philip Prowse, of the Glasgow Citizens' Theatre, directed the highly stylized *Duchess of Malfi*, with a surprised Eleanor Bron in the title role. ('It was the most wonderful and terrifying thing ever proposed to me.') Tom Stoppard was invited to direct his play *The Real Inspector Hound* about two ludicrous theatre critics played by Edward Petherbridge and Roy Kinnear. This was coupled with Sheridan's *The Critic*, directed by Sheila Hancock. McKellen was to play the self-congratulating author, Mr Puff – one of Olivier's minor

185

triumphs in the 1940s. The fourth play was to be directed by the improvisatory director Mike Alfreds, and the play chosen by the actors turned out to be no surprise – *The Cherry Orchard*.

There were company meetings about policy. 'The more actors are involved collectively, the greater the chance of them working to optimum standard,' explained McKellen. 'I have bees in my bonnet about breaking down the division between stars and other members of a company of that size. People arrive here and it might as well be a factory. They run into all sorts of people they don't know. Its size and anonymity need breaking down by fostering the idea of company acting.' Roy Kinnear commented at the time on the company's meetings to discuss its plans: 'We all chip in and it's nice to have the semblance of democracy but, of course, the theatre is a dictatorship and it's got to be.' But Eleanor Bron called the relationship of McKellen and Petherbridge to the actors 'more brotherly than fatherly'.

Three plays in eight months put intense pressure on McKellen, who was already playing the lead in two other plays when the new company was formed. There was one period of little more than a week when he appeared in four leading roles – in *Coriolanus*, *Wild Honey*, *The Duchess of Malfi* and *The Critic* – while also rehearsing *The Cherry Orchard* and running the company. 'I feel like some sort of carthorse,' he complained at the time. Most of the seventeen actors got their chances in one or more of the plays. Nobody was brought in from outside to fill a part, as in the other groups.

All of the group's shows were wildly popular. *The Duchess of Malfi* played to 94 per cent audiences, and the Stoppard–Sheridan double bill to 97 per cent. *The Cherry Orchard*, described by *The Times* critic Irving Wardle as 'the most passionate performance of the play I have ever seen', was further evidence that a company gains in ensemble and cohesion the more it works together, even though by that stage they were all very tired. The company carried the National's flag abroad to the theatre festival at the Odéon Theatre in Paris and the International Theatre Festival in Chicago. Their popularity with audiences suggests that the appeal of a traditional repertory company still worked – people liked coming back to see actors they knew playing a wide variety of parts. Was the group system the solution to overcoming the National's anonymity? The experiment seemed inconclusive. At the end of nine months or little more together each group disbanded, just when they should have stayed together, if the experiment was working. But after nine months at National Theatre rates, actors with mortgages found the need to supplement their income in the richer pastures of television.

The group system was not consistently pursued. The other big hit of the summer was Alan Ayckbourn's *A Chorus of Disapproval* in which

Ayckbourn directed an *ad hoc* cast. It was originally billed as a production by Peter Hall's group, but the company had no members in common with those in *Coriolanus* or Hall's succeeding production, *Yonadab*. The outstanding member of the cast was Michael Gambon, who played the despairing director of an amateur group rehearsing *The Beggar's Opera*. He was to become the mainstay of Ayckbourn's own group which came into existence later.

Peter Wood recruited a group with which he re-staged his famous *Love for Love*, followed by *The Threepenny Opera* and *Dalliance*, a version by Tom Stoppard of Schnitzler's *Liebelei*. Looking back, Wood was not enthusiastic about the group system. 'Rather than giving you a permanent company, it produced what should be called an impermanent company. One company recruited for three productions meant that you were always having to cast wrongly.' Wood believes that the public demands star acting. 'A star is a star and that's what people come to see – a Dench or a McKellen performance. The National is a star arena like the Centre Court at Wimbledon. "Directors' theatre" overtook the National as it had overtaken the RSC because the standard of acting isn't what it was. There just aren't enough good actors to go round. Directors' theatre is often a way of covering up for the dearth of big performers. Concept productions don't require big performances.' Not surprisingly, Wood missed the calibre of cast he had to work with in the Old Vic *Love for Love* – or in his 1983 hit revival of *The Rivals*, which numbered not only Michael Hordern and Geraldine McEwan but Edward Petherbridge and a then unknown Fiona Shaw in the supporting roles of Faulkland and Julia. As the eighties progressed such casts became harder and harder to assemble.

The year 1985 brought a personal crisis to add to the financial one. Alan Bates had been tempted to appear for the first time at the National in the title role of a new Peter Shaffer play, *Yonadab*. As a companion role he chose to play Archie Rice in a revival of *The Entertainer*, with Joan Plowright as Archie's wife Phoebe. It seemed like reconciliation time – between Peter Hall's National Theatre, John Osborne and the Oliviers, putting memories of *Watch It Come Down* and *Who's Afraid of Virginia Woolf?* behind them. Joan Plowright said in a newspaper interview at the time, 'There was a breach to be healed and I thought the time to heal it had arrived. It is, after all, the National Theatre and I think we should be working for it.' They had not reckoned on John Osborne. Two weeks from the beginning of rehearsals, he announced that he would not agree to the casting of Joan Plowright, about which he had not been consulted. An author usually has the right of consent to principal casting and in this case the National appeared not yet to have negotiated the rights, so Osborne had absolute power of veto. His motives remain somewhat inscrutable. He issued a statement that he had 'no animus against Miss Plowright. I have known her for nearly thirty years.' Indeed, twenty-two years earlier he had cast her as Archie Rice's daughter both on stage and screen. For her to play the wife, however, struck him as 'a bizarre notion which was never even put to me'. He may have been more offended that he had not been properly consulted than he was by the casting. He may have felt that Sir Laurence would still not approve of his wife appearing. He had often aired his dislike of 'The Bunker' or 'Colditz-on-Thames', his favourite descriptions for the South Bank institution, while he referred to its director as Dr Fu Manchu. Now he had been as good as invited to make his displeasure in it felt. An embarrassed Peter Hall held crisis meetings between the parties but Osborne's veto remained adamant.

Faced with a nasty gap in the repertoire, Hall took an obstinate course. Instead of recasting the part in *The Entertainer* and dropping Joan Plowright, he dropped the play and asked her to choose another play to appear in instead. Joan Plowright chose *Mrs Warren's Profession*. So, in haste, Shaw's long-banned brothel-keeper Vivie Warren took Archie Rice's place on the National Theatre boards (what would Matthew Arnold have thought of it presenting either?). Joan Plowright prepared herself by meeting with the Contemporary English Collective of Prostitutes and reported that three-quarters of their members were, like Mrs Warren, mothers in need of income.

Alan Bates was destined to further disappointment with *Yonadab*, one of Shaffer's rare outright failures. The failure was squarely written into the leading part. The task of Yonadab – a character referred to twice very briefly in the Book of Samuel – is to be the instigator and interpreter of the biblical story of the incest between King David's son Amnon and daughter Tamar, which was avenged by another of his sons, Absalom, who killed Amnon. In the figure of Yonadab Shaffer saw an embodiment of many of his familiar themes – the outsider's envy of the powerful, the cynic's envy of the believer, the outrage of man at the indifference of God . . . The opportunities for rhetorical soliloquy were many and were taken at length. An illustrated lantern lecture emerged with transparent net-curtains shrouding the stage like an illuminated projection screen. Yonadab, who seemed sophisticated, cynical and modern beyond all likelihood in 1000 BC, spent the evening buttonholing the audience when he was not eavesdropping, spying or lying. His compulsive voyeurism made the audience themselves feel like involuntary peeping toms at the spectacle of a man having intercourse with his sister. This amounted to sensationalism without dramatic justification. The mystery was why the play was put into production in such a clearly unsatisfactory state. Peter Hall's explanation at the time was: '*Yonadab* was fundamentally rewritten from start to finish during the first three weeks of rehearsal. With Shaffer you are banking on how he'll change it in rehearsal. It's an exciting way of working but dangerous.' It was a way of working that had produced *Amadeus* but it was not, in this case, paying off. After giving his final relaxed and reassuring notes to the cast at the end of six weeks of bewildering changes, Hall confessed to me privately that he had been wondering all afternoon whether to cancel the press night, scheduled for the next day: 'When we've got it right, I believe this could be another *Amadeus*, if the notices are good.' But they emphatically were not. 'The play was put on too soon. Another six months would not have been long enough, because in truth the play was not yet ripe,' admitted Shaffer. Three years later he published a new version, 80 per cent rewritten. Whether it solves the play's problems will not be known until it is produced. The episode illustrates the dangers of being over-eager to repeat a winning formula. *Amadeus*, product of the same team of playwright, director and designer (John Bury), had triumphantly proved its many doubters wrong. *Yonadab* (which played to half-empty houses) proved only that one triumph does not guarantee another. As Hall resignedly reflected at the time, 'I still don't know with a new play whether it's going to work or not – and that's after thirty years.'

The 1985–6 season included one more controversial play, Neil Simon's autobiographical *Brighton Beach Memoirs*, only in this case the controversy was whether the National should produce a commercial Broadway playwright, so successful that he was able to buy one New York theatre out of his earnings and have another named after him. Michael Rudman, formerly the resident director at the Lyttleton, had been asked back to direct any play of his choice. Having met Neil Simon in New York and obtained his consent, he was in no doubt. 'You have to have a special reason for doing a highly commercial playwright at the National,' said Rudman. 'The Lyttleton's repertoire is mainly twentieth-century classics in first-class productions. A lot of the time you are trying to find out whether they *are* classics.' Rudman had several such productions to his credit – Maugham's *For Services Rendered*, Miller's *Death of a Salesman* and Rattigan's *The Browning Version*. *Brighton Beach Memoirs* can hardly be ranked with these, but it was Simon's most mature play to date. It was just as well, Simon said modestly, that the National had waited for this one, 'my first full-blown play – all the others were basically two-character plays'. *Brighton Beach Memoirs* presented the ups and downs on a New York Jewish family of seven, living on the anxious underside of the Depression, as seen through the secret memoirs of its fourteen-year-old youngest member.

It was not a typical sentimental family comedy. After nearly 100 performances it transferred to the West End where, curiously enough, it was the first play of Simon's to have a long run. 'You have to remember I'm a very American writer,' Simon told me before the opening. 'More than that, a very New York writer.' It was not such a sure thing commercially.

The National's crisis season of 1985–6 ended paradoxically with over £1 million profit, instead of the £1 million loss that had been expected. It turned out financially to be the best year the company had ever had. Had the crisis been illusory? It would seem so. But no one could have foretold that outcome. The GLC had unexpectedly reacted to the emergency closure of the Cottesloe by suddenly finding – for largely political reasons – that it had £375,000 to spare, to enable the Cottesloe to reopen. On top of that came an unpredictable surge in box office revenue from a flush of popular hits. In the Olivier, *Pravda* (96%), *A Chorus of Disapproval* (86%), and the double bill of *The Real Inspector Hound* and *The Critic* (97%); in the Lyttleton *The Duchess of Malfi* (94%), *Mrs Warren's Profession* (84%) and *Brighton Beach Memoirs* (77%) had boosted takings by £600,000 more than the year before. It had also been a good year for earnings from transfers: *Guys and Dolls* was toured and then presented at the Prince of Wales Theatre, *Glengarry Glen Ross* went to the Mermaid, *The Mysteries* to the Lyceum. These, with substantial royalties from the film of *Amadeus*, earned another £300,000 between them. Meanwhile the economies had taken effect, even though the reopening of the Cottesloe had reduced the saving. Crisis, what crisis? Had Hall's protests turned out to be a case of crying wolf? Not entirely.

The National had itself commissioned an outside scrutiny by management consultants under Lord Rayner, Chairman of Marks and Spencer. In 1985, he gave the administration of the theatre a thorough going-over and suggested savings which could amount to £650,000 or 6 per cent of the theatre's costs in three years' time, mainly through streamlining the operation of the scenery workshops, backstage manning and the box office. This was pretty small potatoes in the way of economies. 'All members of the scrutiny team have been impressed by the scale and complexity of the NT's operation and by the achievements of its artistic and managerial leadership,' ran his report. The 6 per cent saving was forecast only on the assumption that the Cottesloe remained closed. With it open, the potential saving was only 2 per cent. Nobody seriously contemplated the future of the National Theatre without the Cottesloe, the operation of which required £500,000 out of the £650,000 potential saving. The scrutiny suggested that there was only modest scope for increasing box office income by about £220,000 a year, and that sponsorship and patronage (already £250,000 a year) might reach £350,000 in another three years.

What it all boiled down to was that the National was already a tight ship. There was no opportunity or excuse for the Government or the Arts Council to cut back further on the National's grants. 'I share the view that the development of private sponsorship and patronage is unlikely to relieve substantially the NT's requirements from public funding,' declared Lord Rayner. 'I should record support, on the evidence, for increased government support in real terms.' All this had absolutely no effect on the grant allotted for the following year, 1986–7. The GLC, whose last contribution had been £798,000, had been abolished. The Arts Council, combining both grants in one, provided an overall increase of £300,000, a rise of 4 per cent, following a year in which inflation had risen by 6 per cent. If the grant had kept pace with inflation since 1979, it would now amount to £9,241,000, instead of £7,811,000, so the theatre was now going nearly a million and a half short of its previous funding. Clearly it was being penalized for managing to do so well on less money.

The following year, 1986, there was *no increase* in grant at all, although inflation was running at 4 per cent. It was perfectly obvious that there was a deliberate and increasing squeeze on state subsidy to the National. Something had to be done – the farming out of scenebuilding, as well as putting the cleaning and security patrolling of the building out to contract. All processes which go to make a production had hitherto been conducted under one roof. Designers now had to settle the exact detail of their designs much earlier than before and the open spaces of the workshops backstage were henceforward sparsely inhabited, although the paint-frame still functioned and painting of pre-prepared scenery was still done. The paradox was that the building cost so much in maintenance that the National could not afford to use it to the full.

Another paradox was that nobody really knew who owned the building. The freehold was nominally the property of the GLC, now defunct. The South Bank Theatre Board, the quango appointed to get the building put up, had a 200-year lease of the site, with obligations to see that the building was satisfactorily completed and latent defects in it rectified before agreeing final accounts with the contractor, Sir Robert McAlpine. The National Theatre Board itself has no lease, only a licence which does not constitute a legal tenancy. The Board, though responsible for the expenses of running the building, always refused to enter into a full repairing lease. It believed that the building already required substantial structural repairs. The roof leaked – large areas of flat roof always do. In certain places the concrete looked waterlogged.

In rainy weather it looked like a wet shirt – for instance near the base of the main fly tower. The architect, Sir Denys Lasdun, ascribed the dark patches and the stalactites which hang from the underside of the terraces, to the fact that 'it needs a damn good clean' after standing for fifteen years in London air (which he had originally promised would whiten the concrete).

One persistent leak in the Lyttleton roof defies all efforts to locate it. The technologically daring solution was to run a pipe like a gutter across the main foyer ceiling. It collects the drips, which would otherwise fall on the heads of the patrons, in a large jar hanging on the wall. At intervals a man is sent to empty the jar. More serious structural defects in the concrete and its reinforcing steel rods remain a matter of conjecture. In order to examine the problem, the concrete would have to be opened up, causing damage as costly as that which it is designed to investigate. At the time of the Rayner report, estimates put the cost of structural repairs at between £500,000 and £1 million at 1985 prices. Not surprisingly, the NT Board refused to accept the potential liability.

The responsibility remains with the South Bank Theatre Board. But where – and who – is that? Diligent inquiries finally ran it, or its part-time secretary, to earth in an Oxford antique shop. 'The South Bank Theatre Board, *c'est moi,*' said Mr Mark Harrison, now semi-retired from the Office of Arts and Libraries, where the secretaryship had been passed on to him by a man in the same office who was leaving on *his* retirement many years earlier. Mr Harrison is a little-known but key figure in the National Theatre set-up. It is he who holds (or keeps in a safe) the September 1975 exchange of letters which is the Theatre's only legal title to occupy the vast building. One is a letter from Douglas Gosling, then secretary of the National Theatre Board, agreeing to meet certain costs of repair and maintenance and referring to 'the permanent arrangement to be made between us'. No such permanent arrangement has yet been made. The South Bank Theatre Board's letter merely offered the National Theatre occupation 'by way of licence only and not so as to create any tenancy'. Mr Harrison, on behalf of his board, could probably turn them out any time he likes.

There the matter eccentrically rests, and there it will probably continue to rest, unless a large enough chunk of the building falls off or caves in and arouses public interest in who is ultimately responsible. The latest answer to that question is the Arts Council, which took over the defunct GLC's freehold. If the Arts Council decides that there are structural defects (which some experts claim and others deny), who is going to pay to repair them? Its ghostly tenant, the South Bank Theatre Board, has no money – indeed it has no office apart from a shared room and a filing cabinet in the Office of Arts and Libraries. The National Theatre Board, its licensee, is funded by the Arts Council. So if the Arts Council as landlord insisted on structural repairs, in effect it would be charging itself a large capital sum which it has not got – unless Mr Peter Palumbo comes up with the money.

The Rayner scrutiny had found that the National sold an average of 75–80 per cent of its seats, but that the average money yield was much lower – 69 per cent of the maximum in a good year, only 61 per cent in a bad one (1984). The National's average ticket prices were at least £1 less than those of West End theatres. Less than half of its seats were priced in the top range, a quarter in the medium range, and a quarter at the cheapest price. Rayner suggested that the market would bear higher prices and a lower proportion of cheap seats, but, to its credit, the theatre stuck to its principle of leaving 25 per cent of its seats at the cheapest and another 25 per cent at the middle price.

'The principle is that we should offer a range of prices but the differential must not be too big,' said Roger Lobb, the box office manager. 'We don't think we should have the most expensive seats in town, because we want people to keep coming back.' In many commercial theatres the only cheap seats are often in a couple of back rows or in the gallery. The National's policy is to keep a high proportion of its seats comparatively cheap, including the forty seats kept back for sale on the day of performance, plus the unsold seats which are offered at stand-by prices just before the performance. Discounts are offered for group bookings and the very front stalls are always cheap (they are narrower seats without arm-rests) and are called 'ripple seats'. Olivier's belief was that their occupants will be readier to laugh than the patrons behind them who have paid more and that the effect will 'ripple' back through the house. Keeping seat prices down is one of the main justifications of subsidy. But there are also frequent complaints about the difficulty of hearing in the circles, where very few seats are at the top price.

Who makes up the National Theatre audience? Surprisingly little research seems to have been done on this question. The core of it is the mailing list of about 40,000 people, who receive the leaflets giving the programme for the coming two months. About 10,000 of the 40,000 write in to book in advance. These are the regular patrons who come repeatedly (45 per cent of the seats are bought by people who attend four or more shows a year). My analysis of 138 shows put on in the two main theatres from 1976–88 shows that 15 played to audiences totalling over 100,000, 52 to over 50,000, 74 to over 40,000 and 64 to below 40,000. The average audience is between 40,000 and 50,000, which represents a run of eight to ten weeks in a 1,000-seat theatre which is two-thirds full. A play that runs less than three months in the commercial theatre will almost certainly lose money for its management; six months is a reasonable time to break even. Only 10 per cent of its shows attract audiences of over 100,000 (equivalent to a run of six months or more) with an all-time high of 303,000 for *Guys and Dolls*. Strict comparisons with the commercial theatre are impossible to make because the repertoire system requires that shows are often withdrawn when they are still drawing good houses, in order to make way for new productions. But the roughest comparison shows how much smaller audiences are for National Theatre successes – and therefore how few of these would be mounted commercially.

A surprisingly small proportion of National audiences consist of tourists, either foreign or from other parts of the UK. Whereas the West End theatres depend on visitors to London to fill nearly half of their seats, out-of-towners account for only 20 per cent on the South Bank. 'The National has not been successful in attracting tourists,' the Rayner report concluded in 1985. That remains true in 1990. 'The Americans don't know about us,' said Roger Lobb in partial explanation. 'The RSC have been to New York and North America with big hits like *Nicholas Nickleby* and *Les Misérables*. But when *Bedroom Farce*, *Equus* or *Amadeus* were done on Broadway they were presented by the Shuberts and people had no idea they were originally National Theatre shows. Americans believe that the RSC *is* the national theatre.' Perhaps the lack of Americans in the audience is less disturbing than the lack of citizens of other parts of the United Kingdom. Less than one in five is a pretty low figure.

Ironically, the main result of the Rayner Report was the sudden departure of Michael Elliott, the general administrator whose skilful managerial housekeeping over the previous six years was the reason why Rayner had so little to suggest in the way of improvements and economies. Hall and Elliott had worked well together for several years, beginning in the chaos and crisis of the strike-crippled year of 1979, when Elliott was recruited from the industrial firm of Kimberly-Clark. He was mainly responsible for fighting off the strike, removing the trouble-makers and then bringing the many departments of the theatre on to a sound managerial footing. But his differences with Hall had been growing, which was never a recipe for survival. In Hall's increasing absences, Elliott had chaired planning meetings but found that there was no one with the authority to take producer's decisions. Now, in an attempt to fill this gap in artistic command, Rayner recommended a fundamental change in management structure – the appointment of 'a senior executive with the required combination of artistic and administrative experience, who can deputise for the director in his absence . . . The overall direction and management should be shared between two individuals who would work closely together in the office of the Director and be able to act in each other's stead. 'In other words, the job should be split between two virtual equals. This proposal implied that the absences of Peter Hall had to be compensated for by the presence of someone with enough experience of the director's impresario and producer roles to take effective charge of the associate directors. Why the absence was necessary, Rayner did not question.

The proposed reorganisation left no place in the scheme of things for a general administrator, whose post disappeared. Elliott had no alternative but to negotiate his own resignation. His departure was glossed over at the time with little comment as a minor matter, which it was not – for six years he had been the organisation's Number Two. The full story will not be told until the National opens its records to some official historian.

The following year the announcement was made of the appointment of an 'Executive Director' – David Aukin, who was then running the ambitious Leicester Haymarket Theatre, after previous spells in charge of Oxford Playhouse and Hampstead Theatre. Early in his career he had co-founded and run the Fringe companies, Foco Novo and Joint Stock. "He will share with Peter Hall the responsibility for overall direction and management," ran the announcement, "Peter Hall, however, will remain the National Theatre's chief executive." Just how much authority this gave him was not clear, possibly even to Aukin himself. But when he joined, in September, 1986, he knew that Hall had only two more years as director to run. Hall, was a strong believer in one-man rule. 'You'll never have a theatre run by two men,' he told me later. 'You can have one run by one man with a brilliant and loyal lieutenant but once the lieutenant wants to take charge, you're in for trouble.' Aukin settled in to play a waiting game.

The ink was hardly dry on the Rayner report, which so praised the theatre's financial prudence, when in September 1985 *The Observer* revealed that Peter Hall had earned more from the transfers of the production of *Amadeus* than the theatre itself had done. The agreement made by Peter Shaffer with the National Theatre specifically excluded rights to any subsequent American production of the play. An author's rights are his own to dispose of and Shaffer had great bargaining power. The National Theatre, in the person of Peter Stevens, its then administrator, was glad to accept what terms it could get, in order to secure the play. The National stood to gain a percentage (usually about 5 per cent) of the box office takings on any West End transfer or new production in Britain plus a share in the film rights. In addition Shaffer offered it 10 per cent of his earnings from any American production. Since author's royalties are 10 per cent of the box office gross, the theatre's share of the Broadway production worked out at one per cent. The National was not entitled to any share, strictly speaking. The New York production was not a National Theatre production, although it had the same director in Peter Hall and designer in John Bury. The Shubert organization, which had bought the US rights from Shaffer before the play had been presented anywhere, could have appointed any director or designer they chose – just as they had entirely recast the play. 'I didn't have to offer to share my earnings,' explained Shaffer. 'I volunteered to do so. I felt I owed this to the National Theatre because it took the risk of putting the play on first. They gave it eight weeks' rehearsal instead of the usual four. You pay for that at the National by getting fewer performances. You don't make nearly as much money but you are getting the National Theatre's prestige as well as its high standard of production.'

Meanwhile Peter Hall's American agent, Sam Cohn, had negotiated his director's percentage with the Shuberts. It was exceptionally high – 4 per cent of the box office takings rising to 5 per cent after the production had recouped its costs, or passed 'the break-even', plus 5 per cent of the profits. Thereby Hall was bound to make at least four to five times more than the National Theatre itself on the New York production – something in the region of $10,000 a week compared to $2,000, at its peak. This would not have raised eyebrows if Hall had been simply a freelance director. He (through his redoubtable agent) would be getting what his reputation was worth to the Broadway producers, who have no reputation for charity. The fact that he was also the director of the National Theatre made it appear that he had looked after his own interests a great deal more effectively than he had looked after the theatre's. That led to the question, should the theatre's director make himself available to stage Broadway productions while drawing a salary of some £50,000 from public funds? The purists' answer was no. Should the director of the National Gallery take time out to stage an exhibition at the Museum of Modern Art, or the editor of *The Times* put in part of the year editing *Variety* as well? Hall had no inhibitions about his earnings. 'Big money being made out of hugely popular play? Scandalous!' he declared in a defiant letter to *The Observer*, pointing out that when any production transfers from the subsidized to the commercial theatre, those who created it go on to commercial contracts. 'This well-established system has greatly benefited the National Theatre, me and many others. If the system were to change, the subsidized theatre would attract less top talent. It would then cease to attract top writers. And it would then earn less income with which to supplement the declining state grant.' As usual, he had no lack of plausible arguments for doing what his contract permitted. But these arguments sounded self-serving, particularly to those who read his diary entry concerning the Broadway negotiations: 'If I am to do *Amadeus* here, it may be one of my last chances of making money, real money.' Participation in a hit play in the theatre is one of the fastest ways of making real money in show-business. Witness *Amadeus*: Hall's percentage of the Broadway box office over a three-year run amounted to well over $800,000. According to his own figures, he earned altogether over £700,000 – fourteen years' salary. The National Theatre had at that stage made around £500,000, but, unlike Hall, it continued to participate in the profits of the *Amadeus* film, which were considerable. Overall it admits to having received by 1990 over £2 million in royalties, about three times as much as Hall earned. But most of it was from the film, not the play.

On the rare occasions when a subsidized theatre and those who work for it hit a bull's-eye and clean up commercially, what should their respective share-out be? The 1986 Enquiry into Professional Theatre under Sir Kenneth Cork, Chairman of the RSC, recommended that at least half of transfer earnings should go to the theatre, i.e. that the theatre's share of the box office should equal or exceed that of the director and designers added together. Henceforward the National insisted on 5 per cent or more. The most important change recommended was that bargaining on transfers should be carried out including the director in its negotiating team. 'In this way the theatre and its director would have identical interests in any negotiation, rather than the separate interests inherent in the present arrangements.'

This possible conflict of interest had come under the spotlight in a *Sunday Times* investigation of the earnings of Peter Hall and Trevor Nunn published in June 1986, which gave the general impression that both men had made personal fortunes while directing the two main subsidized theatres – and led to libel writs being taken out by both of them. 'Hall and Nunn have been allowed extraordinary freedom by their executive boards to take on extra work in commercial theatre around the world,' the report pointed out, perfectly accurately, and then added: 'There is growing criticism among their colleagues that both Hall and Nunn have used their positions to launch new productions through the subsidized theatre and then, once their success has been established, transferring them into the commercial theatre. They have made far more than their theatres out of this and other commercial work.'

Had shows like *Amadeus, Guys and Dolls, Glengarry Glen Ross, Fool for Love* and *Chorus of Disapproval*, the productions which transferred from the National to commercial theatres in the 1980s, been staged primarily in order to make money on transfer – particularly for their directors? A moment's consideration showed how implausible this was. *Amadeus* was felt to be such a doubtful project that only two members of the planning committee of twenty, besides Hall, were originally in favour of doing it. *Guys and Dolls* was described by Hall as 'the most dangerous gamble I took at the National', partly because it was largely cast from actors already at the National. Two of the other plays were examples of avant-garde American writing, and the Ayckbourn play had a costly cast of fourteen speaking parts. Hall personally stood to benefit as the director of only one of these shows – *Amadeus* – and in that case his earnings were greater than the theatre's because of the way the theatre's contract with the author was drawn. So the *Sunday Times*'s charge of his having deliberately used his position for his own profit was not justified. Had *Jean Seberg* and *Yonadab* been successful, the story might have had some justification.

Hall wondered if the *Sunday Times* special investigation had political motives – that his attacks on government arts policy had provoked someone to 'shut him up'. There is no evidence whatever that the *Sunday Times* was doing a hatchet job for anybody other than itself, neither for the Government nor for Mr Rupert Murdoch, its proprietor, who might not have cared for *Pravda*. The paper was simply following up a tip, gleaned at a dinner party, that if people knew how much money Hall and Nunn had earned by the exploitation of their work, they would be very surprised. They were. The facts about the National given in the *Sunday Times* were obtained from its ex-general administrator, Michael Elliott. It was the interpretation of the facts that was tendentious, as well as the 'Insight' team's wild exaggeration that Hall had made £2 million from *Amadeus*.

The whole *Amadeus* controversy was complicated by the English tradition that public service is normally rewarded at lower rates than the commercial market-place pays for comparable positions. Peter Hall claimed that he would be paid twice as much to do his job in continental Europe and three times as much to direct plays on Broadway. On the opposite side, the Cork Enquiry recommended that a theatre should share in its salaried director's outside commercial earnings, as if his productions were the theatre's. No one takes on running a national gallery, library or theatre to maximize his income. The quality of the institution, the standards of work and the prestige attached are a substantial part of the reward. Until all public servants, from nurses to government ministers, are paid the full commercial rate, such jobs will demand a financial sacrifice. And perhaps they should.

16

The Hall Era Closes

By late in 1985, anyone who knew him must have felt that Peter Hall had had about enough of the National Theatre. He had found a way of devolving his job on to other men's shoulders, while his own were missing increasingly often. His campaign against the erosions of subsidy was not having results. In a long talk at the end of that year he confessed to me: 'I have spent the most miserable year of my life in the theatre. I don't like closing theatres. I don't like sacking people. If our grant continues to fall beneath inflation, we shall be in another crisis soon. Some people will say, how nice, they are managing on less money, but the National Theatre doesn't exist to manage on casts of 17 or 19 actors where we would have used 25 or 30.' He was visibly depressed by his contacts with the Arts Council. 'When I see Rees-Mogg, it's like talking to the headmaster who thinks the boys would be better doing a job of work than putting on plays.' He felt he was campaigning alone – the united theatre front of early 1985 had dissolved. 'All I can do is point out the damage. This place should be the centre of theatre in the country, touring more, receiving regional companies, foreign companies. That's what gets cut. Year by year we are made less productive and therefore give less value for money. It could get to the point of people asking, why give the National £7 million for doing six plays a year?'

He still maintained his punishing schedule on six hours' sleep, arriving at the building by 8.30 a.m. to do the paperwork and dictate his instructions into a tape recorder before rehearsals began at 10.30 a.m. The rest of the planning meetings had to wait until rehearsals ended at 6 p.m. The evenings were often occupied in watching previews and the day always ended with a pile of scripts to read – an average of three a week. Hall's outer office was always crowded with people waiting to grab him as he came out. Some haunted the passage to the rehearsal room hoping to catch him as he passed. The director's morning walk to rehearsal was like the public progress of a medieval monarch or Roman emperor, surrounded by supplicants with their suits and complaints. One almost expected to see him touch some of them to cure them of the King's – or perhaps of the Director's – Evil. Once the door of the rehearsal room closed on him, interruptions were barred, although, during breaks, a messenger might arrive, like the cream-faced loon in *Macbeth*, bearing news of some new crisis. Amazingly, in the midst of a day like this, he would find time to film television interviews. Once it was for a programme called 'A Full Life'.

Something in him relished, perhaps demanded, this urgent atmosphere of crisis. 'He has a natural talent for crisis – the moment one occurs, his whole being goes into a state of relaxation,' his friend from Cambridge days, Peter Wood, said of him. 'When others go into over-drive, he goes into under-drive.' 'I don't think of myself as thriving on crisis, but I must or I wouldn't continue with this job,' Hall confessed to me. 'I'm not as unflustered as I look. I learned to hide my feelings early on.' One thing he was not prepared to do was to devote less time to his passion for directing productions. 'If I couldn't direct plays, I wouldn't want this job.' As for outside work, he had made it clear when renewing his contract from 1984 that if the Board wanted his exclusive services, he wouldn't sign. Rather naïvely the Board 'envisaged' that his outside activities would not exceed four weeeks a year.

He was now also Artistic Director of Glyndebourne Festival Opera, where he directed (or revived) productions of at least two operas a year, often three, sometimes four. The fact that he had been, since 1982, married to the opera singer Maria Ewing (his Carmen both at the Met and at Glyndebourne) gave opera greater priority in his life. 'It *is* a strain to do three jobs – to run this place and direct plays and have a life outside,' he admitted, 'and in five years I shall be sixty. That means there's time to do one more major job.' Fifteen years at the National was approaching its end and he had agreed with the Board that he would 'identify' a successor for 1988 when his contract ran out. In Richard Eyre he named an outstanding candidate for the job, with an excellent record in running the Nottingham Playhouse, followed by five National productions, including *Guys and Dolls*. Although the post was adver-tised and candidates considered, Rayne and the Board seemed content with Hall's recommendation. They did not urge Hall to stay on. His absences had begun to rankle with Rayne. 'He sent me a letter saying he thought he ought to go and we didn't press him to stay.'

Richard Eyre had recently diversified into television and films (he had directed a controversial TV film about the Falklands war, *Tumbledown*, and was known in the cinema for *The Ploughman's Lunch*). The son of a Devon army family, he took up theatre at Cambridge, first appearing in Trevor Nunn's *Macbeth*, and spent his first two years as a jobbing actor outside London, before turning to directing 'in a state of acute boredom'. He did not jump at the National. As he said to me, 'There are only a finite number of people who have run theatres who are willing to do it again. But in the end, I didn't have the courage to say no.'

In contrast with Peter Hall's high, media-oriented profile, Eyre seemed almost self-effacing. He and Hall are alike in their shyness, but different in their ways of dealing with it. Like Hall, Eyre knows the politics of the theatre, is good at persuading people to do what he wants and well able to stand up to the flak that is bound to fly. There was a steely core behind his casual, unassuming manner and youthful (for forty-five) appearance. The outstanding difference in their approach to the job was his insistence on sharing it with a co-director. David Aukin and he had worked together only once before, at Leicester, but Eyre was confident they would make a team, he as artistic director, Aukin as 'executive director', or producer. 'I said I would only do the job in partnership with a producer, so that there was somebody I could talk to about my own work, and who would take over the producer's responsibility.' This enabled artistic as well as administrative decisions to go on being made by Aukin while Eyre was busy rehearsing. The company was no longer to be run partly from the corridors to the rehearsal room or partly on the long-distance telephone from Glyndebourne, Bayreuth or New York. Eyre committed himself to undertake no outside work for three years.

The National which Eyre inherited had changed considerably in the eighties. No longer could it depend on enough state patronage to carry out its full programme. Either the programme had to be trimmed or the funds had to be privately raised. Any means of survival is better than slow death, so the theatre had set up a Patrons and Donors Committee in 1983. This was superseded by a fully-fledged Development Council of more than twenty influential people under the chairmanship of Sir Peter Parker, formerly head of British Rail. Some 80–90 firms and individuals had become regular patrons and corporate members, whose contributions were channelled through the National Theatre Foundation, which funded peripheral activities, especially educational tours and children's programmes. In 1989 began a 'corporate con-tributors scheme' which set out scales of contributions from £2,000 to £10,000 a year, with their appropriate rates of benefit. (For £10,000 the firm got 40 free tickets, for £7,000 only 20.)

Rayne and Hall had strong reservations about sponsorship. They felt that it was demeaning that a National Theatre's work should be credited to sponsors who were expecting a commercial return in publicity. This came up right at the beginning, when a large insurance company proposed a deal by which in return for £250,000 a year it would have its name featured on all NT programmes, posters and stationery and set up a kiosk in the foyer to sell 'National Theatre' life assurance. Rayne turned this down 'with no qualms at all' (it was left to the RSC to put an insurance company's name alongside its logo). 'I don't think we should sell ourselves to anybody for that sum or even a much larger one,' said Rayne. 'We would like to keep our dignity. I am in favour of patronage rather than sponsorship. There is a large group of people who generously give us money without asking for a commercial return.' (Rayne himself was among them. In deep anonymity he was the benefactor behind the series of 'Bargain Nights', on which all seats in the theatre were priced at £2.) Peter Hall made the point that sponsorship is tax-deductible. 'The tax that the sponsors save is our money anyway. I would rather have the Arts Council decide what the country does with it. I don't believe the National Theatre should have to ask for sponsors.' He resisted having sponsors for any normal production, though they were invited to finance the early evening 'platform' performances, the foyer music and exhibitions, Christmas shows for children and educational tours and projects. But in 1986 circumstances forced a change of policy. The theatre accepted sponsorship of *The Threepenny Opera*, from Citicorp/Citibank, and the following year Peter Hall's own production of *Antony and Cleopatra* announced its indebtedness to Ladbroke's, the bookmaking and leisure group, which held a ball on the stage of the Olivier as a sort of sponsor's perk.

Sponsors of productions are asked for a minimum sum of £60,000. Their normal return, besides the publicity, is a large number of free seats for the staff and the opportunity to entertain the company's clients after the performance at a reception, dinner or gala, attended by members of the cast – although no actor is ever *required* to attend (several object to doing so). On average two main productions a year have been sponsored, not a high proportion, because of the long-term planning required by corporate public relations departments. Repertoires cannot usually be planned eighteen months, let alone two years, ahead. It is much easier for a big firm to sponsor a sports fixture or a series of classical concerts, both of which can be relied upon to be 'safer' than plays and to enhance the respectability of the firm. No sponsors could be found for the unfortunately titled *'Tis Pity She's A Whore*, but then no sponsor could be found for the majority of plays produced. Only established popular classics, *Antony and Cleopatra*, *Hamlet*, *The Tempest*, *Cymbeline* and *The Winter's Tale*, Jonson's *Bartholomew Fair* and Molière's *The Misanthrope* were chosen up to 1989. That is not likely to change. There are also sponsored single performances when one auditorium is taken over for business entertainment. The National is nowadays a venue for hire, although it will not sell the entire house, or too large a proportion of it to allow reasonable public access to any production.

Most sponsorship money goes not to productions but to projects, such as the computerized box office installed by Digital, office automation system by Data General, the W. H. Smith Interact programme of workshops and demonstrations at schools, and the Lloyds Bank Young Theatre Challenge competition for youth theatres. The tours sent out by the Education Department, the Studio partly financed by Sainsbury's, and the International Seasons are open to far fewer objections than can be made to the sponsoring of productions. The first night of *Hamlet*, for example, turned into a beano for the sponsor's guests which created a less than attentive atmosphere in the auditorium to which they eventually found their way after the refreshments of the interval.

The theatre has had an Education Department since 1982, when Michael Bogdanov's immensely successful adaptation of *Hiawatha*, which was repeated over three Christmases, showed what a great demand for theatre experience there was among the young, the audience of tomorrow. It sent out its first touring production of Brecht's *Caucasian Chalk Circle* in 1982 followed by many more, ranging from *Hamlet* to Arnold Wesker's *Roots*. The Christmas shows continued with *The Ancient Mariner*, again a Bogdanov adaptation, in 1984, and *The Pied Piper*, adapted by Adrian Mitchell in 1986 and 1987, in which 650 London schoolchildren enthusiastically played the rats and the children of Hamelin in groups of sixty. The Interact programme sends National actors, directors, designers, administrators, stage and front-of-house staff to schools all over the country to spread knowledge of all aspects of theatre and its techniques. Weekend workshops and summer schools are held at the theatre for teachers, students and enthusiasts. With a home-raised budget of £500,000 a year, the National can hardly be accused of neglecting its missionary duties to the young.

When the Cottesloe reopened in late 1985, it did so with a Festival of New Plays, all of them developed from first reading to performance at the National Theatre's new Studio located at the Old Vic Annexe, owned, like the Old Vic itself, by Ed Mirvish, the grocery millionaire and theatre patron from Toronto. He offered it to the National rent-free. Peter Gill was appointed the Studio's first director in 1984. A talented playwright himself, a former Royal Court director and founder of Riverside Studios, he quickly established the Studio as the National's 'new writing' arm, which finds and commissions new plays. Every script submitted is considered by Gill and his assistant John Burgess, and any playwright of promise is offered a reading by a cast of National players. If still promising enough, the work becomes a Studio project, worked on by a director and cast and performed as work in progress to an invited audience of about seventy in the Studio's own performance space. The next stage may be a 'Studio Night' at the Cottesloe before a paying audience, including one or two invited critics. From this process have emerged *Apart from George*, Nick Ward's tragedy about a farm labourer's family set in the Fen country, the same author's *The Strangeness of Others*, Peter Gill's own *Mean Tears*, and Jim Cartwright's *Bed*, which all played in the repertory at the Cottesloe, the Edinburgh Festival or on tour. Tony Harrison's *The Trackers of Oxyrhyncus* began as a Studio production. As a writer's gymnasium, the Studio probably outdoes anything on the Fringe. It is also an exercise gymnasium for the acting company, offering classes for voice and movement and some master classes like one given by the veteran Gwen Ffrangcon-Davies on playing Juliet. Peter Gill regards it as 'a department of the theatre, like the wardrobe'. There is now a group of writers who are encouraged with Studio commissions worth £1,000. There is a writer-in-residence and part of the remit is to find new directors. Directors use the Studio as a workshop for their current productions before putting them into rehearsal and this is done without drawing on the Arts Council grant. Funding is from the National Theatre Foundation and Sainsbury's contribution.

In 1986 the moribund touring side of the National was shaken up by the arrival of Thelma Holt, a producer legendary in her ability to fix the seemingly impossible, who had earlier rescued the Roundhouse. National companies, whose foreign visits had recently been confined to sporadic appearances at festivals, spent seventeen weeks overseas under her aegis in 1986. As a reward Peter Hall invited her to stage an international season in the Lyttleton, of the kind that had not been seen since the World Theatre Seasons mounted by Peter Daubeny at the Aldwych Theatre in the sixties. She went out and raised the funds from her old benefactors at the Roundhouse, the newspaper tycoon, Robert Maxwell, and Cyril Stein, chairman of the Ladbroke leisure group. She scoured world theatre and constructed a season which revived the international status of London and of the National, which in Olivier's day had played host to the Berliner Ensemble and to Jean-Louis Barrault. Now the first visiting company, the Berlin Schaubühne directed by the redoubtable Peter Stein, caused a sensation with its production of O'Neill's *The Hairy Ape*, set on an ocean liner which was built on stage. It took nine days to learn to erect it in the Lyttleton and one hour forty-five minutes to change the scene between acts to begin with. The effect was awesome and opened people's eyes to the scale of the work that more generously state-supported theatres in other countries could do. Ingmar Bergman's Royal Dramatic Theatre from Stockholm, the Ninagawa Company from Japan (with an astonishing *Macbeth*), and the Mayakovsky Theatre from Moscow, for which Vanessa Redgrave spoke the simultaneous translation, made up the season. All the performances were packed, even the *Medea* of Euripides done in Japanese, which gave the lie to English audiences' reputation for insularity of taste. A second season two years later brought over, among others, the Moscow Art Theatre, with Innokenty Smoktunovsky as Uncle Vanya, and the Steppenwolf Theatre Company from Chicago, followed in 1990 by companies from Bucharest and Taiwan.

Meanwhile the building continues to be used far more fully than any other theatre through its programme of 'extras' – early evening performances and talks and exhibitions in the extensive gallery spaces upstairs. There have been over 1,700 'platform' performances as preludes to the evening's plays. Since they were inaugurated by Michael Kustow in 1976, they have brought such authors, or theatre personalities as Arthur Miller, Alan Ayckbourn, Germaine Greer, Stephen Sondheim and Peter Brook before packed audiences, which put questions to them. Short plays and one-man shows have been given, including Simon Callow's reading of all of Shakespeare's Sonnets and Beckett's *Rockaby*, performed by Billie Whitelaw. National theatre-goers can count on its bookshop to stock and display texts of all the plays and playwrights currently being performed as well as programmes and posters for current productions. These have been of consistently high quality throughout the theatre's lifetime, under the supervision of John Goodwin and Lyn Haill. Programmes are, in fact, a profitable sideline, bringing in some £20,000 a year in advertising revenue, while offering a great deal of useful information. Few theatres do them so well.

Peter Hall's last full year as Director, 1987, was a vintage one to be ranked alongside 1982 and 1985 in artistic achievement. Hall's own main production, *Antony and Cleopatra*, showed him back on his best Shakespearean form. It was probably better than anything he had done since he directed at Stratford. He had asked Judi Dench to play Cleopatra at the right time, in her forties, and she gave full value to Cleopatra's overripe charms. In her unforgettable fury at the news of Antony's marriage to Octavia, the depredations of time showed cruelly on the temptress's face. But age had not withered her. The lasting impression of her performance was its speed, its dazzling reversals of mood and its carnality – the deep-throated, darkly inviting voice and husky laugh ('using the gravel' as she put it), giving way in the last act to a voluptuous embrace with death in the form of an evidently living asp (non-poisonous variety). It was a Cleopatra which filled the Olivier to capacity for 100 performances, won all the appropriate awards and was compared by those who saw both with the Cleopatra of Peggy Ashcroft, Dench's mentor, example and friend, at Stratford in 1953.

If a great Cleopatra is rare, so is a great Antony. The full charisma of the role somehow eluded Anthony Hopkins, who at an early stage said he couldn't do it. He had the punch-drunk stupor of a great fighter gone to seed ('somnambulant' was the word more than one critic found for him), but the overall effect suggested an exhausted volcano, flickering but no longer spewing fire or capable of a really dangerous eruption. It was one thing to play Antony as a drunk, but more of the Antony who is occasionally sober, clearsighted and appalled at himself could have been wished for. Sadly, Hopkins had fallen a victim to the National's exorbitant demands on its leading players, which Finney and McKellen had suffered before him. The Hopkins years, which began when *Pravda* brought him back to the stage for the first time in a decade, were for the National the return of the prodigal who had thrown away his earlier success by walking out on *Macbeth* in Olivier's day. What should follow his triumph as Lambert Le Roux but Shakespeare? Not one great tragic lead but two were meted out to him. *King Lear* is taxing enough, but to play Lear while learning and rehearsing Antony and then to play 100 performances of each in repertory is not merely heroic, but foolhardy. It was the longest run of *Lear* yet given in London. Hopkins confessed that for a long time he simply could not get Antony's lines to stick. By the time he was ready to play both roles he was tired. By the time he had performed record-breaking centuries in both parts, he was exhausted and disillusioned. In retrospect he dismissed his Lear as 'a disaster', Antony as 'a dreadful part – you just lumber around the stage in a bad temper and then die', and Shakespeare as an 'overdone' playwright whose work he 'loathed' and was 'just not good at'. This was jaundiced over-reaction, but his term at the National, which began as a revelation, ended unhappily as a disappointment. The *Lear*, directed by David Hare, also making his first foray into Shakespeare at the National, was indeed a production easily forgotten – although it played to 100 full houses and was partly redeemed by Michael Bryant's affecting and natural Gloucester. It aroused some very harsh criticism, the harshest coming from Robin Ray writing in *Punch*: 'Coming from the National Theatre, this slipshod, smug and insolent production reduces me to stunned incoherence – but for that, I could write such things – what they are, yet I know not, but they should be the terrors of the earth.'

This, too, was overstatement but it could not be applied to *Antony and Cleopatra*, which, for once, received a production of exemplary clarity that overcame nearly all the notorious difficulties of staging it and made thrilling and daring use of the entire Olivier auditorium. The battle scenes exploded as if stereophonically all around the audience making use of every Olivier entry and exit, balcony and projection. The play was almost uncut, nearly four hours in playing time, but the pace was neither forced nor dragging and the verse was given extra clarity and rhythm, especially notable in the often underplayed minor parts (there are thirty-six speaking roles). The Octavius, trembling with white-faced tension and neurosis was Tim Pigott-Smith and the Enobarbus was one of Michael Bryant's shrewdest and canniest performances, a deceptively plain man. 'The barge she sat in' he daringly delivered seated at ease in the manner of one of Kipling's old sweats, retailing an almost laughably exotic incident from his overseas service which he had told many times before. But as the power of the imagery took a grip on both speaker and audience, marvelling replaced amusement. This, together with Cleopatra's ravaged, obsessed lamentations for her Antony, gave this great composition its full symphonic impact. It was worth having a National Theatre simply in order to experience it. Really authoritative productions of Shakespeare had been rare on the South Bank, but here was one to put in the record book, garlanded as it was with awards.

The other mainstay of the 1987 season was the company formed by Alan Ayckbourn, who had long experience in directing his 300-seat Theatre in the Round at Scarborough. Ayckbourn began by enlisting Michael Gambon, who readily agreed to play the minor part of the butler in the early Aldwych farce *Tons of Money*, coupled with the lead in a new Ayckbourn yet to be written, which turned out to be *A Small Family Business*. As a third play, for the Cottesloe, they chose in contrast Arthur Miller's sombre tragedy, *A View From The Bridge*. 'After Gambon's agreeing to big and small parts, it was much easier to approach other actors and persuade them to do likewise, to assemble a real company and not a West End two-stars-and-the-rest affair,' explained Ayckbourn. One of the biggest successes of that year, *A Small Family Business* was written, in Ayckbourn's words, 'to conquer the wastes of the Olivier'. An open-fronted two-storey house with elaborate detailing filled the stage. By now the critical voices which once regarded Ayckbourn as too 'commercial' a playwright had fallen silent as his plays grew darker. The small family furniture business in which Jack McCracken (Gambon) takes such pride is progressively revealed to be riddled with corruption. The play could be read as an allegory about contemporary materialistic values, which put profits before people.

Gambon's performance as Eddie Carbone in *A View From The Bridge* took audiences by the throat by its sheer size and emotional devastation. The second act in which the obsessed simple-minded giant of a stevedore stumbles blindly forward to an inexorable tragedy brought the audience to its feet cheering on the first night. 'Thanks to Alan's speedy direction, we got it up into the air,' Gambon recalled. 'I came off to find him in tears of relief and joy that we'd done it.' His performance sold out the transfer to the West End and was described by Arthur Miller as the best Eddie he had seen. Having begun as a spear-carrying walk-on, he had attained that stature thanks mainly to the chances the National had given him, in Pinter, Brecht, Ayckbourn and now Miller. Miller's revived reputation also owed much to the National, this being the fourth of his plays to be given there. Ayckbourn acknowledged that the National had transformed his career. 'It enabled me to write on an ambitious scale for bigger casts than I had ever been able to use before.' As a director, he summarized the experience of working there as 'the excitement of playing in the big league', but he was happy to return to his 300 seats at Scarborough at the end of it.

The National's first attempt at the Beckett masterpiece, *Waiting for Godot*, whose production thirty-two years earlier on the tiny Arts Theatre stage had first brought Peter Hall's name to public attention, was entrusted to Michael Rudman. He had already returned to direct Pinero's farce, *The Magistrate*, with Nigel Hawthorne giving a performance as Mr Poskett, the delinquent JP, of comic desperation. *Godot* put the director and designer, William Dudley, to a severe test. How could you maintain the play's intimate claustrophobic character on the yawning Lyttleton stage? Dudley's solution was to devote three-quarters of it to a landscape of bare uneven earth, rising to a ridge traversed by a main road going who-knew-where. Vladimir and Estragon, two boulders and the single tree were all confined into a small acting area downstage. The wasteland came into its own when the small boy sent by Godot appeared in the far distance and traversed it with agonizing slowness on a zig-zag path while they watched him in total silence. His message delivered – that M. Godot cannot come today – he turned and plodded slowly back. As Estragon, Alec McCowen made a renewed impact at the National (it was fifteen years since *The Misanthrope*). In his crushed top hat, with hollow cheeks, pale glittering eyes, an undernourished moustache, he had the fragile look of mortality, as though he might at any time crumple up like paper and be blown away into the void. John Alderton's Vladimir, by contrast, was all clumsy earthiness and their clowning was a desperate stratagem to fill their spiritual vacuum. They sometimes felt, strangely, that they were not alone. 'From time to time we were conscious that our dialogue was accompanied by a mysterious voice, up above us, which seemed to answer us back, although we could not make out what it said,' McCowen recalled. One day they learned that a real tramp was dossing up above them in the fly tower. 'Looking down from his lodging in the flies, he saw us whom he took to be fellow tramps talking to each other and decided to join in. We thought at first it might be Godot himself.' Beckett would probably have enjoyed this development of the play.

In 1987 the National collected twenty-two theatre awards (its total is higher than any other theatre's). At the end of it Hall announced that his farewell production would be 'The Three Late Shakespeares' in 1988. He proposed to produce *The Winter's Tale*, *Cymbeline* and *The Tempest* simultaneously, with the same company playing each. The plays, with many themes in common, were written during 1611–12 for performance in Burbage's indoor theatre at Blackfriars, which was about the size of the Cottesloe. The ambitiousness of the project was typical of Hall, a stroke of *hubris*. It is difficult enough to cross-cast all three plays from the same company and more difficult for actors to learn and rehearse three such demanding texts simultaneously. This became apparent as rehearsals proceeded and the actors laid down their books. Tim Pigott-Smith, who was playing both Iachimo and Leontes, broke off in a *Cymbeline* rehearsal to ask, 'Where does that line come from – or is it in *The Winter's Tale*? My mind is a hotch-potch of jumbled lines.' Hall devoted a lot of his rehearsal time to his favourite pursuit, teaching Shakespearean verse-speaking. He emphasized Hamlet's advice to the players – to speak it trippingly on the tongue – picking up the half-lines and observing line endings. 'I don't like slow Shakespeare,' he insisted. His devotion to 'text, text, text, before anything else' persuaded him not to cut a single line, even from *Cymbeline* which plays three and a quarter hours. To begin with, he was not intending to allow intervals. The desk of the ASM at rehearsals was piled with alternative texts – one in the original spelling, one with the Quarto variants, and a facsimile of the First Folio, frequently called upon. 'Does the Folio say Britain or Brittany? . . . Does the Folio give that entrance there?' 'Look in the Folio' became a refrain.

Hall's Shakespearean mentors included George Rylands at Cambridge, Edith Evans, John Gielgud and Peggy Ashcroft. 'To speak immodestly, there's a lot to pass on,' he said. Not everyone appreciated it, the silver-tongued veteran Robert Eddison for one. 'I'm not accustomed to being corrected on every line but I'm getting used to it,' he commented wryly in an early rehearsal – but soon afterwards he withdrew from the cast. Meanwhile, actors who were doing their best to absorb Hall's tutelage were distracted in the early weeks by the television crew that accompanied his every move. They were shooting a lengthy programme on Hall at work, down to the bottles of mineral water and the long, slim Romeo and Juliet cigars that sustained him. The crew followed him up on to the raised rehearsal stage so the actors saw advancing upon them not only their director but, over his shoulder, a hand-held camera, microphone boom, television director and crewmen manipulating cable or dropping heavy pieces of equipment. It cannot have improved their concentration. Another distraction that even Peter Hall may have found excessive was that in the middle of it all he was simultaneously rehearsing his wife in *Salome* at Covent Garden. His full life for a time encompassed *Salome* in the mornings and the three Shakespeare plays in the afternoons and evenings.

The part of Imogen – or Innogen, as Hall pedantically insisted on calling her – was recast less than a month before the opening night of *Cymbeline*. Sarah Miles, whose career had been devoted to films for fifteen years, had been persuaded at Hall's insistence to take on one of the longest female roles in Shakespeare just before rehearsals began (the actress originally cast had pulled out for family reasons). It was another of his long-odds gambles and he took an unconscionable time to decide that it was not a winning one. After he announced his change of mind by means of a bald telephone call dismissing her, Sarah Miles not surprisingly gave public vent to her distress. Why did he insist on keeping her in the part for so long? He once admitted to me that he was hoping for a miracle. The desire to play the miracle-worker, to pull the unlikeliest chestnuts out of the fire with Svengali-like skill, was not a sound motive to gamble a production on.

Such were the unhelpful circumstances that surrounded this ambitious, as it proved over-ambitious, experiment, such as only a national theatre could undertake. They help to explain how it turned out to be a grievous disappointment. But the fact that the linked productions left so much to be desired was only partly due to outside pressures and distractions. Hall's singular approach to the culminating play, *The Tempest*, also played its part. In 1973, when Gielgud was his Prospero, he thought him too much of a 'nice old gentleman'. 'I wanted him to break the mould and play Prospero like an older version of Angelo – a terribly neurotic old man trying to order the mistakes of his past life and punish those who had done him wrong. He tried it but he couldn't.' Now, with Michael Bryant in the role, Hall went in for mould-breaking with a vengeance and misdirected a fine actor. Ferocious, turbulent, cantankerous, rough and disturbing . . . all these adjectives were employed to describe a Prospero whose violent urge for personal vengeance seemed so total that one could hardly believe that he ever read a book, let alone that he once thought his library was 'dukedom large enough'. This oversimplifying of one of Shakespeare's most numinous characters unbalanced the play's ambiguities, complexity and mystery and had the effect of coarsening everything else. Caliban, caked in filth and glistening with open sores, had to speak the loveliest verse in the play through a set of distorting Dracula fangs. Ariel, bawled out by his master, shrieked in return, while Miranda was shrilly censorious. The masque was so grotesque that one longed for such revels to be ended. 'We are such stuff as dreams are made on' sounded like an irritable complaint about the use of shoddy materials by the manufacturer.

Above the circular stage in all three plays hung a golden wheel or grid of concentric circles and spokes representing the heavens, with sun, moon, stars and signs of the zodiac disposed around it. This impressive but overwhelming design by Alison Chitty, sometimes compared to a celestial dartboard, could be slowly and noisily tilted at an angle to the audience but at the cost of interrupting the flow of the action. If visually the plays suffered from too much design, on the acting level they suffered from inadequate casting, apart from a few strong performances – notably Eileen Atkins as Paulina in *A Winter's Tale*, Tim Pigott-Smith's Iachimo and Geraldine James as the new Imogen. In a few instances the playing was woeful, despite the lessons in verse-speaking. The opportunity to taste three fruits of Shakespeare's final maturity as a group seemed less interesting than it might have been, since none of them was working as well as it should. The plays demand virtuosity and it was disappointing to realize that the National Theatre simply did not have enough of it available.

By the time his last productions opened, Hall was saying in interviews that he 'couldn't wait' to be gone. Fifteen years was enough for everyone. There was a general feeling that it was time for a change and that the Peter Hall era was over. His heart was already across the river in the West End where the Peter Hall Company was already announcing its first commercially backed production at Robert Adam's beautiful Theatre Royal Haymarket.

In his farewell speech to the National Theatre Company before the 'cathedral window' in the Olivier foyer, he sounded a last defiant call from the battlements: 'This building in solid concrete will be here for ever and ever, whatever successive governments can do to muck it up. The place exists as a necessary part of the cultural scene of this country. If it were taken away now, it would leave a terrible gap.' He was staking his claim to a place in theatrical history: he had established the National on the South Bank as an indispensable institution. There might not be many votes in promoting the performing arts, but there would certainly be none in closing the National down. In a country where traditionally show business is no business of the state, it was an important bridgehead to have secured. 'I've turned this place into something that the public loves,' was another of his claims in a farewell interview. From the opening of the South Bank to Hall's departure, the two main theatres were attended by audiences totalling over 7,000,000, an average of 600,000 a year. As Shaw had observed, the English people 'never want anything', whether a national theatre or a national gallery, but 'once these things stood, they felt the place would be incomplete without them'.

Hall's prime and toughest achievement had been to get the South Bank building open at all, by forcing the company into occupation of it. This took all the determination, ruthlessness and nerve for which he was noted. 'His courage and coolness in 1976 was amazing – I don't know who else could have done it,' said Alec McCowen, who was an onlooker from the wings. 'I believe no one else could have got the South Bank theatre open,' reflected Lord Rayne and Lord Mishcon echoed him: 'No one else could have taken us through those traumatic years as he did.' Going in with the building unfinished was one of Hall's calculated gambles, which on balance paid off. The price was high. For years afterwards the continuing installation of the stage machinery had to be done late at night, with the crews charging costly overtime. The flying systems and revolve might have been made to work much earlier in an empty theatre. But continued delay would have been ruinous for the morale of the National as a whole.

His next most wearing battle was with the logistics of the operation. From the day of opening, the theatre's basic problem was that no one wanted to pay the bill either for the building or for the scale of production that it was geared for. The Arts Council's constant question was 'Can't you manage it on less?' The true answer was No, and Hall went on giving it until some sort of realism obtained in government circles. But, as he was now prepared to admit, the organization was too big for comfort. To fill 2,300 seats a night, 6 nights a week, 52 weeks a year, places an enormous strain on it. It has taken up to 700 people behind the stage to put slightly more than 100 actors on it in a repertoire of 16 plays a year. John Faulkner, the Arts Council Drama Director during the first eight years on the South Bank, calculated in 1983 that for another £750,000 it could have run an additional company, produced more plays and carried out year-round touring. But that money was never there. Touring Britain, whose national theatre it was, was one objective which Hall acknowledged his inability to fulfil. Another was the exchange visits intended with the major regional theatre companies. The third frustration was of large-scale foreign visits to the National and its own visits abroad. Hall believed that with 10 per cent more funding the theatre could have done 30 per cent more, most of it in these areas.

Hall's achievements reflected his character as a risk-loving impresario. His gambling instinct produced the greatest audience successes of his time – *Guys and Dolls* and *Amadeus* – and the biggest mistakes, most obviously *Jean Seberg*, on which he staked more and more of the National's resources as its chances of success receded before him. His taste for public controversy led him astray over *The Romans in Britain* and *Yonadab*. And over-ambition in too much haste marred the three late Shakespeares. But the National also had many fine examples to show of his work as a director.

His worst failing was his inability to stick to running one theatre. He used to reply that he was always reachable by telephone, even if it required an international call to New York or Bayreuth – while Glyndebourne was only a two-hour journey from his desk. If he really believed that none of this mattered to the National team he headed or to the results in the theatre, he was being naive. An army in the field needs to see its commander, not just receive its orders by long-distance telephone. He never appointed a plenipotentiary substitute. So his lieutenants were left with no one with whom to hammer out their disagreements. David Hare, who in other respects admired Hall's leadership, recalled, 'It used to drive us nuts that he was not there to allocate time and resources and to resolve conflicts. You cannot do his job with your left hand only.' It was this rumbling of discontent that prompted the *Sunday Times* to investigate the complaints of absenteeism, among other things. They got the reasons for it wrong. Hall was not doing too much out of financial greed, even if his extravagance, mainly in wives and children, was a strain on his income. He was doing it out of hunger to be directing all the time, especially opera. 'My idea of happiness is to have a Shakespeare play and a Mozart/da Ponte opera to direct every year,' he confessed, but that was nothing like enough. During his later years at the National he had another spur – the demands of the highly-talented opera singer, Maria Ewing, to whom he was then married. He even missed one of his own first nights in order to be present at one of hers. The desire to move, as versatile freelance directors do, from drama to opera and back again, did not combine well with running the biggest theatre complex in the country.

After it was over, he reflected, 'I don't feel that I let the National down in any way. *I didn't make a film.* That occupies the whole of your day and the whole of your mind. But directing an opera doesn't.' Like Bottom the Weaver, who wanted to play the lion's part as well as his own, his attitude was defiant, not repentant: 'I do a lot of things. That's

the kind of animal I am. If you don't like the way I operate, don't hire me.' The National Theatre suffered the consequences. It also reaped the benefits of such unabashed egotism. It enabled Hall to fight on when every man's hand seemed to be against him and the theatre. He not only endured opposition, he gave the organization an aggressive, innovative edge instead of playing safe. Of his 25 productions, a third were memorable – ranging from *No Man's Land* and *Amadeus* to the *Oresteia* and *Antony and Cleopatra*. Those which did not rise to his best level perhaps owed that mainly to the fact that he was so busy. No captain of a flagship as big as the National could afford to spend as much time away from the bridge, down in the engine room, as he wanted to. In retrospect, splitting the job between two men looked inevitable. Perhaps no one man will again attempt to do what Hall did, for the most part, with great success.

17

Our Royal and Revolving Theatre

Hard upon Peter Hall's heels, Lord Rayne departed at the end of the year, to be succeeded as Chairman by Lady Soames (Mary Churchill in earlier life). Since first invited to serve as chairman by Jennie Lee, Max Rayne had offered his resignation to every new minister for the arts and had invariably been asked to stay on, whatever the political complexion of the Government. Coupled with other changes in the Board's composition, notably the dropping of the libertarian John Mortimer, the changes showed that an era was ending at the National. Rayne, like Hall, did not share the Government's enthusiasm for sponsorship and said so to the Arts Council and the Minister. Now, having seen out both Olivier and Hall, he found after seventeen years that his time was also up. Like Olivier, he both wanted to go and hated the thought of it. 'I shall miss it terribly,' he confessed. He had played a much larger part in the theatre's development than was generally realized. While Hall attracted the limelight, Rayne assiduously avoided it, happy to operate in Hall's shadow. There has to be a good working partnership between the Director and the Chairman, who is the theatre's link with the Arts Council, the Minister and his department, the Office of Arts and Libraries. The Chairman and members of the Board are also legally responsible for the solvency – or the debts – of an organization which had no reserves or assets on which to raise money. Unlike Hall, by temperament a big spender, Rayne told me, 'I come from a background where I don't like spending money I don't have. I wasn't always convinced that we couldn't manage on a little less than he was asking for.' Himself a seriously rich man, he did not begrudge Hall's high remuneration and generous allowance of outside work – at first. In any case he felt hamstrung by the precedent set by Olivier. Successive revisions in the terms on which Hall's contract was renewed had limited the amount of outside earnings he was entitled to keep. But with his successor Richard Eyre, Rayne could at last change the formula: the

services of the director were henceforward to be exclusive to the theatre, with provision for a sabbatical leave.

What was important to Rayne was keeping Hall, whose abilities he greatly respected, from open rebellion. Hall's threat to resign if overruled kept the Board's rein very loose. 'I don't think we ever said "No, you can't do that" about anything,' Rayne recalled. This applied even to the issues of blasphemy, obscenity and *lèse-majesté* on which Rayne had expressly reserved the right to say No. He was no Chandos: he was not going to ride roughshod over his artistic executive on matters held to be artistic, even *Jean Seberg*. Rayne's Board lacked theatrical expertise to a surprising degree. Except for one playwright, John Mortimer, and Richard Mills, of the Bernard Delfont organization, its members could claim no inside knowledge of show-business, which was the business it was in. Theatre professionals were unlikely to be impressed by its artistic opinion. The restructuring of the Board when Rayne left brought in another theatrical manager, Michael Codron, a playwright, Tom Stoppard, and at last an actor, Dame Judi Dench, a timely addition of expertise.

It was Rayne's fate to be confronted with an instance of possible *lèse-majesté*, at the very end of his chairmanship and the very beginning of Richard Eyre's term as director. Rayne had renewed his request for 'Royal' to be added to the National Theatre's title for its 25th anniversary and the Palace had agreed to it. Rayne was looking forward to welcoming the Queen at a 25th anniversary gala for the theatre when he discovered that she was about to be impersonated on its stage – an unprecedented liberty to take – in Alan Bennett's short play *A Question of Attribution*. Amazingly, nobody thought it necessary to warn Rayne in advance about the scene in which Sir Anthony Blunt, the former spy who was keeper of the royal pictures, is confronted by his employer in a palace corridor. In so far as his mild manner allowed, Rayne hit the roof. Eyre explained that he had never seen anything to object to in the scene. I knew there wouldn't be a murmur of complaint about it.' Rayne accepted his assurance and took the risk – but not before they had had a 'lively debate' (Eyre's phrase). For about two weeks the fate of the play hung in the balance. Eyre consulted his predecessor for advice on what to do if the Board banned it. Hall advocated his usual tactic – threatened resignation.

It did not come to that. Banning the play would be certain to cause an outcry. It was allowed to proceed in rehearsal, very, very secretly and – amazingly – news of it never leaked out. Unprepared for this theatrical breakthrough – imagine the Lord Chamberlain in years gone by allowing the impersonation of his employer on the stage! – the preview audiences almost audibly gasped at their first sight of Prunella Scales's very convincing characterization of the theatre's patron. They then proceeded to laugh with delight at Bennett's subtly written and far from impudent scene. Whether the original herself was Amused, or definitely Not Amused, is a well-kept secret. When application was made to the Palace for permission to reproduce a painting from the Royal Collection in the programme, the answer was 'In the circumstances, no.'

Knowing nothing of all this at the time, the Queen attended the Royal Gala on 27 October 1988. It was the 25th anniversary of the National Theatre's opening at the Old Vic in 1963 and the 12th of her opening of the South Bank building in 1976. On that occasion it was *Il Campiello*; on this it was Peter Hall's production of *The Tempest*. Small wonder, somebody commented, that she did not come more often. That night people were paying £250 for the best seats; even to sit in the outer darkness at the back of the circle cost £50. The money was to begin a new National Theatre Endowment Fund, Rayne's parting inspiration. With the proceeds of previous royal premières he had set up the National Theatre Foundation. The Endowment Fund was to provide the Theatre for the first time with a capital reserve, as a safety margin and a source of income. He raised a very considerable sum of £1,200,000 by simply writing to donors and asking for contributions of not less than £25,000 over five years. The scale of the response was a mark of respect for his chairmanship. Rayne conducted the Queen into a flower-bedecked foyer where the partygoers included the unfamiliar figures (in that setting) of the Arts Minister Mr Richard Luce and the retiring Arts Council Chairman William, now Lord, Rees-Mogg. Hall, Eyre, Aukin, but not, alas, Olivier were on hand as royal greeters. Twenty-five people represented each of the years that had elapsed since 1963. Several of the Old Vic names were comparative strangers to the South Bank, in which their talents had been used rarely, or not at all. It was a sign of times that even the theatre's birthday party was sponsored.

The augmented title of 'Royal National Theatre', inscribed on a new plaque unveiled by the Queen in the foyer and incorporated unobtrusively in the logo on all publicity, was not embraced with noticeable fervour by most people who worked there. Many of them actively disliked the change and thought it inappropriate to a theatre which should be populist, not privileged. Some people thought that one royal theatre company was enough (not that it had done the RSC's popularity any harm). But the RNT? Would it one day be known as that? It hardly seemed conceivable at that moment.

For all the royal junketing, Eyre and Aukin's regime at the National began quietly, almost dully, but at least it was crisis-free. It took until the second season to build up the feeling that the National was running smoothly on a new, potentially exciting course. But the changeover was noticed within the building. The group system was abandoned and the company became a single body again, appearing in the Olivier and the Cottesloe, while the Lyttleton was given over to individually-cast new plays and visiting productions. The number of associates was reduced from twenty-four to a small group including no more than nine directors. 'Theatres are old-fashioned structures. This large complex needs a common aim under a titular head,' Eyre explained. 'Having five companies was divisive. It also made for an unbalanced repertoire.' The change of leadership style was marked in two ways. Publicly there were no more press conferences or impassioned protests about government funding. Eyre's tactic was to be low-profile. Privately, the company was aware of having a highly visible, casual-seeming director who was approachable and knew just about everybody's name. He abolished the sending of memos in favour of face-to-face meetings.

But it was some time before Eyre found his touch as a director on the stages. He inherited from the previous season *The Shaughraun*, a nineteenth-century Irish melodrama by Dion Boucicault of damsels in the thrall of an arch-villain, defeated by two Irish scamps (the Shaughraun and his dog). This pair were given winning performances by Stephen Rea and the genuine 'Scamp'. But the star of the show was undoubtedly the Olivier stage revolve, rescued from twelve years of inertia and put to spectacular use by designer William Dudley. 'I had asked for a demonstration. I was astonished at its speed, silence and sophistication and was smitten with the desire to use it.' Spectacular effects were made by combining the revolve with its semicircular lifts so that as it swung round, it simultaneously swung the next setting up from the bowels of the under-stage. As rocky exteriors and Gothic ruins of County Sligo came into view, shrouded in smoke and dry ice, the stage resembled a piece of kinetic sculpture. Said Dudley afterwards, 'We have only scratched the surface of what it can do.' At least the production proved that the darn thing worked (except on rare nights when it didn't). It also showed the danger that revolving scenery can upstage the actors. The rollicking melodrama, done with all the polish and production values which the National is capable of devoting to what is really no more than a quaint period trifle, became so popular that it was brought back again and again as a mainstay of the repertoire. So at last there was a return on the huge investment which had been sunk in the revolve – variously estimated at from £500,000 to £750,000.

Each new artistic director feels called upon to do a *Hamlet* and it seems doomed to be an inevitable disappointment. Eyre's production was to prove as dramatic off-stage as on. He had cast the most exciting of the younger generation of film actors as the Prince. Daniel Day-

Lewis came to this most testing stage role straight from filming his Oscar-winning performance as the crippled writer, Christy Brown, in *My Left Foot*. He looked every inch the Byronic, intelligent, neurotic, dangerous Hamlet of popular imagination, but his performance was too uncontrolled (and under-directed) to be as effective as it promised to be. His energy, fury and fits of quivering emotion sometimes overcame clarity and audibility; he received some reproving reviews. There were good things in Eyre's production – Michael Bryant's Polonius, a monument of deaf complacency, was one. John Gunter's overpowering battlements and sliding walls and corridors were effectively claustrophobic. But the casting was so uneven and the central performance so highly strung that the production as a whole felt worryingly precarious and uncertain from scene to scene, although it pulled in the audiences.

Real-life drama struck it after sixty-five performances. Day-Lewis, whose father the poet-laureate, Cecil Day-Lewis, had died when he was fourteen, had been increasingly troubled by the psychological demands of the scenes with Hamlet's ghostly father and had begun to imagine he was encountering his own – as other Hamlets had done before him. On this occasion, after his confrontation with the ghost he froze and was unable to continue the performance. A new cast was already preparing to take over the production, but by the time it did so, Ian Charleson, the new Hamlet, had discovered himself to be HIV positive. With only his fellow-actors aware of this, he went on to give performances of extraordinary power, surely the first Hamlet to play the part knowingly facing his own death. 'He played for three and three-quarter hours every night, dying, and came off, joking,' said Michael Bryant in tribute to Charleson's courage. He died of AIDs shockingly soon afterwards.

Eyre's contacts with playwrights were already close and he had a varied hand of new plays to present. David Hare provided two of the most successful: *The Secret Rapture*, a morality play for three women members of a family at odds, and *Racing Demon*, a morality play for four clergymen jointly running an inner city parish and questioning the objects of their mission. *The Secret Rapture* had a strong feeling of the late nineteen-eighties, not least because of the contrast it draws between a hard-headed, competitive female politician with a Thatcherite philosophy and her sister, who insists on putting personal relations above profit. *Racing Demon* was staged on an immensely long cruciform stage (first in the Cottesloe, later the Olivier) which served as church, vicarage and even the anteroom to the Savoy Grill, where bishops gather for planning lunches while some of the junior clergy let themselves go on Tequila Sunrises. Hare took his exploration of issues confronting the Church of England well outside the pews and pulpits.

He presented clergy as human beings in conflict with one another rather than as subscribers to a woolly brotherhood in Christ. His briskly handled scenes showed a new confidence and sureness of technique. It was a funny play as well as a searching one, on a theme hardly touched on in contemporary drama. Its immediate sell-out popularity (followed by transfer to the Olivier) showed how well he had judged a new desire to hear spiritual issues debated on the stage, as well as political and material themes. He was criticized for writing on the subject from the standpoint of a non-believer, who could not possibly understand the motives of his characters. It could be argued just as well that only a non-believer could write about crises in faith in terms that made sense to an audience that was itself largely uncommitted. Preaching to the converted would only be effective if there were enough of the converted to fill the theatre. A set of excellent performances in which many types of churchmen were convincingly embodied distinguished Eyre's production, which moved the debate along with speed and excitement. By now Hare's position as a National Theatre playwright was pre-eminent and his stage output was entirely written for the South Bank. 'As a playwright, I see this place as a great opportunity to use the same resources that are used in major classical productions.' It used to be said of writing stage plays, 'You can make a killing but you can't make a living.' Now, thanks to subsidized theatres like the National and RSC, says Hare, a playwright can make a living.

Besides David Hare's and Alan Bennett's popular successes, Nicholas Wright, the retiring literary manager of the theatre, scored an intellectual *succès d'estime* with *Mrs Klein*, a study of the Freudian child analyst, Melanie Klein, her estranged daughter and her most fervent woman disciple, locked in rivalry. There was also the return of Harold Pinter, who had become lost to the National during the Peter Hall regime, with a short – too short – and bleak political piece, *Mountain Language*. Abrupt, brutal and Orwellian, it depicts the enforcement of a rule of terror in an unnamed country, where the oppressed are forbidden to use their native language in order to deprive them of any vehicle of protest, even of rebellious thought. David Storey, unpro-duced at the National except for *Early Days* in Ralph Richardson's time, returned with a poetic play, *Jubilee* (first entitled *The March on Russia*). The apparent banality of a Yorkshire family gathering for a diamond wedding at a miner's cosy retirement bungalow on the edge of the moors was the occasion for the slow revelation of a whole past world and way of life. Unshowy but painfully three-dimensional perfor-mances by Bill Owen and Constance Chapman as the couple, nearing the end of their long march yoked together by a mixture of habit, resentment and remembered fondness, generated a rare depth of emotion which filled the impersonal Lyttleton with the still, sad music of humanity. Other new plays included an uncharacteristic David Mamet comedy about Hollywood, *Speed the Plow*, and Joshua Sobol's *Ghetto*, a portrayal of how the heroic, doomed Jewish community of Vilna, Lithuania, and its theatre troupe faced the onset of the Holocaust.

Perhaps the oddest new play, and the most surprising hit, was *The Trackers of Oxyrhyncus*, which Tony Harrison wrote in order to incorporate the fragment of a 'new' play by Sophocles discovered at Oxyrhyncus, a site in Upper Egypt where a whole rubbish heap of ancient Greek writings have been preserved by the aridity of the climate. It was not a tragedy, to place alongside *Oedipus Rex*, but a satyr play, written to round off a trilogy of tragedies and release the audience's emotions. Led by Silenus, the chorus of half-human satyrs took over the Olivier stage with deafening clog-dances, erect phalluses grotesquely waving, and routines and choruses of cheerful rudery that would have done credit to a rugby club. They proved that the sort of ribald and earthy enjoyment that the play provoked in 450 BC is timeless. Harrison's play, which encapsulated Sophocles' lines, debated the cultural gulf which has arisen since Greek times between high and low art, between Apollo's elitists and the satyrs as representatives of populist culture. The fact that his play attracted enthusiastic full houses suggested that the gulf is not as wide as he painted it, after all.

Eyre had brought in a good deal of new directorial blood, beginning with Howard Davies, who was responsible for the filmlike chases in *The Shaughraun*, and for an excellent *Hedda Gabler*, newly adapted by Christopher Hampton, with Juliet Stevenson as a convincingly contemporary-sounding Hedda. The setting by Bob Crowley attempted to create the suffocation of the Tesmans' house in the Olivier with two levels, an upstairs gallery leading to a curving staircase, with iron railings, against which she rattled her pistol as she made her most dramatic entrance. Nicholas Hytner, a young lion of the RSC, did the award-winning production of *Ghetto*, and Deborah Warner, also from the RSC, directed Brecht's *The Good Person of Szechuan*, with an award-winning performance in the dual leading role from Fiona Shaw.

Fuente Ovejuna, which is one of 314 surviving plays by Lope de Vega, is named after a Cordoban town which defied the high-handed oppression of its local grandee in 1476. Resurrected by Adrian Mitchell like a new text, it was the first production for the National by the producing team of Cheek by Jowl, the fringe company, Declan Donellan, and his designer Nick Ormerod. The movement down the whole length of the Cottesloe by the increasingly confident citizens and the evoking of a town seething with rebellion out of a few sticks of furniture was magical; it became an award-winning hit of the season. Donellan and Ormerod went on to create the National's first *Peer Gynt*.

But Eyre did not only engage the new wave, he sensibly invited back some of the directors who had made the Old Vic National what it was. First to return was Lindsay Anderson, one of the Royal Court contingent along with Gaskill and Dexter. He came as the acknowledged expert collaborator with David Storey to direct his new play. He was followed by Gaskill himself, whose appearance under the Peter Hall regime had been minimal. Pirandello's *Man, Beast and Virtue*, a farcical parable of the ironies of sexual pretence, was given a new translation by Charles Wood and an engagingly mannered and manic production by Gaskill. The climax was the painting of the wife in the crude make-up of a sailor's tart, in order to preserve her virtue by tempting her sea-captain husband into bed on his one night of shore leave – and thus account for her irregular pregnancy.

Last of the Old Vic stalwarts to return (for Dexter had already died untimely) was Michael Blakemore. He directed *After The Fall*, part of the celebration of the 75th year of Arthur Miller, who had become the most-produced living playwright at the National. This production and one by Howard Davies of *The Crucible*, put Miller's two most controversial plays before audiences side by side, an unprecedented homage to a playwright. Miller had become a familiar figure around the theatre, attending rehearsals and previews of his work. Not a man to wax lyrical easily, he described the National to me as 'one of the glories of Britain – a demonstration of what civilization can do. To allow it to be destroyed would be to make a mockery of the pretensions of your culture to exist. If the subsidy is in danger, you could be left with what we are left with in America – the end of theatre culture. The commercial theatre in New York is a sensational theatre, operating on the basis that everything it does must run for years. The National can afford to present plays for what they are, instead of being a show-shop. It has a flexibility which no commercial management can dream of. It's the only place in the English-speaking theatre where minor roles as well as major ones are taken by first-class actors. This is a great advantage from a playwright's point of view.'

The standards of classic revival, which had been slipping, were restored by Peter Wood, who had demonstrated his ease and confidence with Restoration and eighteenth-century texts, both under Olivier (*Love for Love*) and Hall (*The Double Dealer, The Provok'd Wife* and *The Rivals*). After staging an elegant touring production of *The Beaux' Stratagem*, he was immediately asked to direct Sheridan's masterpiece, *The School for Scandal*. He agreed on condition that John Neville played

Sir Peter Teazle. Neville, star of the Old Vic in the fifties, had been absent from the English stage in Canada for the past eighteen years. This proved the overdue occasion to lure him back. (Eyre had worked under Neville at Nottingham Playhouse in the sixties.) Wood, a stickler for the traditional disciplines of classical acting, wanted Neville's 'marvellous diction' at the heart of a production which he built up by painstaking casting.

Wood's careful balancing of the malice with the geniality that is also abundant in Sheridan resulted in a stageful of humanity, both ridiculous and touching, discernible even in the most affected characters. As usual, his eye for detail ensured that even the servants were individualized. Besides Neville's combination of Teazle's exasperation with affection for his wife, and the shrewd good nature of Sir Oliver, portrayed by Denis Quilley on his first return since the South Bank opened, there was a smooth, contemporary poseur of a Joseph Surface, who might have stepped straight out of a television chat-show. Jeremy Northam, who played him, had just won an award for his promise as the priggish young hero of *The Voysey Inheritance*, Granville-Barker's plum pudding of a play about an Edwardian family who take their prodigious meals as seriously as their business and themselves, which Richard Eyre's imaginative direction had turned into a popular hit.

The *School for Scandal* set, by John Gunter, turned the stage into a Gillray cartoon. The eighteenth-century Thames skyline was a cut-out papered with contemporary scandal sheets. Scrolled balloons of gossip were being emitted from the open windows and hanging in a cloud above the stage. The production was the second to use the revolve to bring up new settings and dispose of others. It also served neatly to conduct Charles Surface round his picture gallery selling his ancestors, pausing each time before the same suspended empty picture frame to describe a different picture. The general impression was of a return to the most handsome standards of classical production combined with a modern reading of the text; the society Sheridan lampooned affectionately seemed not at all far from our own.

Perhaps the most praiseworthy feature of the Eyre regime was its determined attempt to get the National out of the South Bank bunker. By 1990 no major city with a touring theatre (with three exceptions) had seen a South Bank production for five to ten years. Touring had always been the Cinderella of its operations, partly because the Arts Council awards its grant specifically for South Bank productions only. The ability to tour depends on a further guarantee from the Council against loss and it is the Council which names the venues to be toured. In round figures it cost £50,000 a week in 1989–90 to put a National Theatre show on the road. Given a share of 65–70 per cent of the box office as visitors, it could not hope to cover costs. It was often hard to fill the big provincial Empires, Palaces and Grands (seating 1,500 to 2,000, compared to the Lyttleton's 900) with the sort of plays for which they had no regular public. For this reason some theatre managers were far from keen to book the National. The RSC, known for a much longer period for bringing top-class Shakespeare, had established its drawing power over the years. The National was a fairly unknown quantity in many cities. It had stopped touring altogether in 1986–7 while a new touring agreement was negotiated with the union that had succeeded NATTKE, now known as the Broadcasting and Entertainment Trades Alliance, or BETA. Restrictive backstage practices and special deals for touring had made it prohibitively expensive on the road, where stage-hands sometimes received three times as much as actors. The new agreement on flexible working reduced the staffing by 20 and substituted a single touring allowance, saving an estimated £340,000 yearly.

The new policy was to tour for sixteen weeks or more a year, visiting carefully chosen cities on a regular basis, such as Bath, Brighton, Bristol, Norwich, Nottingham, Wolverhampton, Bradford and Glasgow. The experiment of co-productions with major provincial repertory theatres was initiated at Bristol and Coventry. Peter Wood's *The Beaux' Stratagem* opened at the Belgrade Theatre, Coventry, for a four-week run and did a six-week tour of provincial dates before reaching the Lyttleton. It followed on the heels of *The Misanthrope*, the Tony Harrison version, produced in collaboration with the Bristol Old Vic and directed by its artistic director, Paul Unwin. By this means, regional theatres could originate productions well beyond their normal resources in terms of casting, settings and direction and get them nationally reviewed.

But the biggest development in touring was the return of Ian McKellen to lead a National company, at his own suggestion, on a world tour of two major Shakespeare productions. It was the most ambitious tour in the history of the National, beginning in Tokyo, then touring Nottingham, Cardiff, Leeds, Edinburgh, Belfast and Hamburg, Milan, Madrid, Paris, Cork, Cairo, Prague, Bucharest and Moscow. The company, twenty-three strong, were cast in *Richard III* and *King Lear*, McKellen playing Richard and Brian Cox Lear. The National was at last making good a conspicuous gap, its national and international presence. There are those who will never be reconciled to a national theatre located in London and believe it should be distributed about the entire country in smaller units. Jonathan Miller put this objection memorably: 'I wouldn't concentrate the National Theatre in one place any more than I would concentrate the

National Health Service all at St Thomas's Hospital.' Glenda Jackson put forward another vision: 'I would have opted for a very big comfortable bus, with a tent which could be inflated very quickly and had a constantly touring company.'

What had done most to prevent adequate touring in the past was partly its great expense and partly the great difficulty of taking successful shows out of the current repertoire to tour them. The way round these problems was to mount productions like these, expressly for touring, but to rehearse and launch them on the South Bank so that there was no doubt that they were part of the National Theatre and not in any sense a "B Team". The expense – over £1.25 million in this case – was met by a combination of Arts Council and British Council special funds plus major sponsorship by Guinness.

Touring, so that the whole country regards the National as its own theatre, could be as important to withstanding cuts as anything done in the theatre's London showcase. This also can be applied to sponsorship. Sir Peter Parker, Chairman of the National's Development Council of high-powered figures in industry and business, sees raising money to stop gaps in the budget as only part of its function. 'We have a government which does not see the National Theatre as a national asset. If it closed tomorrow there wouldn't be a moist eye in the cabinet. There are precious few votes in a national theatre but nowadays industry trumpets its concern for all sorts of community schemes. Sponsorship may not provide serious money in terms of our overall needs – £1 million out of a £17 million budget is only six per cent. But in raising it we are focussing the attention of British industry and commerce on the National Theatre. We are getting a constituency of boardrooms interested. In the long run that is as important to us as the money raised.'

By the spring of 1990 the National was near to being at its best again, garnering a sheaf of the annual theatre awards. At this point it risked doing another musical, Stephen Sondheim's *Sunday in the Park with George*. A show about a painting, it depended above all on its visual impact. The full depth of the Lyttleton stage (plus its equally large rear stage, normally a scene dock) came into its own in recreating the painting by Seurat (the George of the title) of parasoled and straw-hatted Parisians enjoying their Sunday afternoon on the island of La Grande Jatte on the Seine. The long perspectives of the pointillist painting were reproduced dot by dot by a team of ten scene painters, using Seurat's own palette of eleven colours, and the living picture was assembled piece by piece to reach completion at the first act curtain. As Act Two began it was hanging on the wall of the Chicago art gallery which owns it – but this too was revealed to be a *tableau vivant* which burst into song. Sondheim said it was his dream to see the musical –

which had done only moderately well on Broadway in 1984 – staged at the Lyttleton, one of the few theatres capable of illusion-building on this scale.

The show, which cost £300,000, was the first reprise in the musical field since the disaster of *Jean Seberg* and risked the same accusation of using the National for unsuitable and commercial purposes. This time there were no deals for transfers or exploitation. The show was seen purely as a National Theatre enterprise for its own sake. In fact the old charges were not made. David Aukin, whose pet project it was, argued that 'At its best, musical theatre ranks alongside straight drama and it is proper for the National to include in its repertoire the finest examples.' Sondheim carried enough artistic and intellectual prestige to justify the theatre's interest in his work. It was an original production which brought another new director, Steven Pimlott, to the National, with a beautifully detailed design by Tom Cairns. Instead of being played in repertoire, its 120 performances in the Lyttleton were a straight run. For over three months theatregoers were not offered any choice. This was contrary to the letter and spirit of the National as an institution, but its critics were silent on this theme. Indeed, criticism was noticeably indulgent to what some found a somewhat static, dare one say dull, entertainment apart from the excellence of its scenic effects. It showed, however, that musicals can more or less pay their way without benefit of a commercial transfer, although this one was helped by a substantial and unsolicited contribution of £100,000 by Cameron Mackintosh, Sondheim's producer in the West End and sponsor of his chair of musical theatre at Oxford. In June 1990 he announced a £1 million further contribution to help finance a series of 'classic' musicals at the National, beginning with *Carousel* in 1991

For some time there was more strain on the Theatre's stretched finances – grants failed to match inflation. The National suffered in unwonted public silence, by comparison with the shouts of protest that had been an annual feature of Hall's directorship. During 1989–90 there were some scary deficits accumulating in the major opera houses and at the RSC: The National too was heading for another deficit – it was estimated at £100,000 in 1989–90, although it continued to sell 80 per cent of its seats and begged a million pounds a year from its corporate patrons. This seemed modest indeed alongside the Royal Opera House deficit estimated at over £5 million or the RSC's £3 million, which led it to announce closure of the Barbican for the winter months. But it was living on a financial knife-edge and the future looked ominous. There had been a slight lifting of the clouds as 1990 began. The Arts Council, under its new Chairman, the property-developer and patron of the arts, Peter Palumbo, seemed to have found some of the fire that had too long been missing from its belly. His declaration that 'the artist is the most important member of society' had an unaccustomed ring in the prevailing money-conscious climate. He also pointed out that according to a recent poll, only 2 per cent of the population actually favoured abolishing subsidy for the arts, which currently employed 500,000 people with a turnover of £12 billion, a third of it invisible earnings for Britain. Meanwhile the chairmen of two companies which are leading arts and theatre sponsors, Barclays and Royal Insurance, made it plain that they were not prepared to make good the constant erosion of Government subsidy. They were in the business of supplementing subsidy, not providing a substitute for it.

Lady Soames, whose appointment as Chairman of the National Theatre Board had caused some surprise, not least to her ('Nobody thought it more peculiar than myself'), had within a year become an effective champion of the National. 'Enjoy it? I love it. It's gripping.' Her theatregoing, she told me, had begun in wartime when as an ATS subaltern she accompanied her father, Winston Churchill, the Prime Minister, to plays such as Terence Rattigan's *Flare Path* ('he sobbed throughout'). Now, recently widowed, she took up the National's cause with energy, creating an office for herself in the building (there had been none before) and concentrating her formidable charm and connections on the Arts Minister, Richard Luce, and Arts Council Chairman, Peter Palumbo. The Arts Minister paid an overdue day's visit to the theatre, discovering in detail what it did with the Council's money and what its problems are. Nobody knew what brought about a degree of repentance on the part of the Treasury for its tight-fisted record in the past, but for 1990 it disgorged £175 million for the Arts Council (a 12.5 per cent increase) which resulted in an 11 per cent lift in the National's subsidy. This went part of the way towards making up recent reductions. 'They suddenly realized we and the other theatres weren't crying wolf,' said David Aukin, whose own departure (for television) was announced soon afterwards. His successor, Genista McIntosh, after eighteen years' service to the R.S.C., was already a very experienced administrator and now became the most powerful woman in British theatre.

Despite the continuing inadequacy of public funding and the likelihood that sponsorship had already reached a plateau, the National entered the nineties in better heart and shape than it had known for five years. This was reflected in its work. Richard Eyre, on taking over the theatre, had bravely declared: 'The real issue is about art, not about money. The only question that matters is: Is what is on the stage any good?'

Granville-Barker and Shaw would have applauded. But they could have had no conception of the pressures in the opposite direction that would be exerted on a national theatre in the political and economic climate of the last two decades of the century. Granville-Barker had visualized a spacious, self-sufficient building – 'a self-contained factory' giving 900 performances a year in two theatres with a repertoire of 40–50 productions. He did not visualize the daunting non-theatrical costs that the self-contained factory would generate – looking after the building not least among them.

It is pointless to compare the Royal National Theatre of Great Britain with the state-supported theatres of other countries because there is nothing like it in scale anywhere else. The best-known and oldest-established of them, the Comédie Française, does not (or did not) stray beyond the French classics. The Berliner Ensemble confines itself almost entirely to the plays of its founder, Bertolt Brecht. The Moscow Art Theatre has a large repertoire but became so large, unwieldy and geriatric that it split into two companies playing in separate buildings. Some state theatres do no more than two or three new productions a year. The Schaubühne in West Berlin spends up to six months preparing one play. The National's problems are different, but with all its problems the important question is, as Eyre said, how good is its work? How well has it fulfilled the hopes and dreams that were made concrete on the South Bank?

The aim of the theatre is given in its programmes as: 'to present a diverse repertoire, embracing classic, new and neglected plays from the whole of world drama; to present them to the very highest standards; to give audiences a choice of at least six different productions at any one time'. This is a more detailed working-out of the Olivier–Tynan motto, 'the best of everything'. Like that piece of shorthand, it does not answer the further question: *how much* of the best of each kind? What should the mix be? Richard Eyre wrote in his own manifesto: 'composing the content of the repertoire will always be a balancing act between adventure and caution . . . but the spine of the work will always be the classics'. Eyre's first seasons amounted to almost 50 per cent classics. Under Peter Hall's regime classics made up just over a third of the total of a hundred and ninety three productions presented from 1976 to 1988 (visiting productions and Christmas shows being excluded). If 'classics' are defined as plays by writers who flourished up to the First World War, and 'modern' plays as those written since 1920 (so that Shaw is a classic, Pirandello a writer of modern plays), the balance of those years then comes out as follows: classics, 69 (35%); modern plays, 48 (25%); new plays, 74 (40%).

These figures bear out Hall's boast to have presented more new plays than any other kind. It was a risky policy. Out of the 74 new plays in all three theatres, 21 could be accounted flops (less than 60 per cent houses) and 31 hits (audiences of 80 per cent or more). This was a creditable score, especially when it is remembered that, in audience terms, the hits include four of the biggest draws to date, *Pravda*, *Amadeus*, *Bedroom Farce*, *A Small Family Business* and the adaptations *On the Razzle*, *Animal Farm* and *Wild Honey*, each of which was seen by over 100,000 people.

Audience numbers are the only quantifiable test we have of the success of a theatre, but it is, of course, only one test. Critical appreciation is another, though it is impossible to assess. There may be five good notices to five bad ones, but is Mr X's good opinion worth more than Mr Y's snub? Of course it is, in some cases. Let us apply another test: whether Harley Granville-Barker's hopes for it have been fulfilled or not.

Granville-Barker, writing in 1930, made the most cogent, clear-headed and practical case ever put for a national theatre as 'a cathedral of the art of drama', drama considered as a fine art, having spiritual functions beyond casual entertainment. 'It need not always be on the heights, any more than art or literature are,' he wrote, 'but they need to have the heights in view.' Shaw said it should be what Westminster Abbey was to religion and 'show what it can be at its best'. Barker, an experienced manager who had presented Shaw commercially when he was the most controversial playwright of his day, was well aware that 'good drama well done' could not be presented by commercially-run theatres at a profit – as people were suggesting then, just as they do today. He analysed the pressures on commercial producers: 'If 100,000 people want to see a play, but over six months, it is a failure. If only 50,000 people want to see it over three or four months, the producer will find himself in the street with a loss. Yet there are quite good plays, quite good performances, that only 10,000 people want to see.' This is as true now as it was then. In its first twelve years on the South Bank, the National had only fifteen productions that played to 100,000 people, spread over nine months to three years. Only the repertory system made them viable, so the National was performing a service that commercial theatres could not attempt. But nowadays, unless audiences average 80 per cent, plays at the National have to be taken off – and smartly too. The pressure to get the patrons in fast is as intense as it is anywhere on Shaftesbury Avenue. Plays that 10,000 people want to see are still given in the Cottesloe, but even there they will be taken off after 40 or 45 performances.

The National cannot now afford to run new plays at what is a perfectly respectable audience level in the commercial theatre (60–70 per cent). 'The minority play has its rights. Some should be nursed to success,' wrote Granville-Barker – but the National cannot now afford to 'nurse' difficult plays, as it once nursed *Plenty* in 1978. 'It became more and more like running a commercial theatre,' Hall reflected, looking back over fifteen years. 'Balancing the books is now a big factor in planning, so that getting the mixture right gets more and more difficult.' Richard Eyre aims at doing work the commercial theatre won't do, but his choice is narrowed by the fact that the theatre must now earn more than its grant (it does), partly by finding hits to exploit by transferring them.

It was as a 'library of standard literature' that Granville-Barker saw a large part of a national theatre's function, and it is arguably its most important *raison d'être*. He visualized classics remaining 'in stock' for several years, as they do at opera houses, but this cannot happen when there is no permanent company. He would be surprised that more standard plays have not been done over the years. Of Tynan's blue book of 400 world-class plays only about 130 have yet been staged. European classics – Racine, Goethe, Schiller, Calderon, Sophocles, Aristophanes, etc. etc. – have been markedly neglected. They need inspired translators and directors with a strong desire to do a particular play because of its present relevance. There has been a shortage of such directors. The National also has to consider the 'alternative national theatre', the RSC, whose primary repertoire must be Shakespeare and the Jacobeans. Competition between them should stop short of presenting contemporaneous productions of the same play. Thanks to an efficient grapevine, there have been few clashes (although in 1988 both companies put on *Hamlet*, *Cymbeline* and *The Tempest*, and in 1990, *King Lear*). There are welcome signs of the Eyre regime giving classics a higher priority than in the past. It is pointless to exhume them out of duty, but the bogey of 'dead theatre' has been much exaggerated. Every ten years or so there is a new generation of young playgoers who need to see the standard repertoire – 'classic' means timeless.

Granville-Barker wrote very warmly of the service a national theatre could do the art of acting and this is the department in which he would probably be most disappointed in the way things have worked out. The English theatre for thirty years, he wrote, had seen 'a succession of actors who, having made a reputation, have done little or nothing thereafter to fulfil it, sagging back into mediocrity masked by an over-increasing emphasis on their popular manner, their successful tricks'. This was because they had little choice of parts. 'A National Theatre would give actors great parts to play in surroundings that would enhance them and we might – who knows? – see a little great acting again.' How much great acting is there at the National nowadays? How many actors never get any better there because after six or nine months have elapsed they have gone away to secure their much higher salary in television? It never occurred to Granville-Barker that the National Theatre would not be able to keep the best actors in the country on a long-term basis because it could not pay them enough. He assumed that they would stay because they enjoyed 'conditions of security and stability such as the older generation of actors could only dream of'.

Neither has the theatre developed an ensemble such as Granville-Barker hoped for, such as we see dangled before us in visits by Stein's Schaubühne company, Yefremov's Moscow Arts Theatre or the Japanese Ninagawa troupe. Since Olivier's company broke up there has been nothing resembling a permanent troupe. The admired names of international theatre, such as Strehler, Bergman, Stein and Brook, are men with permanent groups who are not distracted by complex administration problems or a constant battle for adequate funds. No leading actor except Michael Bryant 'belongs' to the National Theatre. The reason is financial. Granville-Barker assumed that the best seats in the house would cost 10s 6d and top actors would be paid £2,000–£2,500 a year. In 1989 the best seats cost almost thirty times as much and if the top actors were paid thirty times as much, they would be earning £60,000 a year or £1,150 a week. In 1990 it is only the Director who is paid £60,000. The top rate for actors is £450–£500, less than half of what top actors get in a West End production. So far from being encouraged to remain with the National, they are positively forbidden by their union, Equity, to sign contracts for more than a year's duration. Actors at the top of their tree are happy in principle to work at the National, but seldom for as long as a year. Film or television mini-series take priority because the differentials are now too great. Michael Gambon, whose loyalty to the National has brought him back to it many times, admitted that his ability to earn £30,000 a year from voice-overs helped make it possible to do so. Michael Bryant, who refuses voice-overs out of principle, acknowledges that his earnings as an actor could be some eight times higher outside but sticks to the National because 'This is the theatre I love.' Many actors will sacrifice earnings for the sake of a part that stretches them, but not for too long. Peter Hall recalled, 'I would say to actors, can you give me another six months? – and they would reply, sorry. That made it very difficult to do a perfectly-cast production.' But if the National Theatre does not aim to give its audience, at least occasionally, a production that it as near perfection as it can get (as it occasionally does in spite of everything) what does it exist for?

It would be wrong to conclude that there is no company loyalty, no feeling of belonging to the organization, no camaraderie around the dressing-room well. There clearly is. But the sense of pride in playing for England has diminished since Olivier's day. One of his stated objectives was 'to improve the standing and appreciation of acting and to develop in time a company which will be the finest in the world'. Nobody is aiming to do that today.

Would it still be possible? Yes, if the nation was willing to put up enough funding for proper salaries to be paid. But the nation did not choose to make its National Theatre a cathedral of the art of drama, but a theatrical supermarket, where the productions are stocked by the trolleyful. It is very difficult to combine a factory-like production schedule with hand-made goods of the highest quality. Only a small proportion of shows can hope to attain that standard under the pressure to maintain the output.

It has been the task of this book to describe what exists rather than to speculate on what might have been better. Back in 1907, introducing their original proposals for a national theatre, William Archer and Harley Granville-Barker wrote: 'There never was and there never will be an ideal theatre. The theatre is too complex and delicate a machine, depending on the harmonious co-operation of too many talents, ever to reach perfection for more than a passing moment.' They warned us not to let our craving for the ideally desirable blind us to the practical, which would at least be 'an improvement on existing conditions'. At present we have got rather better than the national theatre we deserve. It is not the ideal, but it is the most ambitious 'improvement on existing conditions' yet attempted and it has survived for twenty-five years. Archer, Shaw, Granville-Barker and the rest of the pioneers would be reasonably satisfied with that. During the next twenty-five years, it must strive not just to survive but to become the best national theatre possible. There is still a long way to go, but at least we are fairly launched well down the road.

Sources and Bibiography

The two outstanding published sources on the National and its first 25 years are, of course, Sir Laurence Olivier's *Confessions of an Actor* (Weidenfeld and Nicolson, 1982) and Sir Peter Hall's *Diaries*, edited by John Goodwin (Hamish Hamilton, 1983). Other important sources devoted to the history of the National Theatre movement and its development are: William Archer and Harley Granville-Barker *A Scheme and Estimates for a National Theatre*, (Duckworth, 1907) and Granville-Barker's revision of these proposals, *A National Theatre* (Sidgwick and Jackson, 1930). Geoffrey Whitworth's *The Making of a National Theatre* (Faber and Faber, 1951) carries the story forward and John Elsom and Nicholas Tomalin continued it down to 1976 and the move to the South Bank in *The History of the National Theatre* (Cape, 1978).

The National Theatre publications are further sources: *A Pictorial Record –* the National Theatre at the Old Vic 1963–71; *The Complete Guide to Britain's National Theatre* (1977) and *Britain's National Theatre – The First 25 Years* (1988).

The special issue of the *Architectural Review* for January, 1977, is devoted to a comprehensive review of the building and Judith Cook's *The National Theatre* (Harrap, 1976) is a collection of interviews with the principal people involved at the time it was opened.

Following is a selection of other books consulted or quoted in the text:

Arts Council: Theatre is for All – Report of the Enquiry into Professional
  Theatre in England, chaired by Sir Kenneth Cork (1986)
Conversations with Ayckbourn – Ian Watson, (Faber and Faber, 1988)
Sally Beauman: The Royal Shakespeare Company – A History of Ten
  Decades, (Oxford University Press, 1982)
Michael Billington: Peggy Ashcroft, (John Murray, 1988)
Peter Brook – A Theatrical Casebook, compiled David Williams, (Methuen,
  1988)
Simon Callow: Being an Actor, (Methuen, 1984)
Noël Coward: Diaries, (Weidenfeld and Nicolson, 1982)
Richard Findlater: The Player Kings, (Weidenfeld and Nicolson, 1971)

Richard Findlater (ed.): At The Royal Court, (Amber Lane Press, 1981)

William Gaskill: A Sense of Direction, (Faber and Faber, 1988)

Joy Leslie Gibson: Ian McKellen, (Weidenfeld and Nicolson, 1986)

John Gielgud: An Actor and His Time, (Sidgwick and Jackson, 1979)

Ronald Harwood (ed.): The Ages of Gielgud, (Hodder and Stoughton, 1984)

Logan Gourlay (ed.): Olivier, (Weidenfeld and Nicolson, 1973)

The Guys and Dolls Book, (Methuen, 1982)

Jim Hiley: Theatre at Work, (Routledge and Kegan Paul, 1981)

Anthony Holden: Olivier, (Weidenfeld and Nicolson, 1988)

Jonathan Miller: Subsequent Performances, (Faber and Faber, 1986)

Garry O'Connor: Ralph Richardson, (Hodder and Stoughton, 1982)

      Olivier: In Celebration, (Hodder and Stoughton, 1987)

Olivier: On Acting, (Weidenfeld and Nicolson, 1986)

Prince of Wales: A Vision of Britain, (Doubleday, 1989)

Michael Redgrave: In My Mind's Eye, (Weidenfeld and Nicolson, 1983)

Kathleen Tynan: The Life of Kenneth Tynan, (Weidenfeld and Nicolson, 1987)

Kenneth Tynan: Othello – The National Theatre Production, (Hart-Davis, 1966)

      A View of the English Stage, (Davis–Poynter, 1975):

      The Sound of Two Hands Clapping, (Cape, 1975)

      Show People, (Weidenfeld and Nicolson, 1980)

Franco Zeffirelli: Autobiography, (Weidenfeld and Nicolson, 1986)

Index

NT stands for National Theatre, LO for Laurence Olivier, PH for Peter Hall and RSC for Royal Shakespeare Company.

243